REV UP TO EXCEL 2010

Upgraders Guide to Excel 2010

by

Bill Jelen

Published by

HOLY MACRO! BOOKS

PO Box 82, Uniontown, OH 44685

Written by: Bill Jelen

Technical Editor: Bob Umlas

Copy Editor: Keith Cline

Design & Layout: Fine Grains (India) Private Limited,
                     New Delhi, India.

Cover Design: Shannon Mattiza, 6'4 Productions

Published by: Holy Macro! Books, Box 82, Uniontown OH 44685, USA

Distributed by: Independent Publishers Group

First Printing: July 2010. Printed in USA

ISBN: 978-1-615470-001-3

Library of Congress Control Number: 2010904989

Contents

About the Author

Bill Jelen is the host of MrExcel.com and the author of 32 books about Microsoft Excel, including Guerilla Data Analysis Using Microsoft Excel, Excel Gurus Gone Wild, and PowerPivot for the Excel Data Analyst.

You will frequently find Bill on the road, entertaining groups of accountants with his Power Excel seminar. For a list of upcoming events, visit http://www.mrexcel.com/pressappearances.shtml. To book Bill for your next Professional Development day or Controller's Conference, visit http://www.mrexcel.com/speaking.html.

He has made over 60 guest appearances on TV's Call for Help with Leo Laporte and was voted guest of the year on the Computer America radio show. He has produced over 1100 episodes of his daily video podcast Learn Excel from MrExcel.

Before founding MrExcel.com in 1998, Bill spent twelve years "in the trenches", as a financial analyst for the accounting, finance, marketing, and operations departments of a publicly held company. Since then, his company automates Excel reports for hundreds of clients around the world. The website answers over 30,000 questions a year – for free – for readers all over the world.

Dedication

For George

Acknowledgments

Thanks to Bob Umlas for technical editing on this book. Bob is the smartest Excel guy I know. Keith Cline makes the copyediting process painless. Thanks to Paramjeet Singh for layout and printing.

At MrExcel.com, thanks to Scott Pierson, Schar Oswald, Tracy Syrstad, Wei Jiang, Barb Jelen. My sons Josh and Zeke have been picking up time after school and learning how to produce podcasts. Thanks to the hundreds of people answering 30,000 questions a year at the MrExcel message board.

Thanks to Mary Ellen Jelen for everything.

Introduction

So you are upgrading to Excel 2010.

Since many I.T. departments adopt an "every-other" approach to upgrades, many of you will be upgrading directly from Excel 2003 to Excel 2010. You missed the only version of Excel to not have a menu called "File". You missed the frustration of not being able to move icons around on the menu. You are going directly to a mature version of the ribbon interface.

Chapters 1 through 11 of this book introduce you to all the changes in the Excel interface. I give you strategies for finding things on the ribbon, but also the cool tips and tricks for dealing with the ribbon. You'll see how to unlock the 1.1 million rows in the new Excel. You'll learn about the vastly improved File menu (a.k.a. Backstage view) and all the other Excel interface goodies. You'll also read about why Ctrl+C, Application, V is going to become your new best friend.

Chapter 12 introduces the new functions in Excel 2010.

Chapters 13 through 20 deal with data wrangling and business intelligence. Pivot tables get a makeover and improvements (Chapter 19). And as you'll learn, the new PowerPivot add-in is the best feature to happen to Excel in 20 years (Chapter 20).

Chapters 21 through 34 will make your worksheets look great. You will learn about the new charting engine and data visualization tools. These chapters also cover SmartArt concepts, and they show you how to use document themes and cell styles to quickly format a worksheet. You'll also learn how to remove the background from pictures.

This book is the quick-hit summary of what's been introduced in the past two versions of Excel. In my five others books about Excel 2010, I've already written 3,000 pages covering every feature of Excel. This book is designed for someone who uses Excel 2003 and knows it well. My goal is to get you up to speed with the new interface, show you how to leverage what's new, and then get you back to work.

Introducing the Ribbon

By far, the biggest change when you upgrade from Excel 2003 to Excel 2010 is trying to find commands on the ribbon. Rather than the familiar File, Edit, View, Insert, Format, Tools, Data, Window, Help menu bar, you are now presented with large icons and words such as File, Home, Insert, Page Layout, Formulas, Data, Review, and View.

Where to Find Commands in Excel 2010

Here are some simple guidelines:

The Home tab contains the most frequently used commands. If you want to find something, start looking on the Home tab. Nearly everything from the Excel 2003 Edit and Format menus is located on the Home tab. Everything from the Excel 2003 Formatting toolbar is on the Home tab.

The most-used commands on the Excel 2003 Insert menu are not on the Insert tab in Excel 2010! Instead, commands to insert cells, rows, columns, and worksheets are on an Insert drop-down on the Home tab. Commands to insert a function or a name are on the Formulas tab. Insert Comment is on the Review tab.

The Pivot Tables command has been moved from the Data menu to the left side of the Insert tab.

Most Excel 2003 File menu commands are on the Excel 2010 File tab. This tab is called the Backstage view and is discussed in detail in Chapter 4. A few File commands are elsewhere. For example, Save Workspace is on the View tab. Page Setup and Print Area are on the Page Layout tab.

Everything on the old Window menu and most things from the old View menu are now on the View tab.

Help is now the blue question mark icon at the top right of the window. Everything else that used to be on the Help menu is now under File, Help.

Items from the Data menu are generally on the Data tab, with the exception of the Pivot Tables command.

The old Tools menu has been split among many tabs. You will find these commands spread among the Review, Formulas, Home, Data, View, and File tabs. Table 1.2 shows the break out of individual commands.

Table 1.1 shows where you can find most Excel 2003 menu commands in Excel 2010.

Table 1.1

2003 Menu	2010 Ribbon
File	File
Edit	Home
View	View
Insert	Home, Insert, Formula, Review
Format	Home
Tools	See Table 1.2
Data	Data, Pivot Tables on Insert
Window	View
Help	Question mark on right; or File, Help
Standard toolbar	See Table 1.3
Formatting toolbar	Home

Table 1.2 shows where you can find the commands formerly found on the Tools menu.

Table 1.2

Excel 2003 Tools Menu Commands	Excel 2010 Tab
Spelling, Research, Share Workbook, Track Changes, Compare, Merge	Review
Error Checking and Formula Auditing	Formulas
Speech, Shared Workspace, and AutoCorrect Options	Add to QAT
Protection	Home (Format drop-down) or Review
Goal Seek and Scenarios	Data (What-if drop-down)
Macro	View
Add-Ins and Options	File (Options)

Table 1.3 shows commands formerly found on the Standard toolbar.

Table 1.3

Excel 2003 Standard Toolbar Icons	Excel 2010 Tab
New, Open, Save, Print, Print Preview	File
Spelling & Thesaurus	Review
Cut, Copy, Paste, Format Painter	Home
Undo, Redo	QAT
Hyperlink	Insert
AutoSum, Sort	Home
Chart, Drawing	Insert
Zoom	View (or bottom right)

Ribbon Components

The ribbon is the new interface at the top of Excel 2010. It consists of icons and words grouped into several tabs. Within each tab, icons are further classified into groups. In Figure 1.1, there are 4 icons in the Clipboard group of the Home tab and 10 icons in the Font group.

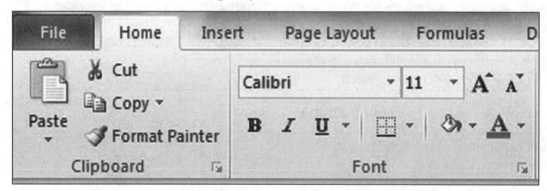

Figure 1.1 - *Icons are classified in logical groups within each ribbon tab.*

Dialog Box Launchers

In the lower-right corner of some groups, you will see a tiny icon showing a diagonal arrow. You can see this in the lower-right corner of Figure 1.1. This icon is a dialog box launcher. Click the icon to open a dialog box similar to the dialogs you are familiar with from Excel 2003.

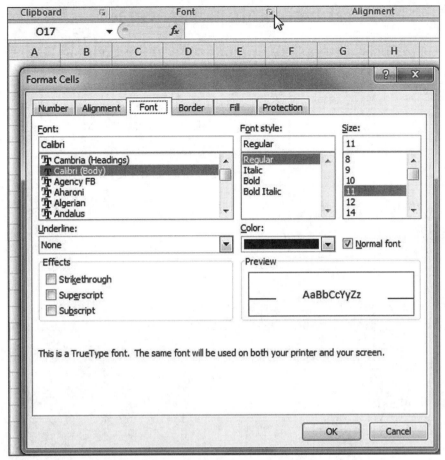

Figure 1.2 - *The mouse pointer is showing the dialog box launcher in the Font group of the Home tab. Dialog launchers are found in many groups.*

Icons That Really Contain a Drop-Down

A lot of large icons look like a single icon until you hover over the icon. You will then see that the top half of the icon is a Paste icon, for example, and the bottom half of the icon is a drop-down with more choices related to the icon.

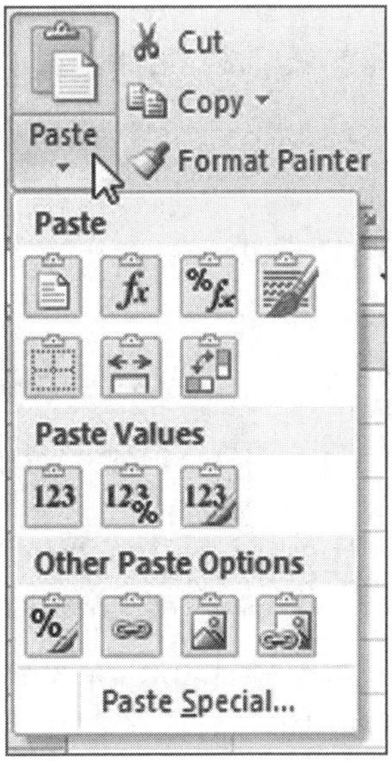

Figure 1.3 - *The Paste icon is really an icon and a drop-down.*

Gallery Icons Fit Many Choices into a Tiny Space

Some ribbon elements consist of a gallery of many different options. In Figure 1.4, the Chart Layouts gallery shows three thumbnails at a time.

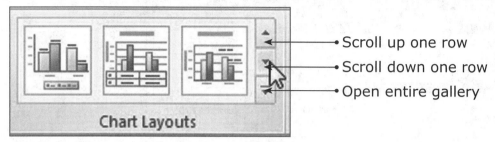

- Scroll up one row
- Scroll down one row
- Open entire gallery

Figure 1.4 - *Three buttons on the right side of the gallery enable you to scroll up, down, or open the entire gallery.*

You can use the Up- and Down-Arrow button to scroll through three thumbnails. Or, click the third arrow to open the gallery and see all the options simultaneously (Figure 1.5)

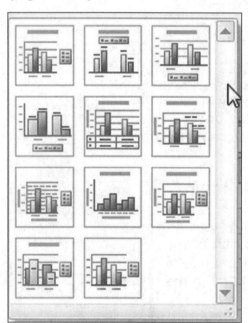

Figure 1.5 – *The third button next to the gallery is the More button. Click that button to see all the choices at one time.*

Making the Ribbon a Bit More Like a Menu

Although there is nothing you can do to bring back the legacy Excel menu and toolbars, you can make the ribbon behave a bit more like a menu.

Press Ctrl+F1 or right-click the ribbon and choose Minimize the Ribbon. When you do so, Excel hides the ribbon, as shown in Figure 1.6.

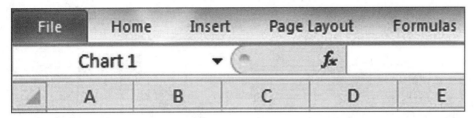

Figure 1.6 - *Ctrl+F1 hides the ribbon, leaving only the tab names.*

After the ribbon is hidden, you have more room to work with your document. You can also later click any ribbon tab name to open the ribbon temporarily. After you choose a command, Excel returns the ribbon back to the view in Figure 1.6. At least this feels more like a typical menu system.

Context-Sensitive Ribbons

Occasionally, new tabs will appear on the right side of the ribbon. These tabs appear when the current selection includes SmartArt graphics, charts, drawings, pictures, pivot tables, pivot charts, worksheet headers, tables, ink, or when you are in the legacy Print Preview mode.

These new tabs will stay visible as long as the object stays selected. If you click outside of your pivot table or chart, the tabs will disappear. If you are looking at an object and cannot find the tools necessary to edit the object, click the object to bring the tools back.

Different Screen Sizes Show Different Icons

If you frequently try to help coworkers over the phone, you want to be aware that the ribbon looks different at different sizes. If you have a massively wide monitor, you will see more icons than someone working on an older laptop.

To demonstrate, Figure 1.7 shows the right side of the Home tab. You see 11 drop-down icons. If you were looking at this screen, you might tell a coworker to open the drop-down next to the word *Fill*.

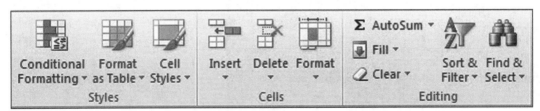

Figure 1.7 - *The Home tab at one screen resolution.*

In Figure 1.8, the Excel window is less wide. The Insert, Delete, and Format icons are now arranged vertically, and the words *AutoSum*, *Fill*, and *Clear* are missing.

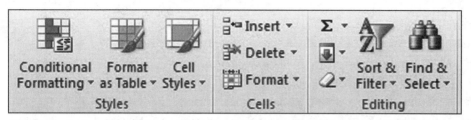

Figure 1.8 - *Your coworker will insist that he doesn't have an icon labeled Fill.*

At an even smaller screen width, the Insert, Delete, and Format icons are combined into a single drop-down called Cells. You have to open the Cells drop-down to see the Insert icon.

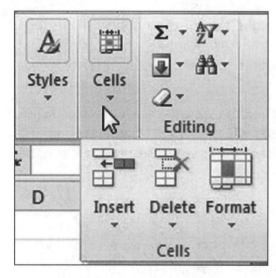

Figure 1.9 - *As the Excel window shrinks, commands are consolidated into one drop-down per group.*

Eventually, if the Excel window gets small enough, Microsoft assumes that you cannot possibly be working in the worksheet and the ribbon disappears completely.

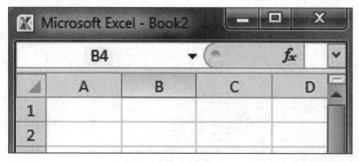

Figure 1.10 - *Eventually, the ribbon disappears completely.*

Introducing the Ribbon

Keeping Some Commands Always Visible on the QAT

In Excel 97-2003, you always had quick access to icons for bold, italic, cut, paste, align right, decrease decimal, sort ascending, print preview, Chart Wizard, and more.

With Excel 2010, these icons are spread across seven ribbon tabs, so the odds are that you will not always have access to the various icons that you might need. Microsoft addresses this problem with the Quick Access Toolbar (QAT).

The QAT is a toolbar that is always visible near the ribbon. It appears on the left side of the screen, above the File tab. Although the QAT initially contains three icons (Save, Undo, and Redo), you can customize the QAT to hold all your favorite icons. One set of customizations can apply to all workbooks opened on the computer, and you can define a second set of icons to open for each specific workbook.

Figure 1.11 - *The QAT starts with three icons and a drop-down menu.*

When you open the drop-down menu at the right side of the QAT, Microsoft suggests some popular icons that you might want to have available all the time. In Figure 1.12, selecting Open Recent File adds that icon to the end of the toolbar.

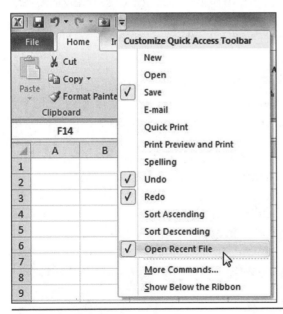

Figure 1.12 - *The drop-down includes a dozen commands you might want to add.*

In reality, you can add any of hundreds of commands to the QAT. Right-click any command and choose Add to Quick Access Toolbar, as shown in Figure 1.13.

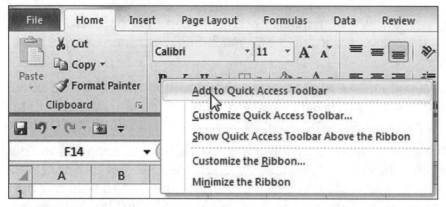

Figure 1.13 - *Right-click any command to add it to the QAT.*

If you find yourself using the QAT frequently, move it below the ribbon, as shown in Figure 1.13, by using the final menu item in Figure 1.12.

You can customize the QAT in even more ways, too, as you'll read about in Chapter 2.

Finding the Elusive Mini Toolbar

If you have used Outlook 2003, you might be familiar with toolbars that fade in. When you receive a new Outlook message, a notifier box starts to appear in the lower-right corner of the screen. This notifier shows the subject line, the first words in the message, and icons to immediately delete the mail or to open the e-mail. If you are busy working on a document and ignore the notifier, it slowly fades away. However, if you move the mouse toward the notifier, it solidifies so that you have time to click the Delete button to eliminate the mail if it is junk.

The Mini Toolbar uses similar technology. I think it will appear much more frequently in Word and PowerPoint than it will appear in Excel. It is possible to use Excel 40 hours a week and never see the Mini Toolbar appear.

> **Note**: During the beta period, Microsoft has variously called this feature a Mini Bar, Mini Toolbar, and a Floaty. Although I prefer visiting the Mini Bar, it looks like Mini Toolbar will win out in the final version. When I write books for Que, the editorial guidelines there state that the T in toolbar is never capitalized. Although I generally agree with this, to me, Mini Toolbar is just a bad replacement for Mini Bar, and so I will capitalize the T. After all, you wouldn't drive a Mini cooper automobile, would you?

The Mini Toolbar is elusive in Excel for two reasons. First, it is relatively hard to select characters within a cell in Excel. It is easier in Excel charts or SmartArt graphics to select characters, but it is relatively rare to select just a few characters inside of a cell. Second, on many computers, the Mini Toolbar initially appears in a completely invisible state! If you don't move the mouse pointer toward the completely invisible Mini Toolbar, it will never appear.

In Figure 1.14, the Mini Toolbar is just starting to appear (as we select characters in a chart title and move up and to the right). The toolbar is so light, it is difficult to guess if it will even show up as this book goes through the printing press. The Mini Toolbar starts just above the *e* in the word *Title*.

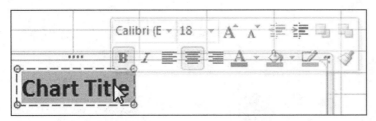

Figure 1.14 - *Select some text, move up and to the right, and a nearly invisible Mini Toolbar starts to appear.*

If you then hold the mouse still, the Mini Toolbar will remain in its nearly invisible state. If you move the mouse left or down, the Mini Toolbar will become completely invisible.

However, if you move the mouse right or up by a few pixels, the Mini Toolbar sharpens completely into view.

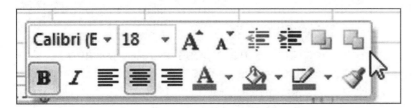

Figure 1.15 - *Move toward the invisible Mini Toolbar and it solidifies.*

The theory behind the Mini Toolbar is that a leading reason for selecting text is that you might be planning on formatting the text. The Mini Toolbar puts 17 popular formatting commands at your mousetip. You can do a fair amount of formatting without ever having to visit the ribbon or the QAT.

Although the Mini Toolbar contains only 17 icons, a few of those icons lead to drop-down menus with significant variations. In Figure 1.16, the paint bucket icon opens to reveal flyout menus for patterns and gradients.

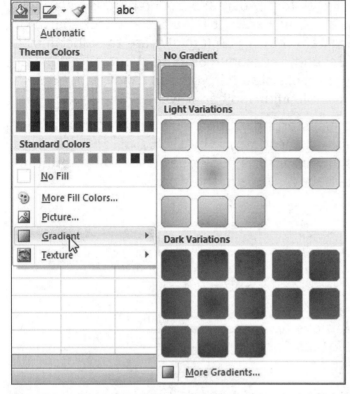

Figure 1.16 - *Some icons on the Mini Toolbar lead to menus with hundreds of options.*

Mini Toolbar Versions

The figures shown previously in this chapter represent the Mini Toolbar when you are formatting a chart title. If you cause the Mini Toolbar to appear when you are editing text within a cell, some buttons do not apply.

Quadruple-click any nonblank cell and move the mouse pointer up and to the right. An abbreviated version of the Mini Toolbar with seven icons will appear. It doesn't make sense to change the indentation of just a few characters in a cell, so Excel produces this version of the Mini Toolbar, shown in Figure 1.17.

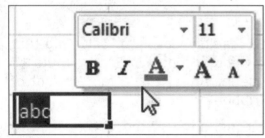

Figure 1.17 - *If you select characters within a cell, a miniature Mini Toolbar appears.*

If you right-click any cell, the full Mini Toolbar appears above the cell. This is by far an easier way to invoke the toolbar than by selecting characters within the cell. In this version of the Mini Toolbar, the Center Across Selection icon replaces the Send Forward icon.

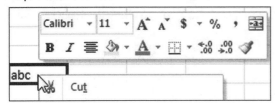

Figure 1.18 - *Right-click a cell to access this Mini Toolbar.*

Customizing the Mini Toolbar

Although you can customize the ribbon and QAT, you still cannot add icons to the Mini Toolbar in Excel 2010.

When Does the Mini Toolbar Completely Disappear?

As discussed previously, if you move toward the Mini Toolbar, it solidifies. If you move away from the Mini Toolbar, it disappears. You can move your mouse back and forth between 7 o'clock and 2 o'clock and cause the Mini Toolbar to fade in and out of view.

However, once your mouse strays a certain distance from the selection, the Mini Toolbar disappears and will not reappear until you reselect the text.

This distance is based on pixels. In general, though, if you move approximately 10 rows away from the selection in a spreadsheet with the default font and zoom, you will have hit the limit and the Mini Toolbar will permanently disappear.

I can see many situations where you would move away from the selection (for example, to respond to an incoming e-mail notification). After you've moved too far away from the selection, you will either have to reselect the text or use the formatting icons in the Home ribbon.

Permanently Disabling the Mini Toolbar

The Mini Toolbar is fairly elusive in Excel and will rarely get in your way. However, if you want to permanently disable the feature, you can do so.

From the File menu, choose Options. The first setting in the Popular category is Show Mini Toolbar on Selection. Uncheck the box shown in Figure 1.19 to disable the Mini Toolbar.

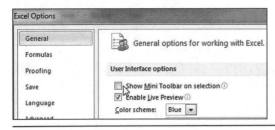

Figure 1.19 - *Use this setting to permanently disable the Mini Toolbar.*

Surely There Is a Classic Mode

I've been told that when Bill Gates saw the ribbon, he asked whether there would be a Classic mode. The Office user interface team convinced Bill that the ribbon would be too different and that there could not be a Classic mode. Bill Gates bought that argument.

Okay, so the largest software company in the world cannot figure out how to do a Classic mode, but a lone programmer named Lin Jie is offering Classic mode for $15.95. Figure 1.20 shows the familiar File, Edit, View menus along with the Standard and Formatting toolbars. To buy the add-in, visit www.mrexcel.com/classicexcelmenu.html

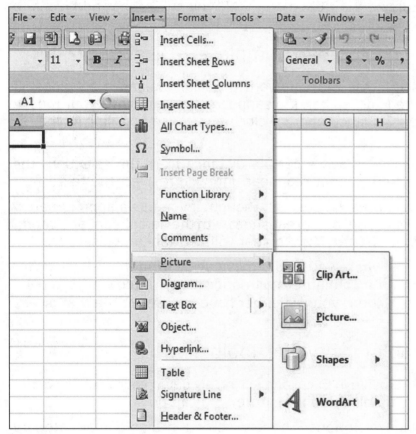

Figure 1.20 - *Bring back the old Excel menus.*

Next Steps

Chapter 2 shows you how to customize the ribbon and QAT.

Customizing the Ribbon and Quick Access Toolbar

Presumably, you are reading this book because you are upgrading from Excel 97-2003 to Excel 2010. You are going to be horribly disappointed with the limited customizations that you can do to the ribbon and Quick Access Toolbar (QAT). During the Excel 2007 era, it was impossible to customize the ribbon using the Excel interface, so the limited tools in Excel 2010 actually seem like a great improvement over Excel 2003.

Adding a New Group to an Existing Tab

You might feel like the Pivot Table command belongs on the Data tab rather than on the Insert tab. You can add a new group to the Data tab to hold the pivot table icons.

First, look at the ribbon and decide where you want the new group to appear. Perhaps a good location would be between the Sort & Filter group and the Data Tools group.

Figure 2.1 - *Decide where you want the new group to appear.*

Right-click anywhere on the ribbon and choose Customize the Ribbon.

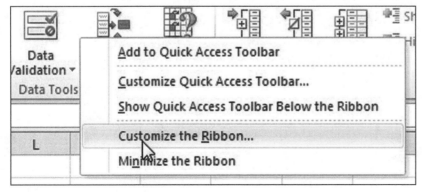

Figure 2.2 - *Right-click the ribbon to access this menu.*

The Customize dialog contains two large list boxes. You will first be working with the list box on the right side of the screen.

Expand the plus sign next to the Data entry to see the groups on the Data tab. If you want a new group to appear after the Sort & Filter group, click Sort & Filter, and then click the New Group button below the list box.

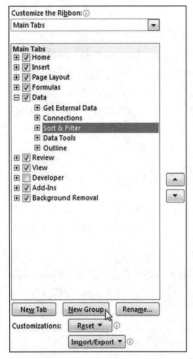

Figure 2.3 - *Choose where the new group should go.*

Excel adds a new group with the name of New Group (Custom). Click the Rename button below the list box.

Figure 2.4 - *Choose to rename the group.*

Type a new name in the Rename dialog. Also, choose an icon. This icon will appear only when the Excel window gets small enough to force the group into a drop-down, as shown later in Figure 2.8.

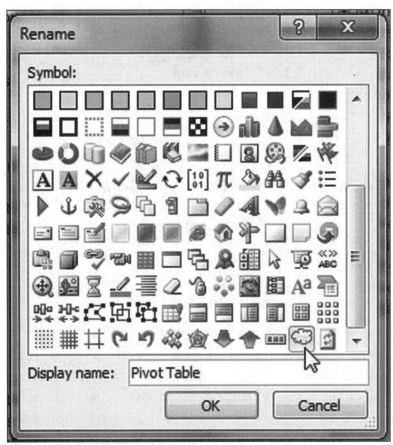

Figure 2.5 - *Type a new name and choose an icon to represent the group.*

> **Note**: The 180 icons available in Excel 2010 are a far cry from the 4096 icons available in Excel 2003. As I pointed out at the beginning of this chapter, toolbar customization took a giant step backward after Excel 2003.

After renaming the new group in the list box on the right side, it is time to turn your attention to the list box on the left side. It starts out showing Popular Commands. Use the drop-down above the left list box to change from Popular Commands to All Commands.

Scroll down to the commands starting with Pivot. You will see a confusing array of commands. Click the first PivotTable icon, and click the Add button in the center of the screen. Click the second PivotChart icon, and then click the Add button. Click PivotTable and PivotChart Wizard, and then click the Add button.

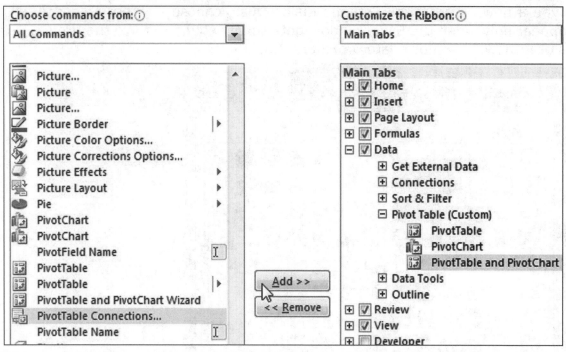

Figure 2.6 - *Choose icons to add to the new group on the ribbon.*

It is sometimes difficult to figure out which icons you want. There are two icons that say PivotTable. The first icon is simply an icon. The second icon is an icon with a rightward-facing triangle on the right side of the list box. That triangle indicates that the second icon is actually a drop-down that leads to more choices. That second PivotTable drop-down icon is the icon at the bottom half of the Insert tab's Pivot Table group. It opens to enable you to choose between PivotTable and PivotChart. You might prefer to use that icon instead.

Two PivotChart icons are available. Hover over each icon to see that the first one is the PivotChart icon available on the PivotTable Tools Options tab. You will also see that the second icon is the one on the Insert tab. The first PivotChart icon will be grayed out unless you are in a pivot table. The second PivotChart icon is the one that is used to create a new pivot chart from a dataset.

Figure 2.7 shows the resulting group on the Data tab.

Figure 2.7 - *The resulting custom group gets added to the ribbon.*

If you are wondering why you had to choose an icon back in Figure 2.5, it is for people who have the Excel window resized to a narrower width. If you make your Excel window narrower, the custom group will eventually get squished down to a single drop-down. Your icon will appear on that drop-down, as shown in Figure 2.8.

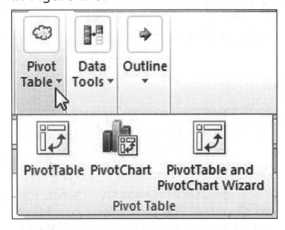

Figure 2.8 - *The icon from Figure 2.4 shows up at a smaller window size.*

Small Icons vs. Large Icons

Note back in Figure 2.1 that the Sort icon appears as a large icon with a caption and that the AZ and ZA icons appear as small icons without a caption. You are probably wondering how you can control your new group. How can you specify that the pivot table icon should be large and the pivot chart and wizard icons should be small? You can't. At least not with the Excel interface.

If you want to start writing some XML and VBA, you can gain control over the size and images used in the ribbon. For an excellent book on this daunting task, look for *RibbonX: Customizing the Office 2007 Ribbon* by Robert Martim, Ken Puls and Teresa Hennig.

Adding a New Ribbon Tab

I find that I spend most of my time on either the Home or the Data tab. If I could combine the left side of the Home tab with the right side of the Data tab, plus pivot tables, I would probably be able to spend all my time on one tab.

Figure 2.9 shows a new MrExcel tab that reuses groups from other ribbon tabs to build a new tab.

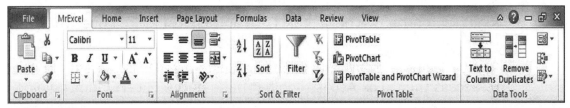

Figure 2.9 - *The MrExcel tab is a custom tab with my favorite groups.*

The general steps for creating a new ribbon tab are as follows:

1. Right-click the Ribbon and choose Customize the Ribbon.

2. Click New Tab at the bottom right of the dialog.

3. Click Rename and give the tab a name.

4. Use the Up and Down buttons at the right side of the dialog to move the new tab into the proper location.

5. From the left drop-down, choose Main Tabs.

6. In the left drop-down, expand an existing tab and find an existing group that you want to add to your new tab. Click that group and click Add.

7. Repeat step 6 to add additional groups.

8. You can reuse a custom group that you created previously. In the left drop-down, choose Custom Tabs and Groups. You can move the Pivot Table (Custom) tab created earlier in this chapter onto your new ribbon tab.

9. Click OK to finish customizing the ribbon tab.

To sum up the customization for the ribbon, you can add new custom groups or a new ribbon tab. You cannot add or remove icons from an existing group. If you have an existing group with six icons and you want to remove two, you will have to build a new custom group with the four icons that you want to keep. You cannot force certain icons to be large and others to be small.

Customizing the QAT

Initially, the QAT is a tiny toolbar with three icons. It appears on the left side of the screen, above the File tab.

There are five ways to customize the QAT:

- Using the drop-down at the right side of the QAT to add any of 12 popular icons

- Right-clicking any icon on any ribbon tab and choosing to add to the QAT

- Right-clicking any icon in the QAT and choosing Remove from the QAT

- Right-clicking the QAT and choosing Customize Quick Access Toolbar to access the Quick Access Toolbar pane of the Excel Options dialog

- Selecting File, Options, Quick Access Toolbar to customize the QAT

Using Excel Options to Customize the QAT

Chapter 1 discussed quick ways to make small customizations to the QAT. If you need to make many customizations to the QAT, you will want to use the full-featured customization tool available in the Excel Options dialog.

The Excel Options dialog box pane to customize the QAT is similar to the pane for customizing the ribbon, with a few changes.

The top-left drop-down still offers choices such as Popular Commands, All Commands, Commands Not in the Ribbon, and Macros. You can find an icon in the left list box and use the Add button to add it to the QAT.

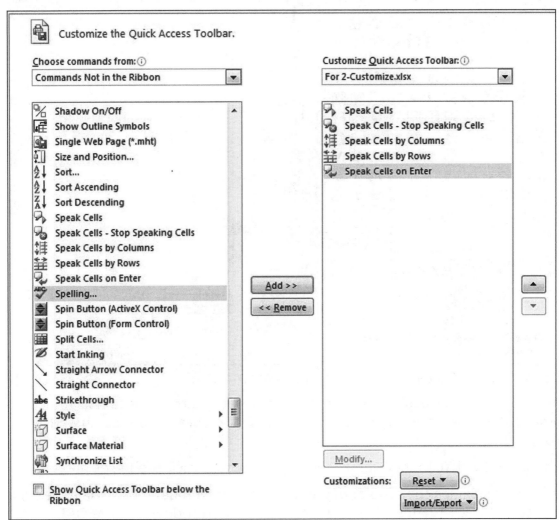

Figure 2.10 - *Select icons to add to the QAT.*

A drop-down above the right list box will allow you to add icons to All Workbooks or to only a specific open workbook. Icons added to a specific workbook appear after the icons added for all workbooks.

The Modify button works only for icons from the Macros category. You can choose a new icon and words to appear in the tooltip.

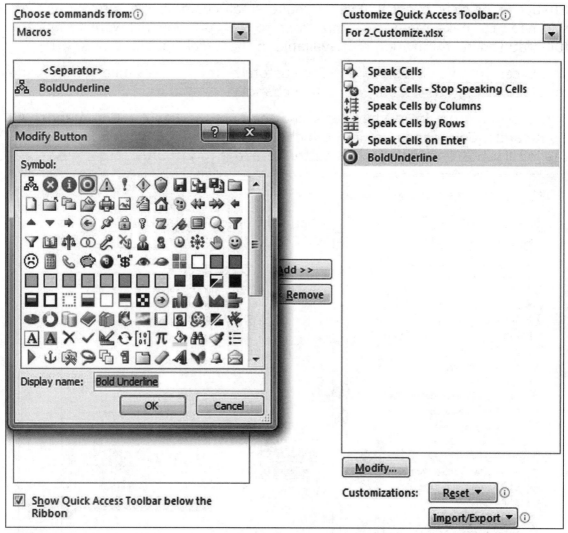

Figure 2.11 - *You can only modify icons for macros.*

The left list box always starts with a <Separator> entry. This is not an actual command, but will draw a vertical bar in the QAT to break your commands into groups.

To restore the QAT to its original set of three icons, click the Reset button.

Any custom groups that you added in the Customize Ribbon tool will appear in the list of All Commands. These will appear as a drop-down on the QAT.

Adding Too Many Icons to the QAT

If you add too many icons to the QAT, only the first row of icons is shown on the QAT. A More Controls icon appears at the right end of the QAT. Click the More

Customizing the Ribbon and Quick Access Toolbar

Controls icon to see a second row of QAT icons. If you have even more icons than will fit on the second row, a scrollbar at the right edge of the second row of the QAT will enable you to scroll through the additional icons.

Caution: Chapter 8 talks about using keyboard shortcuts. Although it might be possible to memorize some keyboard shortcuts, it will be hard to memorize the keyboard shortcuts associated with the QAT. The QAT icons are assigned shortcut keys on-the-fly every time that you press the Alt key. If certain icons are grayed out in the current context, their shortcut keys are shifted right and applied to other icons. If you want to reliably memorize certain QAT icons, be sure to add them to the leftmost section of the QAT, before any icons that may occasionally be grayed out.

Sharing Customizations

Let's say that a coworker has developed a new ribbon tab that has a great set of customizations. You can ask the coworker to export the customizations, and then you can import those to your computer.

Note that exporting customizations is an all-or-nothing proposition. You cannot export only a portion of the customizations. When you export customizations, you will get the new ribbon tabs, the new groups, and any QAT changes.

To export the customizations, use the Import/Export button at the bottom of either the Customize Ribbon or Quick Access Toolbar pane of the Excel Options dialog. The file created will be a UI file. Move this file to another computer, and then use the same button to import on the new computer.

Next Steps

Chapter 3 discusses a new security method called Protected mode.

03

Protected Mode

I like Protected mode.

I am sure that you regularly get files from other people in your company. They arrive via Outlook or you download them from an Internet site. I always worry that those people aren't smart enough to avoid getting viruses or that they actually hate me and would maliciously slip something bad into the Workbook_Open macro to cause problems with my computer.

In Excel 2003, if you opened a file with a macro, it stopped right away and made you choose whether to enable or disable macros. Have you ever thought about this question? How the heck should I know whether I should enable the macros when I haven't even had a chance to look around the worksheet (or examine the macro code, if you are comfortable with that)?

When you answered Enable Macros in Excel 2003, you were really taking a risk.

Now, any file that comes from a potentially dangerous location is open in the new Protected mode in Excel 2010. Here is the cool thing about Protected mode: You can look at the workbook. You can scroll through it or go to other worksheets. You can look at the macros. When you are convinced that the file is safe, you click a button and the workbook is available in regular mode.

This is brilliant. I get to actually look at the workbook, and while doing so it cannot harm my computer. I get to make an educated decision as to whether the workbook may prove harmful.

And, you know what? A lot of the time, you won't even have to leave Protected mode. You can look at the worksheet, see what you need to see, and close the workbook.

If you need to edit the workbook, use the button shown in Figure 3.1.

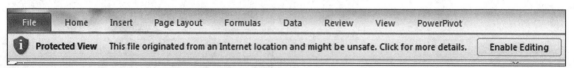

Figure 3.1 - *When you are convinced that the workbook is safe, enable editing.*

Which Workbooks Open in Protected Mode?

Basically, any file that did not originate on your computer can open in protected mode. Specifically, these workbooks open in Protected mode:

- Files that you download from the Internet
- Files in your temporary Internet folder
- Files that you open from Outlook
- **Files that fail validation**

If you want to adjust those settings, click the words in the information bar in Figure 3.1, and then choose Protected View Settings. You can turn off Protected mode for one or more of the situations shown in Figure 3.2.

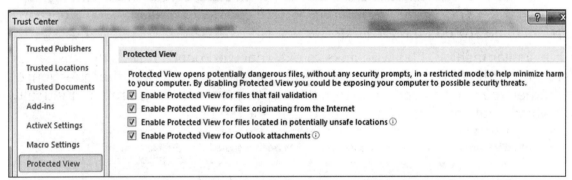

Figure 3.2 - When you are convinced that the workbook is safe, enable editing.

New Rules for Workbooks with Macros and Links

If you frequently use workbooks that have macros or external links, you will like the following improvements.

Normally, if you open a workbook that has macros, you must click the Enable button to use the macros (see Figure 3.3).

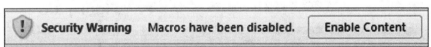

Figure 3.3 - *You have to explicitly enable macros.*

In Excel 2010, when you decide to enable macros for a workbook stored on a local drive, that workbook becomes a trusted document. When you open that same file again, you will not be asked to enable the macros.

This should allow you to keep the setting for Disable All Macros with Notification as shown in Figure 3.4. In Excel 2003, this setting was known as Medium Macro Security.

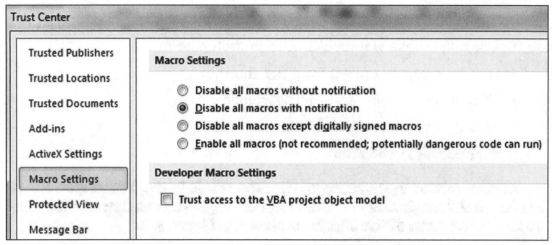

Figure 3.4 - *This setting now forces you to choose to enable macros once for each file stored on a local hard drive.*

In a similar fashion, files with links to external workbooks have a new behavior starting with Excel 2007. Instead of being forced to answer the question of whether you want to update external links, the external links are automatically disabled until someone clicks Enable Content (see Figure 3.5).

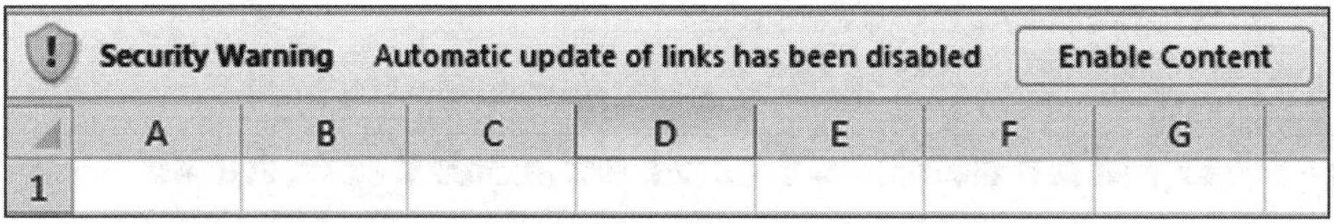

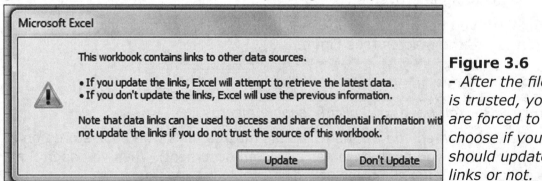

Figure 3.5 - *External links are initially disabled for each file until you click this button.*

In Excel 2010, when you choose to Enable Content the first time for a file stored on a local hard drive, you will no longer be asked to enable content. You will instead be taken directly to a dialog like the Excel 2003 dialog where you get to choose to enable links or not (see Figure 3.6).

Microsoft Excel

This workbook contains links to other data sources.

• If you update the links, Excel will attempt to retrieve the latest data.
• If you don't update the links, Excel will use the previous information.

Note that data links can be used to access and share confidential information with not update the links if you do not trust the source of this workbook.

Update   Don't Update

Figure 3.6 - *After the file is trusted, you are forced to choose if you should update links or not.*

You can control the startup prompt for one specific workbook by choosing Data, Edit Links to display the Edit Links dialog. In the lower-left corner, choose Startup Prompt. In the Startup Prompt dialog, you have the choices shown in Figure 3.7.

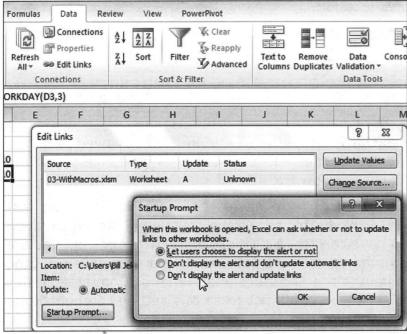

Figure 3.7 - *You can override the behavior for the trusted document.*

Untrusting a Document

If you decide to enable content on one workbook, and then discover that the workbook is doing something detrimental, you don't want those macros or links to automatically work the next time you open the workbook.

You cannot change the trusted status for one workbook. You can reset the trusted status for all workbooks. Choose File, Options, Trust Center, Trust Center Settings, Trusted Documents, Clear (see Figure 3.8)

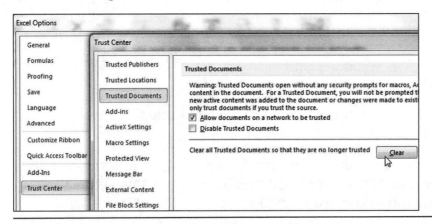

Figure 3.8 -
To untrust one document, you have to untrust them all.

Using Trusted Locations

If you want to trust your own workbooks but not trust the workbooks created by others, you can start saving safe workbooks in one specific folder and set up that folder as a trusted location.

In the Trust Center, use the Trusted Locations item in the left navigation to set up trusted locations.

Beware of Group Policy Settings Set by Your IT Department

If your employer licenses Office 2010, the people in IT are allowed to set up certain defaults in Group Policy. These defaults can be a bit dangerous in the hands of someone who doesn't know Excel.

Overzealous IT people might choose to never show you the message that external links have been blocked. This allows the completely insane situation where you think that you have correct calculations in the workbook but you are not getting the correct numbers from external links. If your IT people want the company to restate numbers to the Securities and Exchange Commission, this is a fine choice. Otherwise, they should not force this setting through Group Policy.

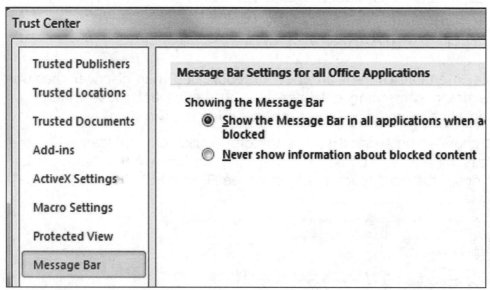

Figure 3.9 - *The IT department can force this insane option on everyone in the company.*

Another setting that you can control through Group Policy is to force certain file extensions to always open in Protected mode. To check this setting, use the File Block Settings tab in the Trust Center.

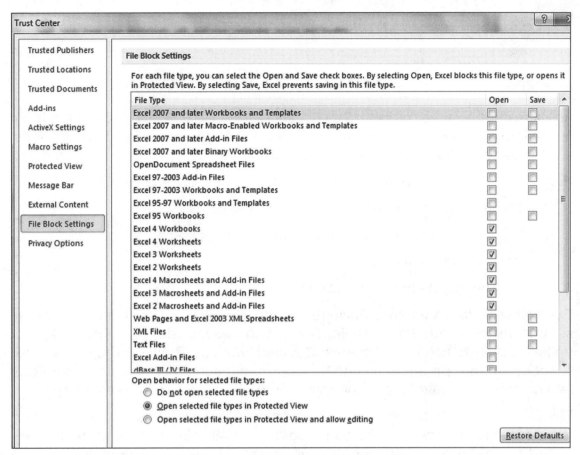

Figure 3.10 - *You or the IT person setting up Group Policy can control which file types open in Protected mode.*

Next Steps

In Chapter 4, you will learn the theory behind the new Backstage view.

Backstage View and the File Menu

As Microsoft prepared for Excel 2007, they started to think about commands as falling into two categories: In commands and Out commands. The In commands are things that you do when you are working in your document.

Here is a typical process when you are working in your document:

1. Decide on a change that you want to make.

2. Find the command in the Excel interface.

3. Perform the command.

4. See the results in the document.

Examples of In commands include changing a cell to bold or creating a summary report with a pivot table. The ribbon was introduced in Excel 2007 to make it easier to use In commands. Coupled with Live Preview, the ribbon was supposed to make it easier to find the command, and Live Preview would often let you see the results of the command before you selected the command.

The Out commands are typically things that you do with your workbook after you have finished creating the workbook. For example, you might need to e-mail the workbook to someone or save the workbook to a SharePoint library. The theory is that once you get to the point where you are using the Out commands, you no longer need to see the results in the document.

Because you no longer need to see the results in the document, Microsoft made the logical leap that you don't even need to see the document. This would allow them to use 100% of the screen real estate when you are invoking an Out command. Thus, the Backstage view was born.

When you open the File menu, Excel fills 100% of your screen with a three-panel Backstage view. The left portion of the screen works like a left navigation bar. The middle portion of the screen contains a variety of commands related to the choice from the left navigation bar, and the right portion of the screen provides a view of the additional settings related to the command.

Commands in the Left Navigation

The left navigation bar of the Backstage view contains six commands and six categories (see Figure 4.1). Four commands appear at the top of the navigation bar: Save, Save As, Open, and Close. Two other commands appear at the bottom of the navigation bar: Options and Exit. When you invoke one of these six commands, the Backstage view closes, and either the command is invoked or a dialog box opens.

If you are a fan of keyboard shortcuts, this means that Alt+F+S, Alt+F+A, Alt+F+O, Alt+F+C, and Alt+F+X will continue to do Save, Save As, Open, Close, and Exit.

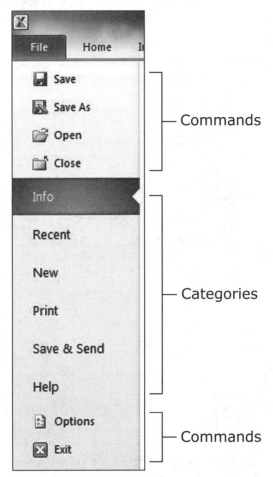

Figure 4.1 - *The left navigation bar offers six commands.*

Closing Backstage View

There are three X icons visible in Backstage view, but none of them close the Backstage view. This is the number one most frustrating thing about the Backstage view. When you click one of those three X icons, you will either close the current document or close Excel.

The proper way to close the Backstage view is to press the Esc key or to click any other ribbon tab with the mouse.

The Info Pane

When you have an Excel document open and you open the File menu, the Backstage view defaults to the Info category. In the Info category, the center pane offers tools for inspecting your document. The right pane offers properties about your document.

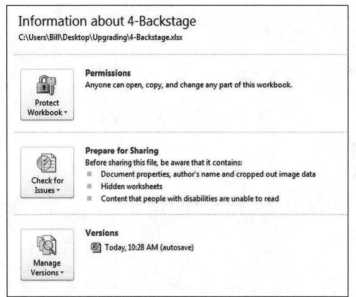

Figure 4.2 - *You can protect, inspect, and recover recent autosaved versions of the document using the center panel of the Backstage view.*

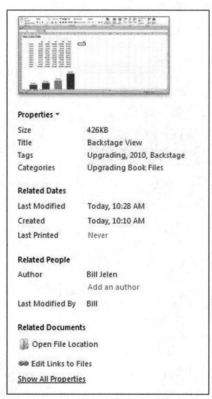

Figure 4.3 - *The right panel of the Backstage view offers information about the workbook.*

The right pane of the Info pane shows properties about your document. You can use the Properties drop-down to change the properties. If you get in the habit of adding tags to your documents, it will be easier to locate the documents in the future.

Changing Permissions

The Protect Workbook icon offers new tools such as Mark as Final. When you mark a document as final, other people will open the document in Read-Only mode. They can easily choose to allow editing, but it provides a bit of information to others that they should not be changing the document.

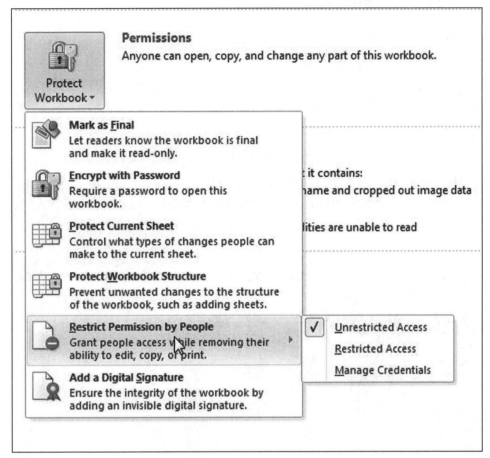

Figure 4.4 - *In addition to the typical protection, you can now mark a document as final or restrict who can print the document.*

Inspecting the Document

The Check for Issues drop-down offers three tools for checking the document. The Document Inspector will look for many types of hidden data in your workbook. The Accessibility Checker will check for issues that might make the workbook difficult to use by someone with special needs. The Compatibility Checker will check for features that you have used that will not work with earlier versions of Excel.

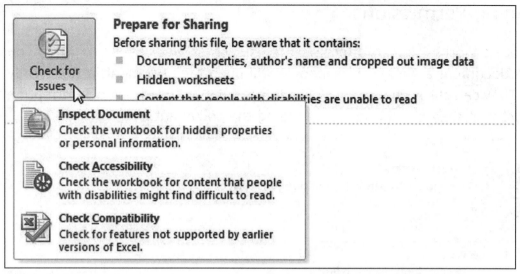

Figure 4.5 - *Three tools help you check for issues.*

Various gaffes have occurred. For example, hidden information in Office documents has been used to reveal lobbyists as the source of some government documents. The Document Inspector alerts you to potential hidden information in your document.

When you run the Document Inspector, you will see a list of all areas that might contain hidden information.

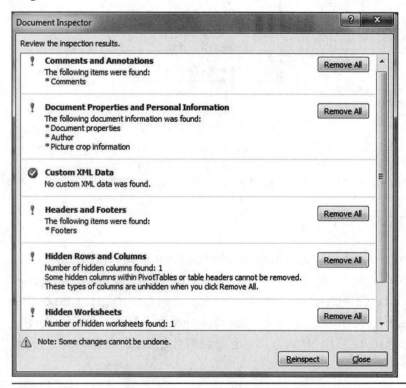

Figure 4.6 - *The Document Inspector alerts you to hidden information.*

When you run the inspector, Excel identifies potential sources of hidden data. The Document Inspector dialog offers to remove all the hidden content. However, removing hidden worksheets, rows, or columns could cause calculation problems with the remaining content. Therefore, take care when removing anything using this dialog.

> **Caution**: The Document Inspector finds many hidden bits of information, but it does not find all hidden information. It will not find cells formatted with a white font, cells formatted with the ;;; custom formatting code, and personal information in the Manage Names dialog box.

The Accessibility Checker will alert you to ways you can change a document to make it more accessible to people with special needs. Figure 4.7 shows some of the suggestions from the checker.

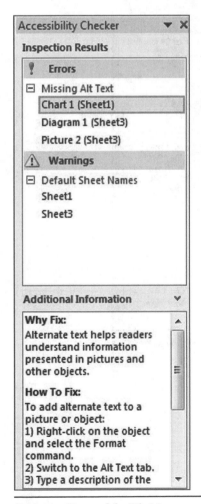

Figure 4.7 - *The new Accessibility Checker looks for ways to improve access by people with special needs.*

The Compatibility Checker checks your current document to see whether people using earlier versions of Excel will encounter any problems. In Excel 2010, you might have some issues that will cause problems in Excel 2007, such as using a new function name, sparklines, or one of the new icon sets.

The problems in the Compatibility Checker are broken down into two somewhat strangely named categories:

Minor Loss of Fidelity means that you might have used a color in the new Excel that wasn't available in Excel 2003. The worksheet is going to calculate just fine, but the appearance might be different. You don't have to worry a lot about these problems.

Significant Loss of Functionality means that there is going to be a calculation error. Either you've used a function that will evaluate as a #NAME? error or you've used more than 65,536 rows. You need to be concerned with these kinds of problems if you are sharing the workbook with people using legacy versions of Excel.

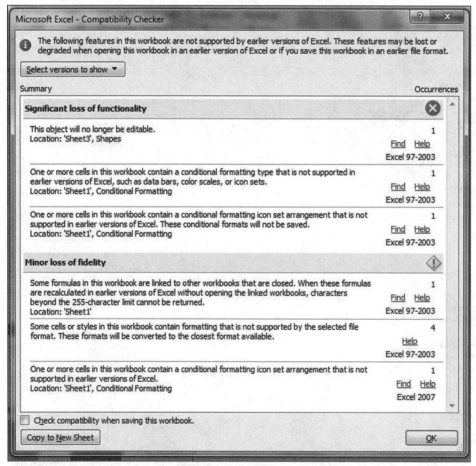

Figure 4.8 - *The Compatibility Checker lets you know which features won't render well in earlier versions of Excel.*

Rolling Back to the Last Autosaved Version

If you realize that you've caused problems in the past 5 minutes and those problems can't be fixed using 64 levels of Undo, you might want to roll back to the last autosaved version. Instead of crashing Excel to go back to the last autosave, you can click one of the autosaved versions in the Info pane to recover that version.

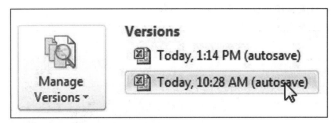

Figure 4.9 - *Click the autosaved version to recover that version.*

Excel will show you the autosaved version and give you a button to choose Recover.

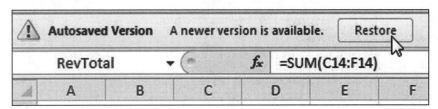

Figure 4.10 - *Recover an autosaved version.*

> **Note**: Also new in Excel 2010, if you close Excel and do not save the workbook, Excel will keep the last autosaved version available after Excel restarts. To find the unsaved version, open the File menu and choose Recent. At the bottom of the right side of the screen, choose Recover Unsaved Workbooks. This feature is not perfect. It has saved me a few times, but there have also been a few times when it clearly should have saved the workbook but didn't.

Accessing Recent Files

If you open the File menu when no workbook is open, you are automatically taken to the Recent category of the Backstage view.

A Recent Files list appears in the center of the Backstage view. Unlike the limit of 9 files in Excel 2003, you can show up to 50 files in the list. To increase the total to 50, choose Options from the File menu. Choose Advanced from the left navigation. Scroll down to the Display heading. The first option under Display is Show This Number of Recent Documents. You can increase this from 25 to 50. The only way to clear the list of recent documents in Excel 2010 is to set this back to 0, and then close the Excel options dialog.

New in Excel 2010, the right side of the screen shows the folders from which files were recently opened. I find myself using this feature a lot. I may be going through all the files in one particular folder. Although I have to open each file only once, I do have to open other files in that same folder.

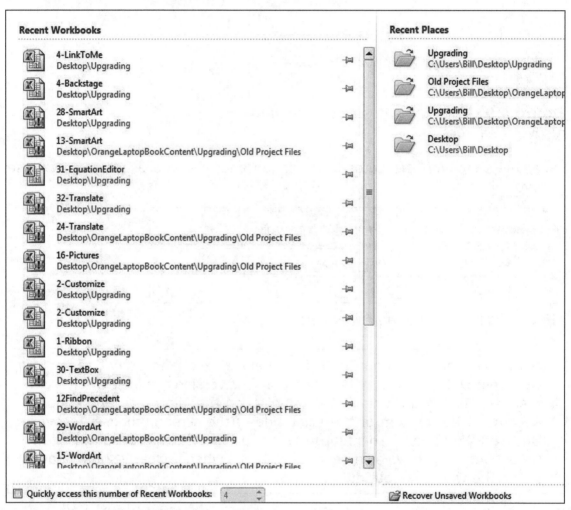

Figure 4.11 - *The Recent Files list now includes folders, too.*

A grayed-out thumbtack appears next to each file. If you click the thumbtack, you will pin the item to the list. This essentially makes the file or folder a favorite item that will always appear in the list.

If you were a fan of using Alt+F+2 to open the second most recent file, use the Quickly Access setting at the bottom of the center pane. This will include a selected number of recent files in the left navigation bar of the File menu, enabling the Alt+F+1 through Alt+F+9 shortcut keys.

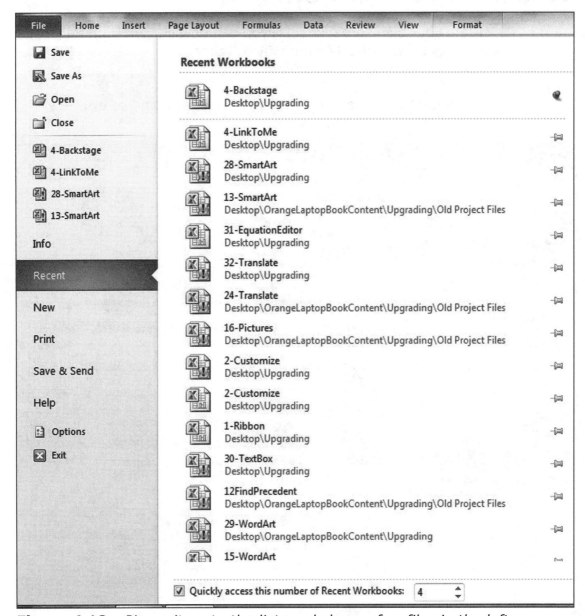

Figure 4.12 - *Pin an item to the list, and show a few files in the left navigation pane.*

When you have another workbook open and you open the File menu, it now requires an extra click to get to the Recent Files. If this extra click bothers you, use the drop-down at the right side of the Quick Access Toolbar. Choose Open Recent File from this drop-down and you will have one-click access to the Recent Files list.

Use the New Command to Download Cool Spreadsheets from Office Online

Rather than create your own spreadsheets, you can now choose from hundreds of free spreadsheets downloadable from Office Online.

From the File menu, choose New.

The Office.com Templates section lists Agendas, Budgets, and so on.

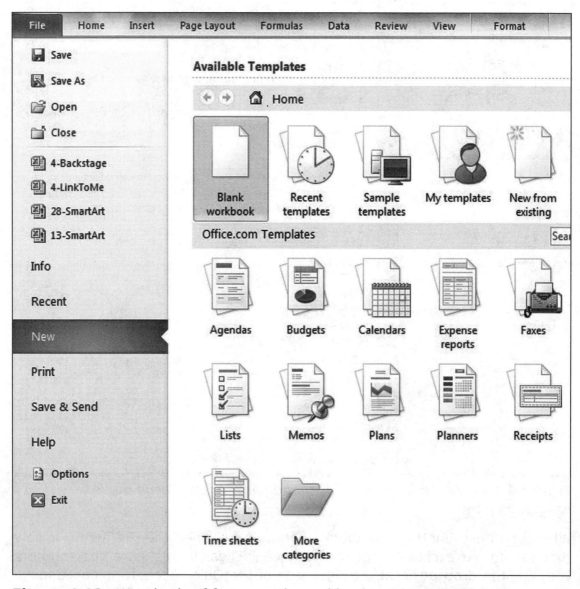

Figure 4.13 - *Hundreds of free sample workbooks are available in the New pane of Backstage view.*

Be sure to check out the More Categories folder, which contains spreadsheets for address books, games, ID cards, itineraries, quizzes, scorecards, tournament brackets, and more.

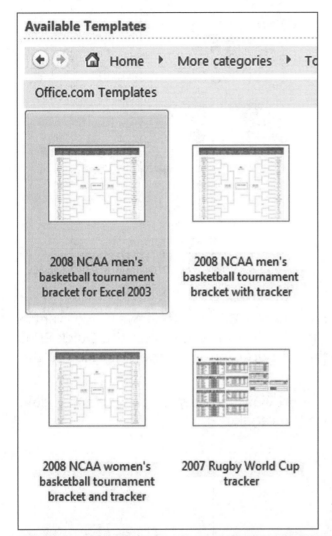

Available Templates

Home ▸ More categories ▸ To

Office.com Templates

2008 NCAA men's basketball tournament bracket for Excel 2003

2008 NCAA men's basketball tournament bracket with tracker

2008 NCAA women's basketball tournament bracket and tracker

2007 Rugby World Cup tracker

Figure 4.14 - *If they have NCAA tournament brackets, they probably have most business applications, too.*

Caution: You must be using a legal version of Microsoft Excel 2010 to download the templates from Office Online.

Printing, Page Setup, Print Properties, and Print Preview

The Print category of the Backstage view attempts to consolidate settings from numerous dialogs into a single place. The right side of the screen shows Print Preview. The center of the screen includes a place to choose the printer and access Printer Properties. A new set of drop-downs shows the current value of certain settings and provides a quick way to change those settings.

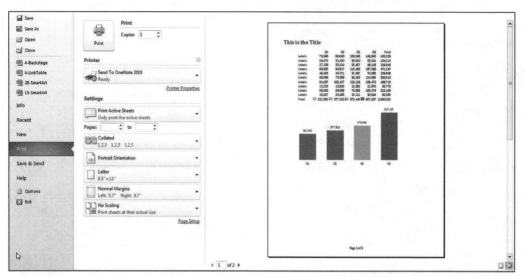

Figure 4.15 - *The Print pane in the Backstage view attempts to consolidate all printing settings in one place.*

Ctrl+P now takes you to the Print pane of the Backstage view. If you want a one-click way to print one copy of the current worksheet, add the Quick Print icon to the Quick Access Toolbar using the drop-down at the right side of the QAT.

Two icons at the lower right of the Print Preview enable you to zoom and toggle the margins just as you could do with the regular Print Preview.

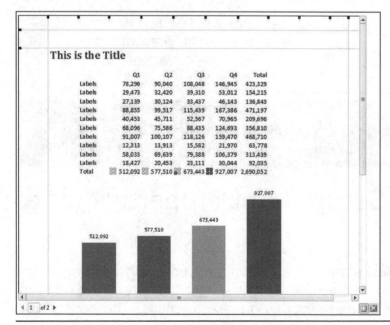

Figure 4.16 - *This Print Preview works well with documents in Portrait mode.*

There are a couple of times when you might want to access the old Print Preview. Documents in Landscape mode don't look that good in the new Backstage view. Also, if you are running a macro and you need the macro to pause while the Print Preview is shown, you will want to customize the ribbon or QAT to add the Print Preview Full Screen icon.

The center pane includes many print and page setup options. These drop-downs are a new type of control in Excel 2010 and show the current value of the setting rather than the name of the setting. Instead of opening the Orientation drop-down to see whether it is currently Portrait or Landscape, the drop-down shows the current setting. This way, you have to open only those drop-downs that require changes.

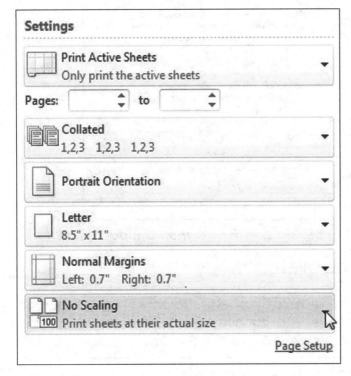

Figure 4.17 - The center portion of the Backstage view's print commands includes a number of drop-downs that affect the printer and page setup.

Using Save & Send to E-Mail or Share the Document

The Save & Send category contains a number of commands:

- You can send the workbook as an attachment to an e-mail.
- You can save the workbook as a PDF file.
- You can save the workbook to a SharePoint library.
- You can save the workbook to your Windows Live SkyDrive.

- You can change the file type, such as switching from XLSX to XLSM or XLSB.

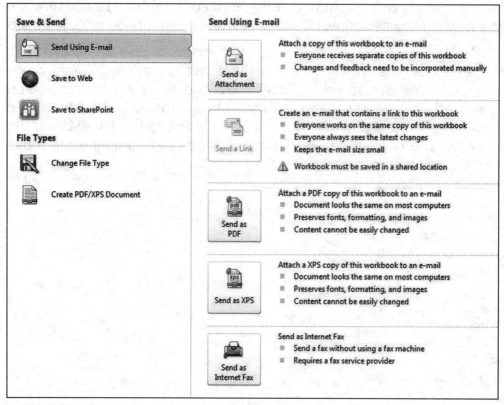

Figure 4.18 - *Use Save & Send to create a PDF or e-mail the document.*

Saving a Workbook to the Web

The SkyDrive service provides you with 25GB of storage on a Microsoft server. Set up an account at Windows Live and choose to activate your SkyDrive. You can then use Save As to save workbooks to the SkyDrive. This works out

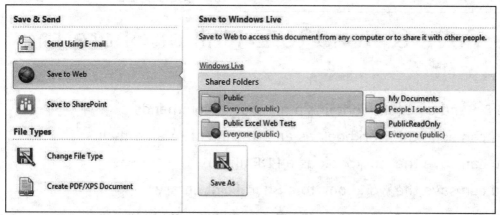

Figure 4.19 - *You can save your workbooks to the Web.*

great when you don't have a USB flash drive available or when you want to share a document with coworkers who don't have access to the network. In the SkyDrive, you can set up a folder as private, public, or shared with certain people. By saving your workbook in the appropriate folder, you can control who can see the workbook.

> **Note**: The new Excel Web Application will let people edit your workbook in a browser. See Chapter 33 for more details.

Working with PDF Files

Excel 2010 will let you save your workbooks as PDF files. Use the Save & Send category to save as a PDF.

Think of Saving as PDF as if you are printing the workbook to a PDF file. In the Publish as PDF or XPS dialog, you can click the Options button to control if you want the selection, active sheets, or entire workbook sent to the PDF file.

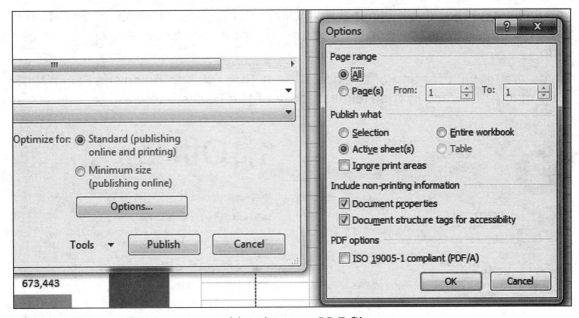

Figure 4.20 – *Print your workbooks to a PDF file, without buying Adobe Acrobat.*

Let's face it. People send you PDF files when they don't want you screwing around with their data. But, let's be truthful here: You need to screw around with that data.

If you have ever tried to select data from a PDF file, copy it, and paste it to Excel, you know that there are three basic kinds of PDF files:

➢ Files that paste amazingly well to Excel

> Files that paste a table into a single column

> Files where the text and numbers have been converted to an image so that you can't copy and paste to Excel

You would think that a PDF file created by Microsoft Excel would automatically create a file that would round-trip beautifully to Excel. Unfortunately, they use the second type of file that will not paste nicely back into Excel. This isn't as evil as converting everything to images, but it is almost as bad.

If you have to regularly take data from PDF files to Excel or Word, I highly recommend a product called Able2Extract from InvestInTech. You can get a free 30-day trial to try it out. The standard version handles either of the first two types of PDF files. The deluxe version can also handle PDF files where everything has been converted to an image. For more details, see www.mrexcel.com/tip107.shtml.

Using Help in Excel 2010

You will notice that there is not a Help tab in the Excel 2010 ribbon. You should use the question mark icon at the top-right of the Excel screen to access Help.

If you are looking for any of the other items that used to be on the Excel 2003 Help menu, they are in the Help category of the Backstage view.

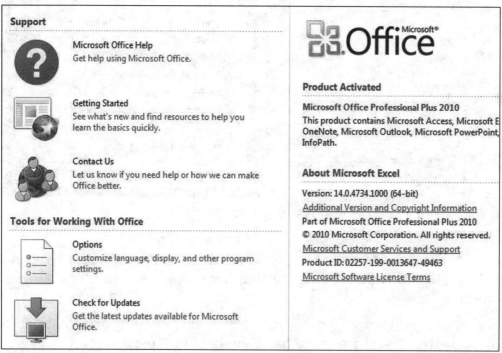

Figure 4.21 - *Contact Us, About, and other Help-related items are found here in Backstage view.*

Excel Options and the Trust Center

The old Excel 2003 dialog box for Excel Options was incredibly packed with 13 different tabs. The Excel 2010 dialog box contains only 10 categories in the left navigation bar, but Microsoft achieved this trick by making the Advanced category contain 13 different sections. The result is that the Advanced category has a long vertical scrollbar.

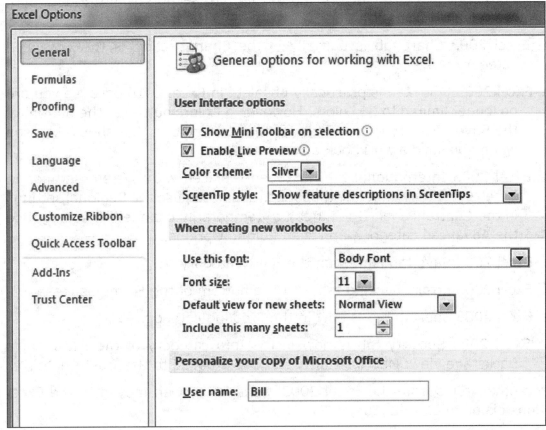

Figure 4.22 - *The Excel 2010 Options dialog contains 10 categories down the left navigation bar.*

Rather than cover all the various Excel options in this book, the following list provides a mapping from the old Excel Options dialog to the new Excel Options dialog. After that, you can read about some of the interesting new options:

The Excel 2003 View tab is now mostly found in the Advanced tab. Scroll down to the sixth through eight sections of the Advanced tab. One improvement is that Excel 2010 is clear whether the change affects only the worksheet, the entire workbook, or all workbooks.

The Excel 2003 Calculation tab is now found in the Formulas category.

The Excel 2003 Edit tab is at the top of the Advanced category.

The Excel 2003 General tab does not correspond to the Excel 2010 General category. In Excel 2007, the General category was called Popular. The Default File Location is in the Save category. The User Name is in General. Most of the other settings are spread throughout the Advanced tab.

The Excel 2003 Transition tab is at the bottom of the Advanced Category.

The Excel 2003 Custom Lists tab had been in the Popular category in Excel 2007, but was strangely moved to the third section from the bottom of the Advanced category.

The Excel 2003 Chart tab is partially in the Chart section of the Advanced category.

The Excel 2003 Color tab is practically obsolete in Excel 2010 because you are no longer limited to 56 colors. However, a Colors button at the bottom of the Save category lets you specify the color palette that should be used when you save a workbook as an XLS file.

The Excel 2003 International tab has been replaced with system settings in Excel 2010. To change the thousands separator, use the Regional settings in the Control Panel. If you need to temporarily change the setting, use the Advanced category, and then Editing Options.

The Excel 2003 Save tab is now on the Save category.

The Excel 2003 Error Checking tab is at the bottom of the Formulas category.

The Excel 2003 Spelling tab is now in the Proofing category.

The Excel 2003 Security tab is now in the Info category of the File menu's Backstage view. Macro security has been moved to the Trust Center.

Some other items from the Excel 2003 menu have been moved to the Excel Options dialog in Excel 2010:

The old Tools, Customize choices are reduced and found in the Customize Ribbon and Quick Access Toolbar categories of Excel Options.

The old Tools, AutoCorrect choices are now in the Proofing category of Excel Options.

The old Tools, Add-Ins dialog can now be accessed by using the Add-Ins category of Excel Options. Use the Manage drop-down at the bottom to choose Excel Add-Ins, and then choose Go. Alternatively, if you have chosen to show the Developer tab, you can access add-Ins from that tab.

Tools, Macro, Security is now in File, Options, Trust Center, Trust Center Settings, Macro Settings.

Some New Options in Excel 2010

Here are a few of the new options added since Excel 2003:

If you have a slower PC, you can turn off Live Preview or the Mini Toolbar by using check boxes in the General category.

There are three color schemes for Excel 2010: silver, black, and blue. Change the scheme on the General tab.

Chapter 6 covers the new Paste Options menu. If you hate this, you can turn it off using the Cut, Copy, and Paste section of the Advanced category.

With the grid size of 17 billion cells rather than 16 million, there is the chance that you will invoke a command that is going to take a long time. The Editing Options section of the Advanced category has a setting where you can be warned if a command will change more than 33.5 million cells. You can change the number of cells before you are warned, however, even while the spin button is showing numbers in thousands.

Accessing the Trust Center

The Trust Center category in Excel Options leads to a button where you can choose Trust Center Settings. That button leads to a new dialog with 11 additional categories.

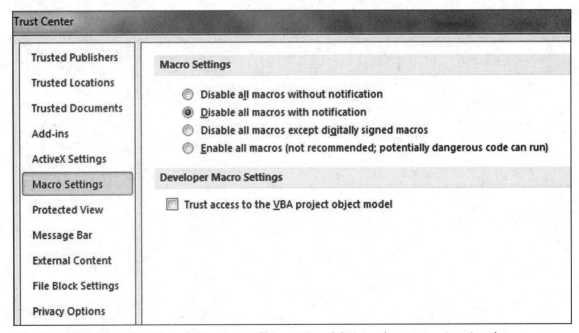

Figure 4.23 - *The Trust Center offers 10 additional categories in the left navigation bar.*

Items that you can control in the Trust Center include the following:

Trusted Locations are folders on your local hard drive where you are the only author of content. Excel will not nag you about macros or external links in these workbooks.

Macro Settings offer the same four choices as in Excel 2003 but with completely new words. If you were a fan of the Medium setting in Excel 2003, this is now Disable All Macros with Notification.

Protected mode is covered in Chapter 3. You can control which types of documents open in Protected view using the Protected View category of the Trust Center. Items in the File Block section might also be forced into Protected view.

File Block Settings is new in Excel 2010. You can prevent people from opening or saving certain types of documents.

Next Steps

Chapter 5 talks about the big grid in Excel 2010.

05

Unlocking the Big Grid

Excel 2010 offers more rows and columns than Excel 2003.

That is an understatement.

Table 5.1 shows the magnitude of the increase, but I am not sure that numbers do it justice.

Table 5.1

	Excel 97-2003	Excel 2010	% Change
Rows	65,536	1,048,576	1,500%
Columns	256	16,384	25,500%
Cells	16.7 Million	17.2 Billion	102,300%

In case you are wondering how Microsoft comes up with numbers such as 16,384 and 1,048,576, these are powers of 2. There are 2^20 rows and 2^14 columns.

In Excel 2003, you could not have daily dates for 1 year stretching across the columns. In the new version, you can show weekdays for 46 years before you run into the last column (XFD).

This chart helps you visualize how large the new grid is. The green area is the size of one worksheet in the new Excel. The tiny yellow box in the lower-left corner is the size of one worksheet in the old Excel.

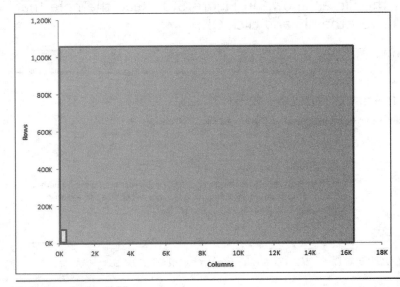

Figure 5.1 - *The yellow is the size of the old Excel grid. The green is the size of the new Excel grid.*

Unlocking the Big Grid

I was excited to see this new, larger grid in Excel 2010. The first thing that I did was open one of my old workbooks. After pressing Ctrl+Down-Arrow key and Ctrl+Right-Arrow key, I was disappointed to see that I was only at cell IV65536. Here, I am in Excel 2010, yet the grid only has the old limits!

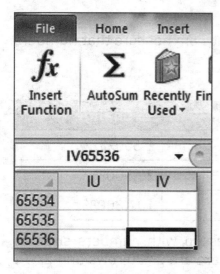

Figure 5.2 - *What gives? Excel 2010 is showing only 65,536 rows?*

This problem happens when you open an Excel 2003 workbook in Excel 2010. It is opened in Compatibility mode. When you are in Compatibility mode, you cannot access any rows beyond 65,536 or columns beyond IV.

To exit Compatibility mode, follow these steps:

1. Open the File menu to access the Backstage view. You should see the Info category.

2. Choose to Convert the file as shown in Figure 5.3. Read the note that you are about to convert the file and click OK.

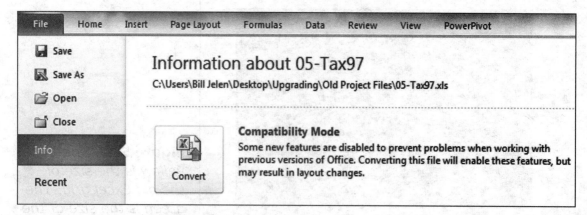

Figure 5.3 - *Choose to convert the file to unlock the extra rows.*

3. Read the note that the conversion was successful. To access more rows, you need to close and reopen the workbook. Click Yes to do this.

Caution: When you perform the preceding steps, Excel will erase the XLS version of the file and replace it with an Excel 2010 version of the file. If you prefer to keep both versions, you would instead use File, Save As to save an Excel 2010 version of the file.

After converting the file, you can see cell XFD1048576:

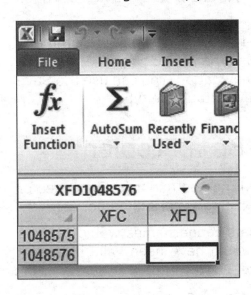

Figure 5.4 - *The new final cell in the big grid is XFD1048576.*

Excel 2010 Supports Three New File Types

The XLS file type has been the standard file type for more than 20 years. The file specification changed over time, but Microsoft had kept the same file extension. This actually created a bit of confusion because XLS files created in Excel 97 could not be opened in Excel 95.

To accommodate 1.1 million rows, the file type was going to have to change. Microsoft decided to change the file extension so that everyone could tell whether they had a new or old file type.

The old XLS file type was known as a binary file. If you look at an XLS file with a text editor such as Notepad, it is difficult to make out any information inside the file. One problem with XLSB files is that if a few bits become corrupted, it can be difficult to open the file and you potentially lose your whole worksheet.

Excel 2010 does continue to support a binary file type with the .xlsb extension.

However, the new fascinating file type is XLSM. This file type consists of a series of XML text files zipped into a single package. The .zip extension is renamed from .zip to .xlsm. This results in a file that is small and less prone to corruption. In Windows Explorer, try renaming your file to add a .zip extension to the end. You can now use WinZip or any other zip utility to look at the files inside your ZIP file.

Every XLS file had the potential of including macros. The XLSB and XLSM file types have the ability to store macros. If you are a person who would never turn on the macro recorder to record a small utility macro, or if you work with a bunch of paranoid coworkers who think that everyone is out to get them, you might be interested in the XLSX file type. This is the same as XLSM, but all macros are stripped out of the file.

By default, Excel 2010 saves files as the macro-free XLSX file type. I recommend changing to the XLSM file type as the default file type. If you go to File, Options, and then choose the Save category in the left navigation, you can use the Save Files in This Format drop-down to choose a new default file type.

Named Ranges That Can Be a Problem

It is possible to name a range in Excel. Useful names might be Expenses or TaxRate. A range name cannot duplicate an existing Excel cell name.

A lot of three-letter words that used to be safe range names would now be a problem. For example, Tax97 or ROI2011 would have been valid names in Excel 2003, but are now cell addresses in Excel 2010.

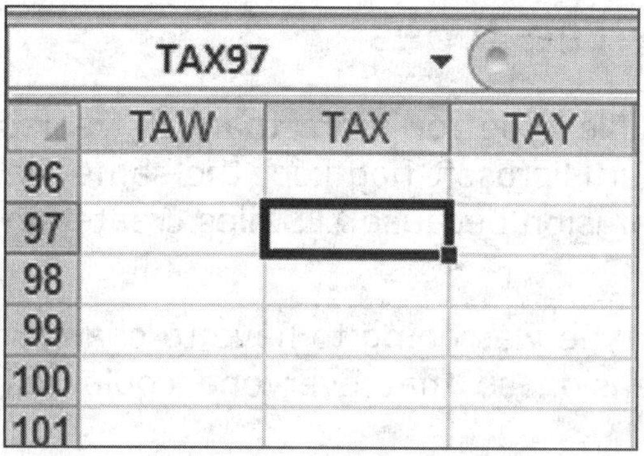

Figure 5.5 - *In Excel 2010, Tax97 is a cell address.*

If you attempt to convert an existing file that uses a name such as Tax97, Excel will alert you and convert the range name to _Tax97.

Although all references in formulas will automatically update, you should check any VBA macros or INDIRECT functions to see whether they explicitly referenced the old range names.

Who Needs This Many Cells?

After using the big grid for 5 years, I've never had an occasion to use 17 billion cells. However, I have run into datasets that filled A1:S675000. I've also run into CSV files from QuickBooks that had more than 500 columns.

So, while you may never need 17 billion cells, you will sometimes need more than 65K rows or 256 columns. Microsoft realizes that changing the grid size causes a change in the file format. The new grid size is designed to get you through the next several versions of Excel.

If you happen to need more rows than the 1.1 million, check out the new PowerPivot add-in for Excel 2010. See Chapter 20 for details about using PowerPivot.

Next Steps

Chapter 6 introduces the new Excel 2010 Paste Options menu.

■

06

A Faster Way to Paste Special

The new Paste Options menu could be one of the biggest time savers in your hour-to-hour use of Excel.

Microsoft took a look at data to see which command is the most frequently undone command. It turns out that it was Paste.

Yes, Paste seems simple enough, but there are myriad Paste Special options, and many people were confused about which elements of the copied cells would get pasted.

Even if you are an absolute pro at using Paste Special, you are going to love the new Paste Options menu because it will let you perform tasks that you perform several times an hour with far fewer keystrokes.

Ctrl+C, Ctrl+V, Ctrl, V Is Your New Favorite Shortcut

Do a normal copy and paste. As in Excel 2003, a little Clipboard appears onscreen. This Clipboard has been in Excel for a while, but because I had to grab the mouse to open the drop-down, I never used that menu.

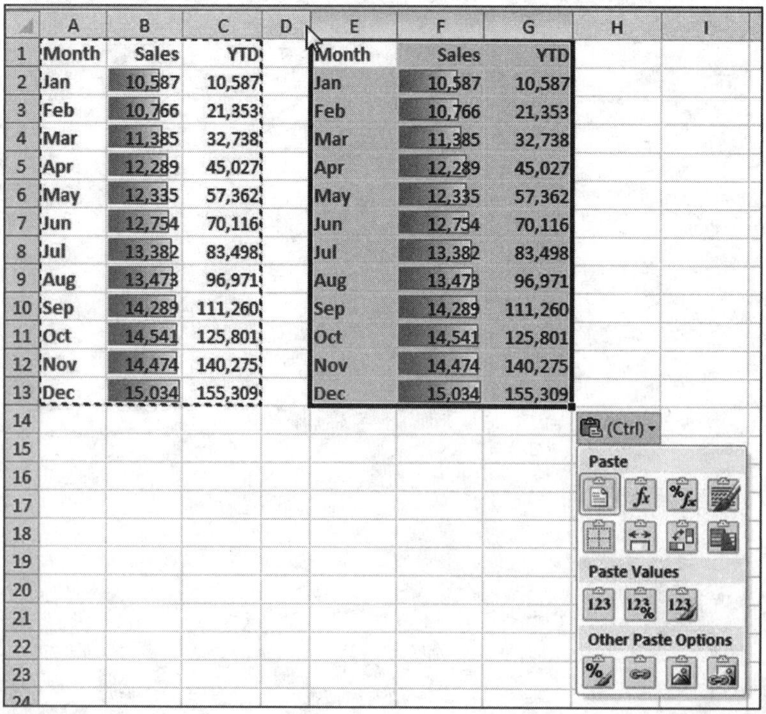

Figure 6.1 - *Press Ctrl after doing a paste to open the Paste Options menu.*

In Excel 2010, the little Clipboard icon also indicates that you can open the drop-down by pressing the Ctrl key one more time.

When you press Ctrl again, you see a series of icons that let you change the type of paste that you just performed. For example, you could click the first icon in the third row to paste as values.

Furthermore, if you hover over that icon, you will learn that pressing V is the shortcut key for pasting values.

So, if you are a keyboard person, you might find yourself doing the following:

> Ctrl+C to copy
>
> Ctrl+V to paste
>
> Ctrl to open the Paste Options dialog
>
> V to change the paste to values

For keyboard-centric people, this is a pretty fast way to convert formulas to values.

The Right-Click Context Menu Includes the Same Icons

If you usually paste by using the right-click menu, you will see that the right-click menu includes icons for Paste, Paste Values, Paste Formulas, Transpose, Paste Formats, and Create Links.

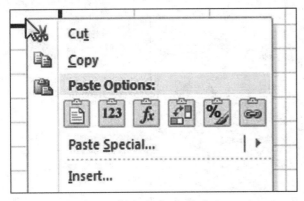

Figure 6.2 - *The right-click menu offers 6 options.*

When you hover over one of those icons, the rest of the context menu disappears so that you can see the effect of the paste in Live Preview. In Figure 6.3, hovering over the Transpose icon shows you that transpose would turn the pasted data on its side.

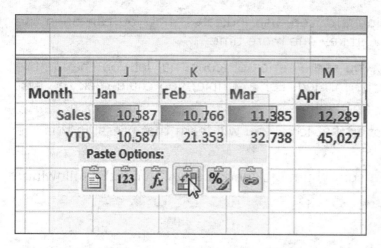

Figure 6.3 - *When you use an option, the menu is hidden so that you can see the Live Preview of the paste.*

If you hover over Paste Special in the right-click menu, the menu will disappear and you have access to all 15 icons. In Figure 6.4, you might be able to see the outline of the temporarily hidden right-click menu in columns I through L and also the outline of the temporarily hidden Mini Toolbar above the column letters for J through M.

Month	Sales	YTD
Jan	10,587	10,587
Feb	10,766	21,353
Mar	11,385	32,738
Apr	12,289	45,027
May	12,335	57,362
Jun	12,754	70,116
Jul	13,382	83,498
Aug	13,473	96,971
Sep	14,289	111,260
Oct	14,541	125,801
Nov	14,474	140,275
Dec	15,034	155,309

Paste

Paste Values

Other Paste Options

Paste Special...

Figure 6.4 - *If you choose Paste Special from the right-click menu, the menu disappears so that you can see Live Preview.*

If you regularly use the Paste icon in the Home tab, the drop-down at the bottom of the tab now leads to a menu with the 15 icons. There are still some options in Paste Special that are not available in the icons. You can access those commands by using the Paste Special menu item at the bottom of Figure 6.5.

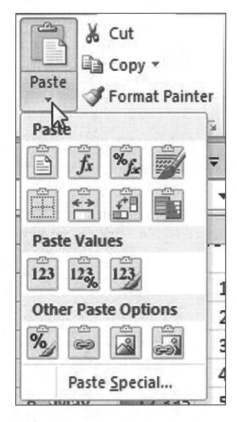

Figure 6.5 - *The Paste drop-down in the Home tab offers the new icons.*

Fast Keyboard Access to Paste Commands

Many times each day, I convert formulas to values by using Ctrl+C, Alt+E+S+V, Enter.

Sometimes, I need to copy values and formats to a new place. In the new place, I have to do Alt+E+S+V, Enter, Alt+E+S+T+Enter.

As mentioned previously, you can use Ctrl+C, Ctrl+V, Ctrl, V to change formulas to value.

To paste values and formats, you now use the new Ctrl+V, Ctrl, E to paste values and number formatting.

There might be an even faster way.

If you have a newer computer, you might have a rarely-used key on your keyboard. Usually located between the right Alt and Ctrl keys, this Application key shows a mouse pointer over a menu. This key opens the right-click menu.

To convert a range of formulas to values, I have now started using this shortcut sequence:

> Ctrl+C to copy

> Application+V to convert to values

If you need to paste values and formats, the Application+E keystroke combination will do it.

Decoding the Tiny Icons

The one complaint that I have heard about the Paste Options menu is that it is tough to figure out what the icons mean.

Photocopy Figure 6.6 and hang it up by your desk. I used a similar image next to my computer for the first month to remind myself to start using the new shortcuts.

Icon	Key & Action
	P - Paste
	F - Formulas
	O - Formulas & Formatting
	K - Keep Source Formatting
	B - No Borders
	W - Column Widths
	T - Transpose
	G - Merge Conditional Format
	V - Values
	A - Values & Number Format
	E - Values & Formatting
	R - Formatting
	N - Paste Link
	U - Static Picture
	I - Linked Picture

Figure 6.6 - *Shortcut keys and meanings for each icon in the Paste Options menu.*

The following list describes each of the 15 items in the Paste Options menu:

Paste is a regular paste. You get all formulas, borders, and formats.

Formulas will paste only the formulas and will not disturb the existing formatting.

Formulas & Formatting will paste the formulas and any numeric formatting. Borders, comments, and fills are not pasted.

Keep Source Formatting is similar to a regular paste.

No Borders pastes everything except for the borders.

Column Widths duplicates the column widths from the source range.

Transpose turns row-wise data into column-wise data and vice versa.

Merge Conditional Format is for the few people who liked a default behavior in Excel 2007. Conditional formatting now consists of Icon Sets, Data Bars, 2-Color Color Scales, 3-Color Color Scales, and the traditional conditional formatting rules. Something new in Excel 2007 is the ability to apply two different conditional formats to the same range. For example, you might combine an icon set and a traditional formatting rule. That makes sense. Unfortunately, a lot of people would inadvertently combine a two-color color scale and a three-color color scale, leading to a lot of brownish-colored cells. In Excel 2010, when you paste, the conditional formats in the source range will overwrite the conditional formats in the target range. If you know what you are doing and you want the conditional formatting from both the source and target range to stay, use this icon. Note that you won't see this icon unless the source range had conditional formatting.

Values eliminates the formulas and paste their current values.

Values & Number Format converts formulas to values, but brings along any numeric formatting applied to the source range.

Values & Formatting converts formulas to values, but brings along the cell formatting, too.

Formatting pastes only the formats. If you have a report nicely formatted for January and you want to build a blank report for February, you might want to paste the formats.

Paste Link will create formulas in the pasted range that point back to the source range.

Static Picture pastes a picture of the copied range. This picture might include cells, SmartArt, charts, and so on. When the original range changes, this picture does not change.

Linked Picture pastes a live picture of the copied range. When something changes in the original range, the picture reflects that change. This used to be called the Camera Tool in Excel 2003.

Next Steps

Chapter 7 talks about the new Page Layout view, a way to view your workbook while seeing margins, headers, and footers.

■

0 7

Page Layout View

Before you print your document, you will often need to adjust margins, heading rows, and so on. The new page layout tools make the job easy.

Legacy versions of Excel offered two views, either Normal or Page Break Preview. Many people hated the slow Page Break Preview. Excel 2010 includes a better view called Page Layout view. You will find that Page Layout view makes it easy to visualize the printed page as you are adjusting margins, headers, and footers. When you are in Page Layout view...

Excel draws in the margins of each page as white space.

You can edit headers and footers.

You can continue to work in your worksheet, adding new data, new rows, and new columns.

Look for a row of three icons in the lower-right side of your Excel window. The three icons are for Normal, Page Layout view, and Page Break Preview, as shown in Figure 7.1.

Figure 7.1 - *Whereas most commands are on the ribbon, these three view icons are in the lower-right of the screen as well as on the View tab.*

To the right of the icons, a zoom slider allows you to adjust the zoom from 10% to 400%.

Figure 7.2 shows a worksheet at 50% zoom in Page Layout view.

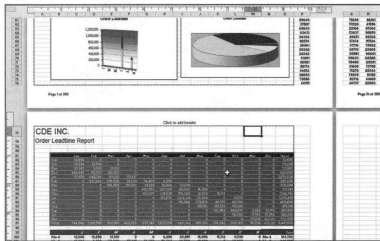

Figure 7.2 - *See margins and headings in Page Layout view.*

Adjusting Page Layout

Many popular page layout settings are now in a series of drop-downs on the Page Layout tab. Adjustments made in this tab while you are in Page Layout view will appear in the worksheet.

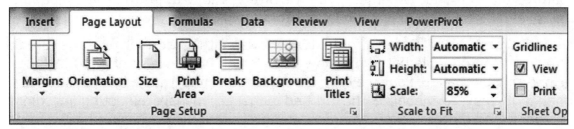

Figure 7.3 - *Many popular settings from the old Page Setup dialog are on the Page Layout tab.*

Adjusting Margins

You have many choices for adjusting margins. I find that I still use the old Excel 2003 method, with one slight adjustment.

A ruler appears at the top and left side of Page Layout view. The margins appear as a gray section at the end of each ruler. You can drag the edge of the gray background to adjust the margins.

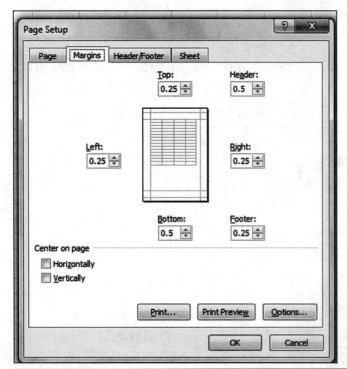

Figure 7.4 - *You can have complete control over margins in the legacy Page Setup dialog.*

The Margins drop-down on the Page Layout tab offers predefined margins of Normal, Wide, and Narrow. If you are not a person who has to be in complete control, you can choose one of these settings.

The last item in the Margins drop-down is Custom Margins. Choose this setting to access the old Excel 2003 Page Layout dialog box (see Figure 7.4), where you can explicitly set the margin, header, and footer location.

A small diagonal arrow in the lower-right corner of the Page Setup group of the ribbon will take you back to the Excel 2003 Page Layout dialog.

Out of habit, I always set my top, left, and right margins to 0.25". My bottom margin is at 0.5", and my footer location is at 0.25". I don't use headers, so I never set that location. Here is the beautiful thing about Excel 2010: Once you use the Custom Margins dialog to set some custom margins, the last custom setting that you used will always be available at the first item in the Margins drop-down (see Figure 7.5).

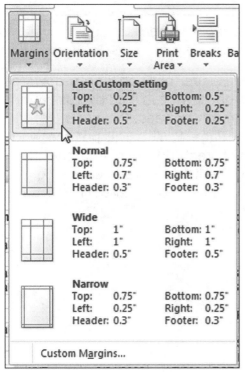

Figure 7.5 - *Once you choose your favorite margins, they will be available in the dropdown.*

This means that you can set you favorite margins once, and then return to those by choosing the Last Custom Setting choice from the Margins drop-down.

Controlling Headers and Footers

In Page Layout view, words appear in the top and bottom margin encouraging you to Click to Add Header or Click to Add Footer. There are actually three click

---

zones for headers and three click zones for footers. In Figure 7.6, a click would edit the left footer.

Figure 7.6 - *Click to add a left footer.*

When you click in a header or footer zone, a new Header & Footer Tools Design tab appears, as shown in Figure 7.7.

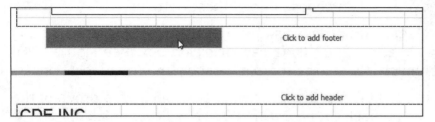

Figure 7.7 - *This contextual ribbon tab appears only when you are editing a header or footer in Page Layout view.*

You can choose from built-in text by using the Header or Footer drop-down at the left side of the ribbon. Be aware that this drop-down can lead to frustration. Some of these entries include values separated by commas. For example, the fifth item in the list is Confidential, 1/8/2010, Page 1. This will put the word *Confidential* in the left footer, the date in the center footer, and the page number in the right footer. The second item in the list is Page 1. Choosing this item will always put the page number in the center footer, even if you have clicked into the left or right footer.

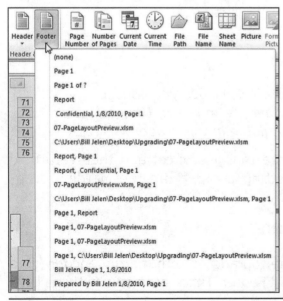

Figure 7.8 - *Beware the items in this list with a single value. They will always appear in the center footer or header.*

To avoid the frustration of where data will appear in the header and footer, you can design your own footer by using the Header & Footer Elements icons.

Excel 2010 enables you to have a different header on odd/even pages, or a different header on the first page. To use these settings, you must be in Page Layout view and click in a header or footer zone. You can then use the Header & Footer Tools Design tab to indicate that the document should have a different header on the first page or on odd/even pages.

> **Tip**: If you are a fan of Scale to Fit, you might notice that your heading font changes size from worksheet to worksheet. If Sheet 1 contains 5 columns, it might print at 100% and your header will be 10 point font. If Sheet 2 contains 12 columns, it might print at 75%, and your header will also scale down to 7 or 8 point font. If you are stapling all of these sheets together into a single report, it looks really strange to have the header font change from page to page. In Excel 2010, uncheck the Scale with Document check box (see Figure 7.9) to stop the headers from resizing.

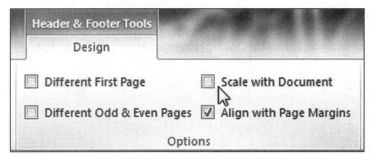

Figure 7.9 - *Force the header font to be the same for all worksheets by unchecking this box.*

When you click outside of the header or footer area, Excel returns you to the Page Layout tab.

Inserting a Watermark Using a Picture Header

The center header is the gateway to adding a semitransparent watermark image that will print behind your document.

To effectively use this trick, you need to create a graphic that has a fair amount of white space at the top of the picture. Figure 7.10 shows a DRAFT stamp at the bottom of some white space. You can create this graphic in Photoshop or any photo-editing tool. I actually created this in Excel as WordArt. On the Page

Layout tab, uncheck view Gridlines to create the white space. I then used the Snag-It utility from TechSmith to capture a region of the screen.

Figure 7.10 - *To get a watermark in the center of the page, include some whitespace at the top of the image.*

Follow these steps to create the watermark:

1. Select the Page Layout view icon in the bottom-right corner of the Excel window.

2. Click in the Center Header zone at the top of the worksheet. Excel displays the Header & Footer Tools Design tab.

3. Click the Picture icon on the Header & Footer Tools tab. Browse for and select your picture. Excel inserts &[Picture] in the header.

4. If your graphic is too large or small, use the Format Picture icon. You can adjust the size, but not the location. If you need more or less white space, you will have to go back to Photoshop to change the graphic.

Figure 7.11 shows the resulting graphic drawn in behind your numbers.

ShipDate	Customer	Quantity	Revenue	COGS
1/1/2004	VWX GMBH	1000	22810	10220
1/2/2004	MNO COR	100	2257	984
1/2/2004	MNO COR	500	10245	4235
1/3/2004	HIJ GMBH	500	11240	5110
1/4/2004	HIJ GMBH	400	9204	4088
1/4/2004	FGH, CO	800	18552	7872
1/4/2004	RST PTY L	400	9152	4088
1/5/2004	CDE INC.	400	6860	3388
1/7/2004	RST S.A.	400	8456	3388
1/7/2004	LMN LTD.	1000	21730	9840
1/7/2004	RST PTY L	600	13806	6132
1/9/2004	RST S.A.	800	16416	6776
1/9/2004	XYZ GMBH	900	21015	9198
1/10/2004	HIJ GMBH	900	21465	9198
1/10/2004	RST INC	900	21438	9198
1/12/2004	HIJ GMBH	400	9144	4088
1/12/2004	CDE INC.	300	6267	2541
1/14/2004	OPQ, INC.	100	1740	847
1/14/2004	OPQ, INC.	100	2401	1022
1/14/2004	RST INC.	1000	19110	8470
1/15/2004	MNO COR	500	9345	4235
1/16/2004	WXY, CO	600	11628	5082
1/16/2004	RST INC.	900	21888	9198
1/17/2004	LMN INC.	300	5961	2952
1/19/2004	MNO COR	100	2042	984

Figure 7.11 - *The header picture appears behind your document.*

What Happened to Print Preview?

Print Preview has been moved to the Print category in the File menu's Backstage view. That new Print Preview is fine for portrait documents, but it is not ideal for landscape documents.

You can still get to the old Print Preview window, although you will have to add a new icon to the ribbon or the Quick Access Toolbar (QAT). Right-click the QAT and choose Customize Quick Access Toolbar. In the top-left drop-down, choose All Commands. Scroll down through the left list box until you find Print Preview Full Screen. Click Add to add this to the QAT.

Figure 7.12 - *Add the Full Screen Print Preview icon to the QAT.*

After you've added the Print Preview Full Screen icon to the toolbar, you can access the old Print Preview, as shown in Figure 7.13. In Print Preview mode, you have only one ribbon tab available.

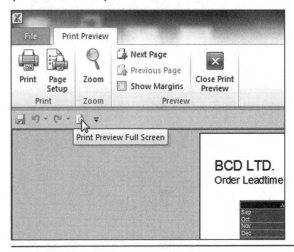

Figure 7.13 - *The Print Preview tab.*

Tip: People who write macros will still want to use the old Print Preview icon. Record a macro that uses the Full Screen Print Preview and the macro will pause until you close the Print Preview. Record a macro that goes to the Print Preview pane of the Backstage view and the macro will not show the Print Preview.

Next Steps

Chapter 8 introduces keyboard shortcuts.

08

Keyboard Shortcuts

When Excel gurus hear that Microsoft changed the menu system, they are often most concerned about all the shortcut keys that they previously learned.

In Excel 97 and Excel 2003, most menu items had a single letter underlined. If you wanted to select Edit, Fill, Justify from the menu, you just had to hold down the Alt key while pressing the underlined letter from each menu selection. Thus, Alt+E+I+J would enable you to quickly select the Justify command.

There are a few menu commands that I have memorized and I can type those shortcuts in my sleep.

In 80% of the cases, Excel 2010 will support your knowledge of legacy shortcut keys.

All Ctrl Key Shortcuts Continue to Work

Any Ctrl key shortcuts will continue to work. Some of the popular Ctrl shortcuts are as follows:

Ctrl+B for Bold

Ctrl+I for Italics

Ctrl+U for Underline

Ctrl+A to Select All

Ctrl+C to Copy

Ctrl+X to Cut

Ctrl+V to Paste

Ctrl+Z to Undo

Most Alt Shortcuts for Edit, View, Insert, Format, Tools, and Data Will work

When you press Alt+E, Alt+V, Alt+I, Alt+O, Alt+T, or Alt+D, Excel 2010 enters a special Office 2003 Compatibility mode. A box appears in the top center of the screen showing the Office 2003 access keys that you have entered so far. When you enter enough keys to invoke a menu command in Excel 2003, the command will be invoked in Excel 2010.

In Figure 8.1, two-thirds of the keystrokes for Edit, Fill, Justify have been selected. When you press J, Excel will invoke the Justify command.

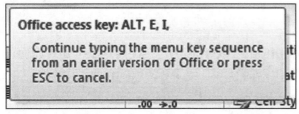

Office access key: ALT, E, I,

Continue typing the menu key sequence from an earlier version of Office or press ESC to cancel.

Figure 8.1 - *When you use the old Alt keys, this tip shows the keys you have pressed so far. It would have been helpful if they would have shown Edit, Fill.*

Note: This feature was a little slow in Excel 2007. If you typed the Alt shortcut quickly, you would often find that Excel had missed the second shortcut key. Therefore, when you thought you were pressing Alt + Format + Column, AutoFit, Excel would only see the keystrokes for Alt + Format, AutoFormat. (You would press Alt+O+C+A, Excel would only get Alt+O+A.) This delay has been reduced in Excel 2010. If you had been using Excel 2007 and actually slowed your shortcut key sequences down to account for the delay, you can go back to normal speed now.

Tip: Alt+F (File), Alt+W (Window), and Alt+H (Help) behave differently. You'll read about these keys later in this chapter.

Using the Office 2010 Keyboard Shortcuts

If you are a fan of using the keyboard, you might have noticed one problem in Excel 2003. There were often menu items that did not have a keyboard shortcut. In Excel 2010, every menu item can be selected from the keyboard.

To access the new keyboard shortcuts, press and release the Alt key.

Excel displays a single-character keyboard shortcut for each tab of the ribbon.

If any contextual ribbon tabs are visible, they will have a two-character shortcut key.

All the icons on the Quick Access Toolbar (QAT) are assigned a numeric keyboard shortcut. The first nine items are assigned the keys 1 through 9. Icons after that are assigned a two-character shortcut starting with a 0.

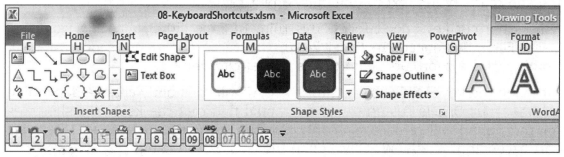

Figure 8.2 - *Press and release Alt to see the new shortcut keys.*

When you press F, H, N, P, M, A, R, or W, Excel will display the appropriate tab of the ribbon. The original shortcut key tips will be replaced with new key tips that will enable you to select any of the items in the ribbon. Figure 8.3 shows the key tips for the Data tab.

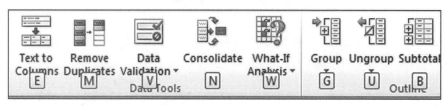

Figure 8.3 - *Press a shortcut key for the Data tab and you will see the Data shortcut keys.*

Some of the key tips make sense. W for What If, V for Validation, R for Refresh, FW for From Web. Excel 2003 typically used the second consonant sound when the beginning letter was already taken. Therefore, because C is already in use for Clear Filter, the Consolidate command uses N as the shortcut key rather than C.

If you press W to select What-If Analysis, you now have three new shortcut keys to select the items from that drop-down.

Figure 8.4 - *As you type additional shortcut keys, new shortcut keys appear until you finally actually select a command.*

Some of the Excel 2010 shortcut keys bow to tradition. E had traditionally been the shortcut key for Text to Columns, and it remains the shortcut key.

Other shortcut keys don't follow this rule. In Excel 2003, Alt+DFA would do Data, Filter, Advanced. In Excel 2010, the same command is now Alt+AQ. Some of these shortcuts seem to use the leftover letters.

Although the keyboard shortcuts for the QAT will constantly change depending on how your QAT is customized, you should find that the keyboard shortcuts for the ribbon will remain constant. You can memorize that Alt+A+S+A will sort ascending. Alt+A+W+G will open the Goal Seek dialog.

Accessing the Old File and Window Menus

In Excel 2003, Alt+F would open the File menu. Alt+W opened the Window menu. In Excel 2010, these keystroke combinations do not show the Office 2003 keyboard shortcut window. Instead, Alt+F opens the File menu. Alt+W opens the View tab.

Many of the keyboard shortcuts in the File menu match the same shortcuts as in the File menu.

Figure 8.5 - *Alt+F opens the File menu.*

Thus, Alt+F+S was File, Save in Excel 2003 and will execute a Save in Excel 2010.

Alt+F+D+A in Excel 2003 was File, Send To, Mail Recipient as Attachment. In Excel 2010, Alt+F+D will get you to the Send menu, but now E is used to send an e-mail instead of A to send as an attachment.

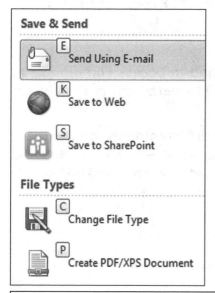

Figure 8.6
Some of the old keystrokes don't quite work. If you had memorized Alt+F+D+A, it is now Alt+F+D+E.

Tip: In Excel 2003, Alt+F+2 would open the second file in the Recent File list. To enable this shortcut as shown in Figure 8.6, go to File, Recent. At the bottom of the screen, check the box for Quickly Access This Number of Recent Workbooks. (see Figure 8.7)

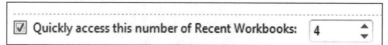

Figure 8.7 - *Show a few recent files in the left navigation bar of the File menu.*

Pressing Alt+W in Excel 2003 opened the Window menu. The commands on the old Window menu were New Window, Arrange, Compare Side by Side, Hide, Unhide, Split, and Freeze Panes.

Pressing Alt+W in Excel 2010 opens the View tab. All the keyboard shortcuts (N, A, B, H, U, S, and F) perform identical actions in Excel 2010.

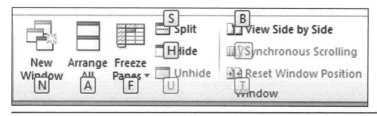

Figure 8.8 - *All the Alt+W shortcuts from Excel 2003 will work.*

> **Note**: In Excel 2003, Alt+W+2 would switch to the next open workbook. To do this in Excel 2010, use Ctrl+Tab or Alt+W+W+2.

Accessing Commands on the Excel 2003 Help Menu

Microsoft has simply abandoned the Alt+H command to access commands on the Excel 2003 Help menu. Instead, the Office 2010 paradigm is that Alt+H takes you to the Home tab in all applications.

This is not a horrible loss because there were not many commands on the Excel 2003 Help menu that you would have accessed using Alt+H. Alt+H+H would open Help, but the F1 key was faster. While you could relearn that Alt+F+H+H will access Help, you can continue to use the F1 key to access Help.

Next Steps

Chapter 9 takes a look at the expanding formula bar.

Formula Bar Tricks

Long formulas were frustrating in Excel 2003. Figure 9.1 shows a screen shot from Excel 2003. When you select cell Q2, the formula for Q2 is so long it spills over from the formula bar and you can no longer see the result of Q2!

Q2	▼	fx	=ROUND('Figure 22.1'!$P$2:$P$1956*0.75,
	M	N	$O$2:$O$1956*0.75^2/2.904+'Figure 22.1'!
2	208.05	214.2	2.904+'Figure 22.1'!$M$2:$M$1956*0.75^4/
3	112.3	115.6	$L$2:$L$1956*0.75^5/2.904+'Figure 22.1'!$
4	215.66	217.8	2.904+'Figure 22.1'!$J$2:$J$1956*0.75^7/2.
5	65.32	68.5	$I$1956*0.75^8/2.904+'Figure 22.1'!$H$2:$I
6	223.62	232.5	'Figure 22.1'!$G$2:$G$1956*0.75^10/2.904+
7	89.86	91.6	$E$1956*0.75^11/2.904+'Figure 22.1'!$D$2
8	170.71	174.12	2.904,2)
			182.83 188.31 173.28

Figure 9.1 - *In Excel 2003, a long formula would cover the grid, often obscuring the cell you are trying to see.*

Figure 9.2 shows a similar formula in Excel 2010. Initially, Excel only shows you the first part of the formula.

fx	=ROUND('Figure 22.1'!$P$2:$P$1956*0.75/2.904+'Figure 22.1'!$O$2:$O$1956*0.75^2/								
	K	L	M	N	O	P	Q	R	
	July	August	September	October	November	December	Forecast		
9.9	212	214.12	216.26	222.75	224.98	227.23	218.96		
93	114.38	117.81	122.52	123.75	128.7	135.14	123.31		

Figure 9.2 - *Initially, you see just the first line of the formula bar.*

Three buttons at the right end of the formula bar enable you to either scroll the formula one line at a time, or to expand the formula bar.

Notice that the formula bar expands without covering the Excel grid. You can also drag the horizontal bar just below the formula bar to allow more or less room for the formula.

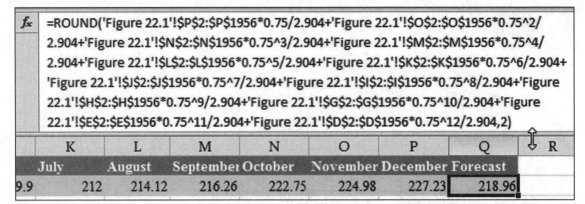

Figure 9.3 - *As the formula bar expands, it does not cover the Excel grid.*

To collapse the formula bar, click the up-arrow icon at the right side of the formula bar.

Next Steps

Chapter 9 takes a look at the expanding formula bar.

1 0

Quick Zoom

The Excel 2003 Zoom drop-down was difficult to use. It offered arbitrary zoom levels of 100%, 150%, 200%, 75%, 50%, 25%, and a choice to Zoom to Selection. If you wanted anything else, you had type the zoom amount in the drop-down box.

> **Tip**: If you have a wheel mouse, you can abandon the zoom interface. Hold down the Ctrl key while rolling the wheel away from you to increase the zoom. Hold down the Ctrl key while rolling the wheel toward you to decrease the zoom.

Use the slider in the lower-right corner of the window to adjust the zoom from 10% to 400%.

Figure 10.1 - *The zoom slider allows you to drag to a particular zoom level.*

There are three controls in the zoom slider. Clicking the − or + icons will move the zoom to the nearest 10%. In Figure 10.1, clicking the minus icon would change the zoom to 160%. Clicking the plus icon would change the zoom to 170%. Although this works okay, if you are really trying to fit just columns A:H on the screen, you will need to tweak to a value somewhere between perhaps 120% and 130% zoom. You can grab the actual pointer and nudge it in 1% increments.

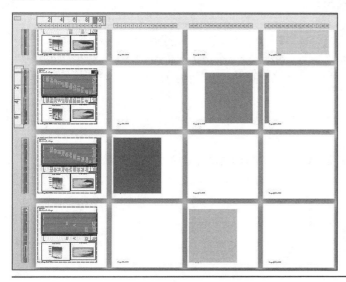

Figure 10.2 - *See your document from a 50,000 foot view.*

At a 10% zoom, you can get a 50,000 foot view of your workbook. Figure 10.2 shows a worksheet at a 10% zoom. You can see approximately 30,960 cells at this zoom. You can't make out any of the values, but you can get an overview of your worksheet.

At the opposite end of the spectrum, a 400% view will show you about 40 cells.

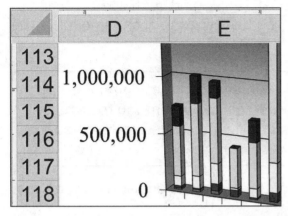

Figure 10.3 - *At the maximum zoom, you can make out details in drawings and charts.*

The old Zoom to Selection command has been moved to the View tab in the ribbon. To type a specific percentage, left-click the percentage to the left of the zoom slider to access the legacy Zoom dialog box (Figure 10.4)

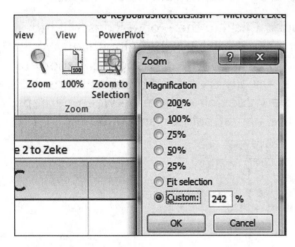

Figure 10.4 - *Zoom to Selection is now on the View tab of the ribbon.*

Next Steps

Chapter 11 shows you how to quickly do math using the status bar.

11

See Totals in the Status Bar

You can figure out totals without ever entering a formula.

Just select some cells that contain numeric data. Excel's status bar will show you the total of the selected cells.

57	3.42	7	67.42
45	8.7	9	162.7
84	5.04	7	96.04
64	3.84	6	73.84
40	8.4	8	156.4
72	4.32	6	82.32
99	5.94	7	111.94
84	5.04	8	97.04
38	2.28	6	46.28
15	6.9	9	130.9
72	10.32	8	190.32
40	8.4	8	156.4
25	1.5	5	31.5
81	4.86	7	92.86
60	9.6	8	177.6
20	7.2	7	134.2
40	8.4	9	157.4

Average: 115.5976471   Count: 17   Sum: 1965.16

Figure 11.1 - *At the bottom of the screen, you can see the total of these cells is 1965.16. There are 17 cells, with an average of 115.59.*

The status bar has been doing this for a dozen years, yet few people ever noticed. In earlier versions of Excel you could choose to have the status bar show either a Total, Min, Max, Count, or Average. Now, in Excel 2010, you can have the status bar show you all of those statistics.

Simply right-click the status bar and you can choose to turn on or off any of these settings.

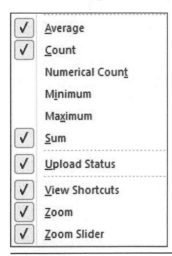

- ✓ A̲verage
- ✓ C̲ount
- Numerical Coun̲t
- Mi̲nimum
- Ma̲ximum
- ✓ S̲um
- ✓ U̲pload Status
- ✓ V̲iew Shortcuts
- ✓ Z̲oom
- ✓ Zoom Slider

Figure 11.2 - *Have Excel show you many statistics for the current selection.*

> **Note**: The statistics in the status bar appear only when more than one numeric cell is selected.

With the exception of the count statistics, Excel will ignore text cells in your selection. As soon as your selection includes one error cell, such as #N/A!, Excel will stop displaying statistics in the status bar.

> **Tip**: Suppose you have 5,000 rows of data and you need to know whether any of the values are #N/A! errors. Select the range. If Excel will not show you the total, you know that you have at least one error cell in the range. If you find that your range contains an error cell and don't want to sort the data, use this technique. Start in the first cell. Hold down the Shift key while repeatedly pressing Page Down. As soon as the status bar stops showing a total, you know that an error cell was encountered in the most recent page.

Next Steps

This chapter completes the section on the Excel interface changes. Chapter 12 introduces the new functions in Excel.

12

New and Improved Functions In Excel 2010

Excel 2003 offered 262 functions with an additional 89 functions enabled if you activated the Analysis Toolpak.

Excel 2010 offers 400 functions. The new functions fit into these categories:

Excel 2007 formally added the 89 Analysis Toolpak functions to Excel.

Excel 2010 renamed most of the statistics functions for dealing with probability distributions. You will see new function names with periods in the name. Suffixes such as .LT and .RT indicate that you are getting the left-tailed or right-tailed probability distribution.

Excel 2007 introduced the new IFERROR function as a fast way to deal with #N/A and #DIV/0! errors.

Excel 2007 introduced plural versions of SUMIF and COUNTIF.

Excel 2010 offers international versions of WORKDAY and NETWORKDAYS functions. These international versions can handle weekends other than the western Saturday-Sunday. Along the same lines, Excel 2010 offers ISO standard versions of CEILING and FLOOR.

Excel 2010 offers new ways of calculating mode, quartile, percentile, and rank.

Excel 2010 introduces the new AGGREGATE function. This is similar to SUBTOTAL, but with 19 calculations rather than 11.

Excel 2007 introduced seven new CUBE functions for retrieving data from an OLAP cube. If you use the new PowerPivot add-in described in Chapter 21, you can convert your pivot table to cube functions.

Microsoft also invested in improving the accuracy of certain scientific and financial functions. There had been a number of academic papers critical of Excel's calculation of scientific functions. In many cases, Excel did fine in the normal range of input values, but started to deviate when you were near the outer boundaries of the input range. Microsoft hired three mathematical consulting firms to propose new algorithms for several functions. Two firms actually proposed algorithms, and then the third firm chose between the two proposed algorithms. Forty functions were improved for Excel 2010.

Handle Error Formulas Using IFERROR Function

Error values are occasionally returned in Excel spreadsheets.

In Figure 12.1, a division by zero error occurs in cell C4, and an N/A error occurs in the VLOOKUP formula in C12.

◢	A	B	C	D	E	F	
1	Revenue	Profit	GP%				
2	12552	5271.84	42%				
3	11236	4044.96	36%				
4	0	-3415	#DIV/0!				
5	15705	5496.75	35%				
6							
7							
8	Inv	SKU	Description			SKU	Desc
9	1001	BG33-3	14K Gold Bangle Bracelet with '			BG33-3	14K
10	1002	Cross50-5	14K Gold Onyx Cross with Whit			CR50-3	14K
11	1003	ER46-29	14K Gold Hoop Earrings			RG75-3	14K
12	1004	BG33-18	#N/A			RG78-25	14K
13	1005	ER46-22	14K Gold Hoop Earrings			W25-6	18K
14	1006	ER46-14	14K Gold Fish Hoop Earrings			BR26-3	18K

Figure 12.1 - *Error cells interrupt the flow of the worksheet.*

In earlier versions of Excel, people would write complicated formulas to prevent the error values. To prevent the division by zero error in Excel 2003, you might have tried the following:

=IF(A4=0,"",B4/A4)

To prevent an error in the VLOOKUP formula, you had to enter an absolutely insane formula that actually performed the VLOOKUP twice. The IF function tested to see whether the result was #N/A, and if so, it would provide alternate text. If the original result was not #N/A, Excel would calculate the VLOOKUP again, resulting in the function taking twice as long to calculate:

=IF(ISNA(VLOOKUP(B12,PT,2,False)),"", VLOOKUP(B12,PT,2,False))

Excel 2010 offers a new function to help handle errors. If you have a calculation that you think might generate an error, enter the calculation as the first argument in the =IFERROR() function. For the second argument, enter a value that should be used in case the first argument generates an error:

=IfError(Value, Value If Error)

The advantage of this function is that the original calculation is performed only once. For example:

=IFERROR(B4/A4,"")

=IFERROR(VLOOKUP(B12,PT,2,False),"")

This is a fast solution. In a dataset, you probably have 95% or more of the formulas that do not generate an error. The only time that Excel has to move to the second argument is in the rare 5% of cases that generate an error.

New Conditional SUM Functions

Excel has provided SUMIF and COUNTIF functions for a decade. These functions enable you to count or total records that meet one criteria.

	F3		▼		fx	=SUMIF($A$2:$A$20,E3,$C$2:$C$20)					
▲	A	B	C	D	E	F	G	H	I	J
1	Region	Product	Quantity							
2	East	XYZ	1000		Region					
3	Central	DEF	100		East	6000	=SUMIF($A$2:$A$20,E3,$C$2:$C$20)			
4	East	ABC	500		Central	3500				
5	Central	XYZ	500		West	1000				
6	Central	XYZ	400							
7	East	DEF	800		Product					
8	East	XYZ	400		ABC	2500	=SUMIF($B$2:$B$20,E8,$C$2:$C$20)			
9	Central	ABC	400		DEF	1900				
10	East	ABC	400		XYZ	6100				

Figure 12.2 - *The SUMIF function allows you to total records that meet one condition.*

COUNTIF and SUMIF are easy functions to replace the complicated SUMPRODUCT or array formula solutions when you need to calculate conditional sums.

After someone learned about SUMIF, they often wondered how to sum the records that met two conditions. You might want a function in F13 to find the units of ABC sold in the East. This was not possible with SUMIF.

In Excel 2007, Microsoft has added the plural S versions of SUMIFS, COUNTIFS, and AVERAGEIFS. These functions enable you to enter up to 127 different criteria. The syntax is slightly reversed from SUMIF. You start with the range of numbers to be summed, and then enter pairs of arguments, criteria range, criteria value, and so on:

=SUMIFS(Sum Range, Criteria Range 1, Criteria 1,)

For example, here is the formula in F13 in Figure 12.3:

=SUMIFS($C$2:$C$20,$A$2:$A$20,$E13,$B$2:$B$20,F$12.

Copy the formula to the rest of the table to find total sales by region and product.

| F13 | | | fx | =SUMIFS($C$2:$C$20,$A$2:$A$20,$E13,$B$2:$B$20,F$12) |

▲	A	B	C	D	E	F	G	H	I
1	Region	Product	Quantity						
11	East	DEF	1000						
12	West	XYZ	600			ABC	DEF	XYZ	
13	Central	ABC	800		East	900	1800	3300	
14	East	XYZ	900		Central	1600	100	1800	
15	Central	XYZ	900		West	0	0	1000	
16	East	XYZ	900						
17	Central	ABC	300						
18	West	XYZ	400						
19	Central	ABC	100						
20	East	XYZ	100						
21									

Figure 12.3 - *The SUMIFS function makes it simpler to create a sum based on two or more conditions.*

COUNTIFS and AVERAGEIFS work in the same manner.

Note that although it was possible to do the same calculation as SUMIFS using SUMPRODUCT in legacy versions of Excel, the SUMIFS function is up to a hundred times faster than the equivalent SUMPRODUCT function!

Like SUBTOTAL, but Better: AGGREGATE()

Excel 97 introduced the SUBTOTAL function, which would look through the visible rows in a dataset and do one of 11 functions. The AGGREGATE() function is similar, with two nice improvements:

Aggregate supports 19 functions rather than 11. The first 11 functions are the same as those in the subtotal function: Average, Count, CountA, Max, Min, Product, StDev.S, StDev.P, Sum, Var.S, Var.P. The new functions are Median, Mode.Sngl, Large, Small, Percentile.Inc, Quartile.Inc, Percentile. Exc, and Quartile.Exc.

Where the Subtotal function ignore hidden row and other subtotal functions, the options argument in aggregate allows you to ignore (a) nothing, (b) hidden rows, (c) error values, (d) both hidden rows and error values, (e) any of the above and other Subtotal and Aggregate functions.

Consistent Naming for Statistical Functions

The statistical functions had been inconsistently named. Depending on the distribution that you are using, the naming conventions varied. For the chi squared distribution, the inverse function was called CHIINV. For the binomial distribution, the inverse function was called CRITBINOM.

There had been a few function names previously that included a period in the name. In an effort to create consistent names in Excel 2010, Microsoft made significant use of a dot followed by a suffix. Suffixes that appear frequently include the following:

.DIST is used for the probability density function (PDF) and for the left-tailed cumulative distribution function (CDF). An argument specifies whether the function is the PDF or the CDF.

.INV is used for the inverse cumulative distribution function.

.RT is used for right-tailed.

.LT is used for left-tailed.

.TEST is used for hypothesis testing functions.

.P is used for functions based on a population.

.S is used for functions based on a sample.

Table 12.1 shows the new names of distribution functions.

Table 12.1

Distribution	PDF/CDF	Right-Tailed CDF	Inverse Left-Tail CDF	Inverse Right-Tailed
Beta	BETA.DIST		BETA.INV	
Binomial	BINOM.DIST		BINOM.INV	
Chi squared	CHISQ.DIST	CHISQ.DIST.RT	CHISQ.INV	CHISQ.INV.RT
Exponential	EXPON.DIST			
F	F.DIST	F.DIST.RT	F.INV	F.INV.RT
Gamma	GAMMA.DIST		GAMMA.INV	
Hypergeometric	HYPGEOM.DIST			
Logonormal	LOGNORM.DIST		LOGNORM.INV	
Negative binomial	NEGBINOM.DIST			
Normal	NORM.DIST		NORM.INV	
Standard normal	NORM.S.DIST		NORM.S.INV	
Poisson	POISSON.DIST			
Student's t	T.DIST	T.DIST.RT	T.INV	
Student's t (2 tailed)		T-DIST.2T		T.INV.2T
Weibull	WEIBULL.DIST			

For hypothesis testing, the functions are F.TEST, T.TEST, and Z.Test. Confidence tests are CONFIDENCE.NORM for the normal distribution and CONFIDENCE.T for the student's t distribution.

Variance and standard deviation have always been available as functions for a sample (VAR, STDEV) and a population (VARP and STDEVP). Microsoft renamed these to be VAR.S, STDEV.S, VAR.P, STDEV.P. The also formalized the fact that the old COVAR function is based on a population by renaming it to COVARIANCE.P, and they added a sample version named COVARIANCE.S.

The old names will continue to work for backward compatibility, but they will appear with a red "do not use" icon in the Formula Autocomplete list. Of course, if you are sharing your workbook with people who still use Excel 2007 or earlier, you will want to keep using the old names.

New Variations of Existing Functions

Eight functions were extended in Excel 2010 to improve consistency with either best practices or with international needs.

Dealing with multiple modes: In descriptive statistics, three key figures are the mean, median, and mode. The mean is the average. The median is the value that occurs in the middle. The mode is the value that occurs most often. Sometimes, a dataset will have a tie and two different values occur the same numbers of times in the dataset. The old MODE function would return the first of such ties. The new MODE.MULT returns an array with all the tied values.

Averaging ties in rank: It seems that everyone hated the old RANK function. Excel tricksters used RANK to sort with a formula, and we hated the way that ties were treated. Mathematicians and statisticians wanted rank to treat ties in a different way. The mathematicians won that argument.

In the old Excel, if two values were tied, RANK would return the same rank for both items. In column C of Figure 12.5, there are two values ranked 2. The next item is ranked as 4. This is typically how the sports world shows ranks. If you like that method, the old RANK function is now renamed to RANK.EQ and continues this method.

The new RANK.AVG will assign any tied values as an average of the ranks. Because Flo and Helga are tied for second and third place, they are both assigned the rank of 2.5.

fx	=RANK.AVG(B2,$B$2:$B$11)		

◢	A	B	C	D
1	Name	Score	Rank.Eq	Rank.Avg
2	Adam	90	4	4
3	Betty	89	5	5
4	Carrie	76	9	9
5	Donna	80	8	8
6	Eddy	85	6	6
7	Flo	93	2	2.5
8	Gareth	96	1	1
9	Helga	93	2	2.5
10	Ike	81	7	7
11	James	70	10	10
12				

Figure 12.4 - *The new RANK. AVG still creates two values with the same rank.*

If you really need to have a name assigned to each rank from 1 through 10, use =RANK.EQ(B2,$B$2:$B$11.+COUNTIF(B$1:B1,B2).

Ceiling and floor for negative values: The CEILING function is a way to always round up to the next highest multiple. =CEILING(2.9,1) is 3, and =CEILING(2.1,1) is also 3. Similarly, the FLOOR function will always round down.

This works great for positive numbers.

Without thinking about it, what is the ceiling of -2.1?

Did you say -3? If you did, this seems somewhat logical. You would think that CEILING should always round away from 0, and -3 is the next number. The old CEILING and FLOOR functions would operate in this way.

Mathematicians pointed out that if you want to go up from -2.1 to the next highest number, you should go to -2 and not -3. Excel 2010 introduced CEILING. PRECISE and FLOOR.PRECISE to work with negative numbers in this way.

Workdays for nontraditional workweeks: Two functions in the old Analysis Toolpak were designed to calculate workdays between two dates. These functions were great if you worked in a company where the workdays were Monday through Friday with a weekend of Saturday and Sunday.

Excel 2010 adds WORKDAY.INTL and NETWORKDAYS.INTL to allow for other weekend dates.

In Figure 12.5, the formula in C4 is as follows:

=NETWORKDAYS(B$1,B4,$G$4:$G$14)

This will calculate the number of Monday through Friday dates that fall between

January 14 and January 24, ignoring any company holidays in G4:G14.

To use different workdays, use this formula from D4:

=NETWORKDAYS.INTL(B$1,B4,11,$G$4:$G$14)

The new third argument of 11 defines the weekend as Sunday only. The tooltip at the bottom of the image shows values for the third argument.

	A	B	C	D	E	F	G
1	Today:	Friday, January 14, 2011					
2							
3	Project	Due Date	Work days	6-day weeks			Holidays
4	A	Monday, January 24, 2011	6	8			Sun, January 2, 2011
5	B	Thursday, March 24, 2011	48	58			Mon, January 17, 2011
6	C	Monday, January 31, 2011	11	14			Mon, February 21, 2011
7	D	Friday, May 27, 2011	94	113			Mon, May 30, 2011
8	E	Friday, July 15, 2011	127	153			Mon, July 4, 2011
9	F	Friday, January 21, 2011	5	6			Mon, September 5, 2011
10	G	Friday, April 08, 2011	59	71			Mon, October 10, 2011
11							Fri, November 11, 2011
12		=NETWORKDAYS.INTL(B1,B10,					Thu, November 24, 2011
13							Fri, November 25, 2011
14				☐ 1 - Saturday, Sunday			Mon, December 26, 2011
15				☐ 2 - Sunday, Monday			
16				☐ 3 - Monday, Tuesday			
17				☐ 4 - Tuesday, Wednesday			
18				☐ 5 - Wednesday, Thursday			
19				☐ 6 - Thursday, Friday			
20				☐ 7 - Friday, Saturday			
21				☐ 11 - Sunday only			Sunday is weekend day
22				☐ 12 - Monday only			
23				☐ 13 - Tuesday only			
24				☐ 14 - Wednesday only			
25				☐ 15 - Thursday only			

Figure 12.5 - *The new NETWORKDAYS.INTL allows for alternate weekends.*

Similar new arguments are available for the WORKDAY.INTL function.

Calculating quartiles for small datasets: The quartile and percentile functions in Excel will break the dataset into percentiles or quartiles. If you have 100 values and you need to calculate a quartile, just about everyone can agree on where each quartile occurs. However, if you need to figure out the quartile for a dataset with few values, you are going to have to extrapolate to find a value between two values in the dataset. Scientists didn't like the way that the old QUARTILE function would extrapolate. A new method is now available in QUARTILE.EXC and PERCENTILE.EXC. The old method is still available in QUARTILE.INC and PERCENTILE.INC.

Almost New Functions

In earlier versions of Excel, you could install an add-in called the Analysis Toolpak to enable 89 new functions in Excel. Many of these functions were specific to engineers or bond traders. However, there are a couple of really useful functions among the 89 functions in the Analysis Toolpak (ATP).

If you tried to use a function from the ATP and shared the workbook with someone who had not installed the ATP, the formula would return the NAME! error. Subsequently, some companies had rules against using the ATP functions.

Starting in Excel 2007, all the ATP functions have been included in the core Excel function list.

A few examples of useful ATP functions are described in this chapter. At the end of this chapter, you will see the complete list of functions that have been promoted from the ATP to be true members of the Excel function fraternity.

Convert Units with CONVERT

The CONVERT function can convert between different units of measurement. The versatile function can handle mass, distance, time, pressure, force, energy, power, magnetism, temperature, and volume:

=CONVERT(Number, From Unit, To Unit)

Excel help provides a complete list of abbreviations available for the CONVERT function. A few sample conversions are shown in Figure 12.6.

D4			f_x	=CONVERT(A4,B4,C4)
A	**B**	**C**	**D**	**E**
1 Quantity	From	To	Result	Notes
2	1 kg	lbm	2.204623	*kilograms to pounds*
3	180 lbm	kg	81.64662	*pounds to kilograms*
4	1 mi	ft	5280	*feet in a mile*
5	1 mi	yd	1760	*yards in a mile*
6	1 mi	km	1.609344	*kilometers in a mile*
7	5 km	mi	3.106856	*miles in a 5K run*
8	100 yd	m	91.44	*meters in an American football field*
9	1 Nmi	mi	1.150779	*miles in a nautical mile*
10	1 yr	hr	8766	*hours in a year*
11	1 mi	Pica	4561920	*picas in a mile*
12	98.6 F	C	37	*Convert Farenheit to Celsius*
13	1 qt	tsp	192	*teaspoons in a quart*
14	1 tbs	tsp	3	*teaspoons in a tablespoon*
15	2 l	qt	2.112917	*quarts in a 2 liter bottle*
16	2 l	oz	67.61333	*ounces in a 2 liter bottle*
17	1 lbf	N	4.448222	*Newtons in 1 pound force*
18	1 BTU	kev	6.59E+18	*kiloelectron volts in a BTU*
19	455 HP	kW	339.294	*kilowatts in a 455 horsepower engine*

Figure 12.6 - *The CONVERT function makes conversions simple.*

Help Your Kids with Their Math Homework

When your middle school student has homework that requires calculating greatest common denominators, least common multiples, or Roman numerals, you can depend on Excel. Excel has functions to make checking this homework a breeze.

▲	A	B	C	D	E
				D3	fx =GCD(B3:C3)
1					
2		Greatest Common Denominator (GCD)			
3		312	456	24	=GCD(B3:C3)
4		306	204	102	
5		289	323	17	
6					
7		Least Common Multiple (LCM)			
8		13	7	91	=LCM(B8:C8)
9		54	90	270	
10		36	250	4500	
11					
12		Roman Numerals (ROMAN)			
13			2010	MMX	=ROMAN(C13)
14			2011	MMXI	
15			2012	MMXII	
16			44	XLIV	
17			45	XLV	
18			46	XLVI	
19			47	XLVII	
20			48	XLVIII	
21					

Figure 12.2 - *This brings back memories of junior high math.*

Tip: The ROMAN function is useful for filmmakers who want to figure out the proper copyright date for the end of the film credits and for NFL commissioners who need to figure out the names of upcoming Super Bowls.

New ATP Functions

This chapter describes just a few of the new functions now in the core Excel product. In all, 89 functions have been promoted from the ATP to Excel.

The following is the complete list of functions that are now part of the core Excel functions: ACCRINT, ACCRINTM, AMORDEGRC, AMORLINC, BESSELI, BESSELJ, BESSELK, BESSELY, BIN2DEC, BIN2HEX, BIN2OCT, COMPLEX, CONVERT, COUPDAYBS, COUPDAYS, COUPDAYSNC, COUPNCD, COUPNUM, COUPPCD, CUMIPMT, CUMPRINC, DEC2BIN, DEC2HEX, DEC2OCT, DELTA, DISC, DOLLARDE, DOLLARFR, DURATION, EDATE, EFFECT, EOMONTH, ERF, ERFC, FACTDOUBLE, FVSCHEDULE, GCD, GESTEP, HEX2BIN, HEX2DEC, HEX2OCT, IMABS, IMAGINARY, IMARGUMENT, IMCONJUGATE, IMCOS, IMDIV, IMEXP, IMLN, IMLOG10, IMLOG2, IMPOWER, IMREAL, IMSIN, IMSQRT, IMSUB,

INTRATE, ISEVEN, ISODD, LCM, MDURATION, MROUND, MULTINOMIAL, NETWORKDAYS, NOMINAL, OCT2BIN, OCT2DEC, OCT2HEX, ODDFPRICE, ODDFYIELD, ODDLPRICE, ODDLYIELD, PRICE, PRICEMAT, QUOTIENT, RANDBETWEEN, RECEIVED, SERIESSUM, SQRTPI, TBILLEQ, TBILLPRICE, TBILLYIELD, WEEKNUM, WORKDAY, XIRR, XNPV, YEARFRAC, YIELD, YIELDDISC, and YIELDMAT.

Bonus Tip: Using the Keyboard to Enter Formulas

This trick is not new, but it is a faster way to enter formulas. In fact, the trick originated with Lotus 1-2-3 back in the 1980s. If you are a fan of using the keyboard, you should learn this method for entering formulas.

Suppose you need to enter a formula in B8, as shown in Figure 12.8.

⊿	A	B	C	D	E
1	Sam had 7 donuts. He gave 2 to Sydney				
2	and bought 4 more at the store. How many				
3	donuts does Sam have?				
4					
5		7			
6	-	2			
7	+	4			
8					

Figure 12.8 - *The fastest way to enter this formula is the arrow key method.*

1. Start in cell B8. Enter either an equals sign or a plus sign. If you regularly use the numeric keypad, it is easier to enter a plus sign.

2. Press the up arrow three times. Excel shows a flashing cursor around cell B5. The provisional formula in B8 shows =B5.

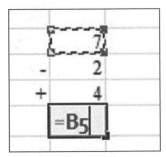

Figure 12.9 - *B8 is still the active cell (thick border), but you are pointing to B5 (dashed border).*

---

3. Type a minus sign to continue the formula. The flashing box disappears. The focus returns to cell B8. If you want to point to cell B6, press the up arrow two times. The provisional formula now shows =B5-B6.

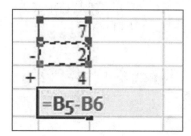

Figure 12.10 - *When you type a math sign, the focus returns to the original cell. It required two presses of the up arrow to arrive at B6.*

4. Type a plus sign.

5. Press the up arrow to move to B7.

6. Press the Enter key to accept the formula.

B8		▼		f_x	=B5-B6+B7	
◢	A	B	C	D	E	F
1	Sam had 7 donuts. He gave 2 to Sydney					
2	and bought 4 more at the store. How many					
3	donuts does Sam have?					
4						
5		7				
6		- 2				
7		+ 4				
8		9				
9						

Figure 12.11 - *The final formula.*

Try it. You'll find that pressing =↑↑↑-↑↑+↑<Enter> is much faster than using the mouse to enter the formula.

Next Steps

Chapter 13 introduces a new concept of structured tables in Excel.

Tables Make Excel a Bit More Like a Database

Many spreadsheets in Excel contain a two-dimensional table of data. You have headings in the first row, and each row of the worksheet represents a different record in a table.

Because a common task in Excel is dealing with tables, Excel 2010 has added several features for working with tables. One of the best benefits of the table functionality is that charts and pivot tables based on a table will automatically grow with the table.

Figure 13.1 shows a typical table in Excel.

	A	B	C	D	E	F	G
1	Region	Product	ShipDate	Customer	Quantity	Revenue	Profit
2	East	I881	1/1/2011	Amazing Yardstick Partners	1000	22810	12590
3	Central	J690	1/1/2011	Inventive Opener Corporation	100	2257	1273
4	East	M144	1/1/2011	Magnificent Jewelry Inc.	500	10245	6010
5	Central	R543	1/2/2011	Magnificent Tackle Inc.	500	11240	6130
6	Central	P154	1/3/2011	Leading Yogurt Company	400	9204	5116

Figure 13.1- *You frequently encounter table-like datasets in Excel.*

To turn on the features, select a single cell in the dataset and press Ctrl+T. Excel will assume your table extends to either the edge of the spreadsheet or to a blank row and blank column. The Create Table dialog will ask you to confirm the range for the table.

Figure 13.2 - *Excel guesses the current region as the address for the table.*

Note: Instead of using Ctrl+T, you can use the Format as Table drop-down on the Home tab or the Table icon on the Insert tab.

When you apply a table, you will notice the following features:

Excel applies a default table formatting. You can change to another style using the Table Styles gallery on the Table Tools Design tab.

Excel turns on the Filter drop-downs on each heading (Figure 13.3. You can use these drop-downs to sort by a column (Chapter 15) or to filter a column (Chapter 16).

If you are in the table and scroll so the headings are not visible, the headings will replace column letters A, B, C and so on. New in Excel 2010, the Filter dropdowns will remain available after the first row out of view.

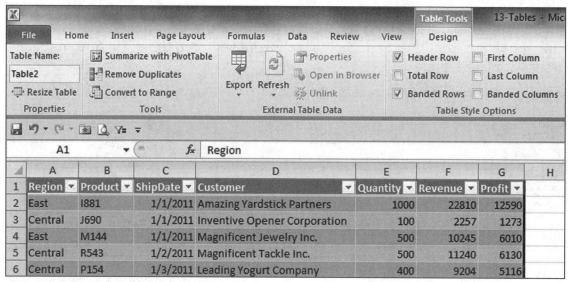

Figure 13.3 - *Excel formats the table.*

You can add totals to the bottom of the dataset by using the Total Row check box in the Table Tools Design tab.

The following features are not immediately visible, but will work:

Any new data typed in the blank row below the table will be made part of the table. This means that any charts, pivot tables, or formulas that refer to the table will automatically apply to the new data.

A resize handle in the bottom-right corner of the table allows you to drag to manually extend the table to include additional columns.

You can use the Table Style Options check boxes to turn on alternate formatting for the first column, last column, header row, total row, or to apply alternating shading to rows or columns.

Any formulas that point to columns in the table will be written in a new table nomenclature. Enter a formula once and Excel will copy it to all rows of the table.

Working with Table Formulas

Excel can greatly automate the process of entering formulas for a new column in a table. Suppose you want to add a Profit % column to the table created earlier in this chapter. Follow these steps:

1. Enter GP% in H1. Excel adds column H to the table.

2. Format cell H2 as a percentage. I realize that in Excel 2003, you would normally format the cell after entering the formula. You need to get in the habit of formatting the cell before entering the formula.

3. In cell H2, type an equals sign. Click the Profit in G2. Type a divide sign. Click the Revenue in F2. You will already notice something different: Excel is building a formula of =[@Profit]/[@Revenue].

E	F	G	H	I	J
Quantity ▼	Revenue ▼	Profit ▼	GP% ▼		
1000	22810	12590	=[@Profit]/[@Revenue]		
100	2257	1273			
500	10245	6010			

Figure 13.4 - *The table formula nomenclature is similar to the old natural language formulas. By the way, those formulas were deprecated after Excel 2003.*

4. Press the Enter key to complete the formula. Excel automatically copies the formula down to all the rows in your dataset!

The automatic copying of the formula is a great feature. However, there will be a few times when you do not want this to happen. If so, find the AutoCorrect drop-down and open it. You will have choices to turn of the calculated column or to turn off the feature permanently.

G	H	I	J	K	L	M
fit ▼	GP% ▼					
12590	55%					
1273	56%					
6010	59%	↺ Undo Calculated Column				
6130	55%					
5116	56%	■ Stop Automatically Creating Calculated Columns				
10680	58%					
5064	55%	⅀ Control AutoCorrect Options...				
3472	51%					
5068	60%					
11890	55%					

Figure 13.5 - *Override automatic formula copying.*

Working with Table Styles

There are 60+ built-in table styles in the gallery. The styles in the gallery will change depending on the six checkboxes to the left of the gallery. For example, if you turn on Banded Columns and open the gallery, you will see that many of the styles support banded columns.

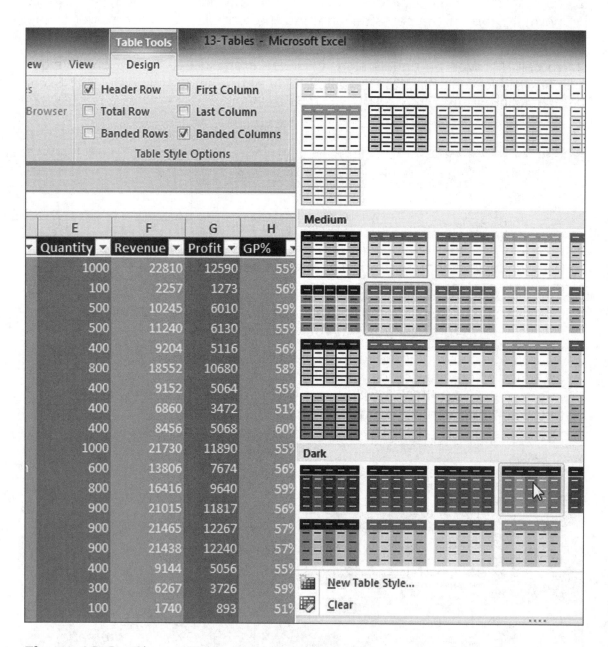

Figure 13.6 - *Choose Table Style Options before opening this gallery.*

Tables Make Excel a Bit More Like a Database

If you instead turn on Banded Rows and open the Table Styles gallery, you will see that several styles support banded rows.

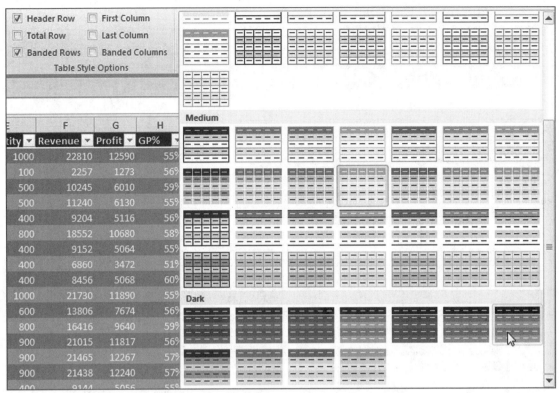

Figure 13.7 - *The gallery looks different when Banded Rows is turned on.*

The gallery supports Live Preview. Just hover over a style in the gallery and the worksheet will redraw to show you that table style. When you find a style that you like, click the style to apply that formatting.

Choosing a Table Style as the Default

Right-click any table style and choose Set as Default to make this the default style used by Ctrl+T in the future.

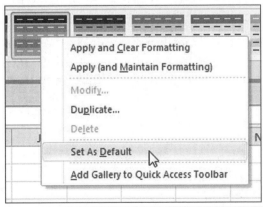

Figure 13.8 - *Set a style as the default table style.*

Creating a Custom Table Style

You can edit any of the built-in table styles. Right-click a style and choose Duplicate. The Modify Table Quick Style dialog appears. You can enter a new name for the table style and then micromanage every element of the table.

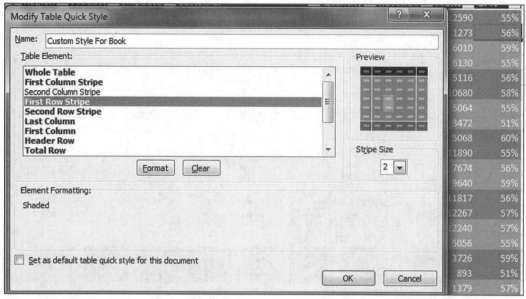

Figure 13.9 - *Edit the stripe size.*

In Figure 13.9, the Stripe Size for the First Row Stripe is increased from 1 to 2. After a similar change to the Second Row Stripe, a new Custom table style is available in the gallery.

The table features row banding that is two rows tall.

Dealing with Table Annoyances

The table functionality is pretty cool. There are two annoyances.

First, the filter drop-downs cover up some of the headings. You will find that you end up left-aligning headings so that you can read the headings. You can turn off the filter drop-downs by using Data, Filter.

Second, sometimes I just turn on the table functionality to quickly apply a format to the table. It is okay to use Ctrl+T to create and format a table and then immediately use Table Tools, Convert to Range to turn the table back into a normal range. The table formatting remains!

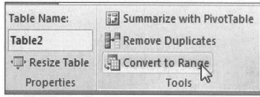

Figure 13.10 - *Change a table back to a range. The table formatting remains, but the other table features go away.*

Tables Make Excel a Bit More Like a Database

Charts and Pivot Tables Grow with the Table

In Figure 13.11, a chart is based on a table that contains 4 weeks and 3 months.

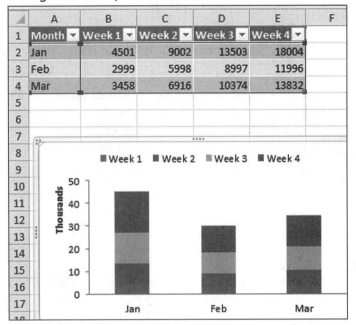

Figure 13.11 - *This chart is based on a table.*

If you enter new data next to the table, the rows and columns will be added to the table and automatically added to the chart.

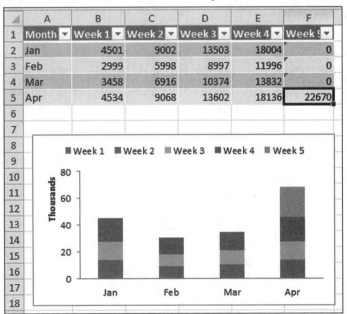

Figure 13.12 - *The chart automatically grows because it is based on the table.*

Next Steps

Chapter 14 covers some fill handle improvements in Excel 2010.

Smarter Fill Handle Double-Click

Suppose have a 50,000 row dataset in A2:F50001 and you enter a new formula in G2.

For many versions of Excel, the fastest way to copy that formula down to all the rows is to select the cell with the formula and double-click the fill handle. (The fill handle is the square dot in the lower-right corner of the cell.) Excel would look at the cell to the left, figure out how many rows were filled in that column, and copy the formula down to the last row.

=2*F2/E2				
D	E	F	G	
dings	Headings	Headings	Headings	
326	276	381	2.76087	
261	239	355		
225	329	237		

Figure 14.1 - *Double-click the square dot in the lower-right corner of the cell to copy the formula down.*

This trick always gets a gasp in my Power Excel seminars, because the process of dragging the fill handle down to row 50,000 is so tedious.

Excel 2010 Improvements

The trick of double-clicking the fill handle had one problem in earlier versions of Excel. If there was a blank cell in the column to the left, Excel would stop copying when it reached the blank cell. You could override this behavior by hiding the column with a few blanks and having a column without any blanks as the visible column to the left.

=2*F2/E2			
D	E	F	G
245	262	256	1.954198
437	211	168	1.592417
261	385	321	1.667532
344	131	428	6.534351
478	242	315	2.603306
343	393		0
237	225	279	2.48
202	115	130	2.26087
310	298	417	2.798658
356		455	#DIV/0!
207	271	268	1.97786

Figure 14.2 - *The automatic copy no longer gets interrupted by a blank cell in the column to the left.*

However, this problem has been fixed in Excel 2010. In Figure 14.2, you will see that the copy had no problem automatically skipping over the blank cell.

Are you familiar with the VBA concept of CurrentRegion? This is the region that would be selected if you press Ctrl+* from a cell. The selection will extend outward in all directions until it hits the edge of the worksheet or a blank edge of the data. Excel 2010 takes a look at what would be the CurrentRegion and copies the formula down to the last row in that region.

In Figure 14.3, the formula would copy down to row 13 because of the data in column B.

	A	B	C	D	E	F	G
	D2			=2*C2			
1	Headings	Headings	Headings	Headings	Headings	Headings	Headings
2	123	123	123	246	123	123	123
3	123	123	123		123	123	123
4	123	123	123		123	123	123
5	123	123	123		123	123	123
6	123	123	123		123	123	123
7	123	123	123		123	123	123
8	123	123	123		123	123	123
9	123	123			123		123
10	123	123			123		123
11		123					123
12		123					123
13		123					
14							
15							

Figure 14.3 - *When you double-click the fill handle, Excel looks for the last row with data in the adjacent region.*

The selected cell will be copied down to the last row in the current region as shown in Figure 14.4.

	A	B	C	D	E	F	G
	D2			=2*C2			
1	Headings	Headings	Headings	Headings	Headings	Headings	Headings
2	123	123	123	246	123	123	123
3	123	123	123	246	123	123	123
4	123	123	123	246	123	123	123
5	123	123	123	246	123	123	123
6	123	123	123	246	123	123	123
7	123	123	123	246	123	123	123
8	123	123	123	246	123	123	123
9	123	123		0	123		123
10	123	123		0	123		123
11		123		0			123
12		123		0			123
13		123		0			
14							

Figure 14.4 - *Excel will copy the formula down to the last row, even if that last row is not in the column to the left or right.*

When Double-Clicking the Fill Handle Won't Work

The improved operation of double-clicking the fill handle works only if the cells below the current cell are completely blank.

In Figure 14.5, a nonblank cell in G3 will override the normal behavior of the fill handle.

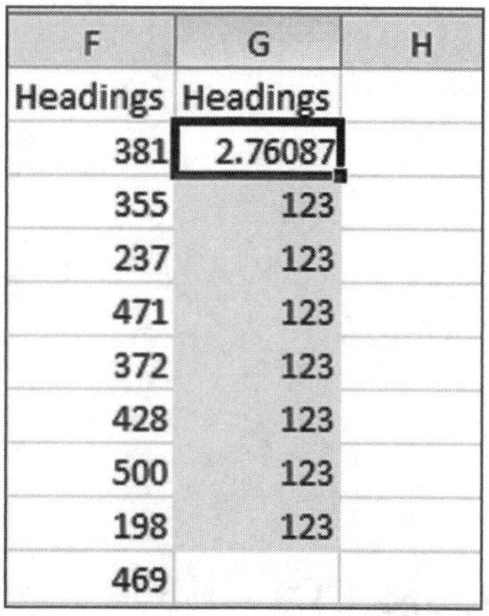

F	G	H
Headings	Headings	
381	2.76087	
355	123	
237	123	
471	123	
372	123	
428	123	
500	123	
198	123	
469		

Figure 14.5 - *The nonblank cell in G3 changes everything.*

When the cell below is nonblank, the data will copy only down until a blank cell in the current column is reached. In Figure 14.6, the formula is copied down to cell G8 only.

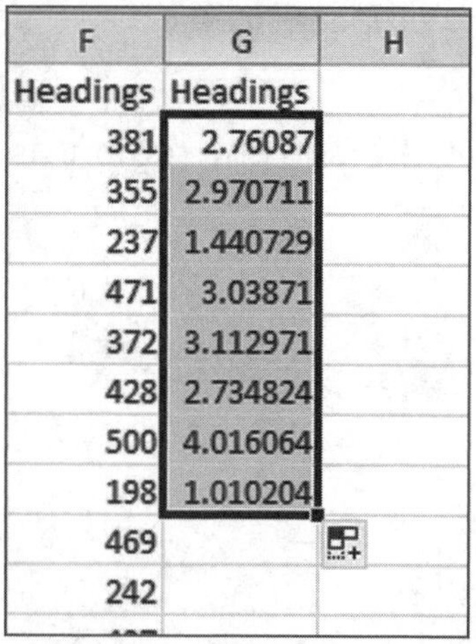

F	G	H
Headings	Headings	
381	2.76087	
355	2.970711	
237	1.440729	
471	3.03871	
372	3.112971	
428	2.734824	
500	4.016064	
198	1.010204	
469		
242		

Figure 14.6 - *The nonblank cell in G3 causes the copy to stop at the first blank cell.*

If G3 is blank, but another cell in column G has data, the copy will stop immediately above the nonblank cell.

Next Steps

Chapter 15 talks about the new sorting options in Excel 2010.

15

Sort by Color

Do you ever use color to mark problem cells?

▲	A	B	C	D	E
1	Project ID	ProjMgr	Start Date	Due Date	% Complete
15	P114	Scott	3/13/11	4/11/11	99%
16	P115	Bill	3/26/11	7/16/11	67%
17	P116	Scott	3/27/11	5/8/11	100%
18	P117	Bill	4/3/11	5/21/11	82%
19	P118	Scott	4/4/11	7/19/11	62%
20	P119	Scott	4/9/11	6/18/11	100%
21	P120	Scott	4/10/11	7/26/11	56%
22	P121	Tracy	4/12/11	7/18/11	71%

Figure 15.1 - *Red projects are really behind; yellow projects are a little behind.*

Although it is easy to use the paint bucket icon to color cells, it is difficult to then do anything with the colors. Now, in Excel 2010, you can sort the data by color.

1. From the Data tab, click the Sort icon.

2. In the Sort dialog, change the Sort On drop-down from Values to Cell Color.

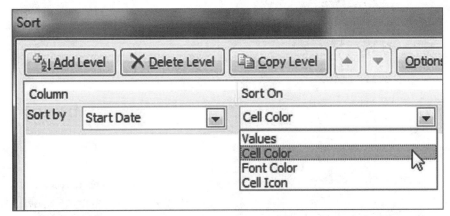

Figure 15.2 - *You can sort by cell color, font color, or conditional formatting icon.*

3. A drop-down appears in the Order column. Choose the appropriate color from the drop-down.

Figure 15.3 - *The drop-down shows colors present in the range.*

4. If you want an additional color to appear after the first color, click Copy Level. Repeat steps 2, 3 for each additional color. Your dialog might look like Figure 15.4.

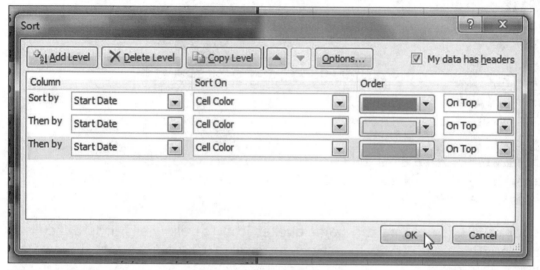

Figure 15.4 - *If you used 50 colors, filling out this dialog would take forever.*

5. Click OK to perform the sort. All the red cells will come to the top.

9	P123	Bill	4/17/11	6/29/11	70%
10	P124	Tracy	4/17/11	6/7/11	89%
11	P127	Bill	4/24/11	6/6/11	83%
12	P132	Bill	5/2/11	6/21/11	78%
13	P103	Bill	2/7/11	5/7/11	94%
14	P115	Bill	3/26/11	7/16/11	67%
15	P120	Scott	4/10/11	7/26/11	56%
16	P125	Schar	4/18/11	6/21/11	88%
17	P130	Tracy	5/1/11	7/9/11	65%
18	P131	Bill	5/1/11	6/19/11	95%
19	P136	Scott	5/21/11	8/28/11	22%
20	P140	Scott	6/6/11	7/31/11	16%
21	P121	Tracy	4/12/11	7/18/11	71%
22	P128	Scott	4/25/11	7/9/11	78%

Figure 15.5 - *The data is sorted by color. Any cell with no fill color appears at the end of the dataset.*

Quick Sort by Color

If you are interested in one particular color, you can sort that color to the top using the right-click menu. Choose a cell with the appropriate color. Right-click and choose Sort, Put Selected Cell Color on Top.

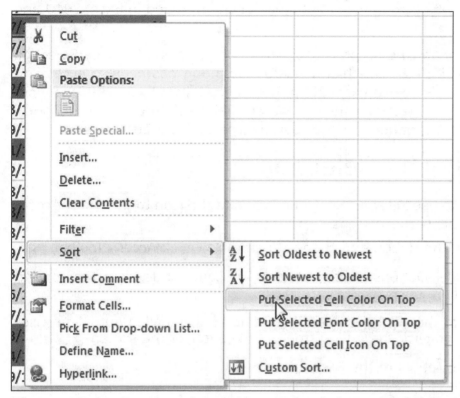

Figure 15.6 - *For a quick sort, just right-click a cell with the color you want to bring to the top.*

Next Steps

Chapter 16 covers several new filter techniques available in Excel 2010.

16

Improved Filter Tricks

The old AutoFilter feature in Excel 2003 has been improved in Excel 2010 and renamed Filter.

First, you will probably be surprised to learn that there is a Filter by Selection command in Excel 2010. This highly useful command has been in Access for many releases and is now in Excel 2010. It was actually in Excel 2003, too, but no one discovered it because the icon was mislabeled. To preserve historical accuracy, Microsoft continues to mislabel the icon in Excel 2010.

Using Filter by Selection

The easiest way to use Filter by Selection is to add the icon to the Quick Access Toolbar (QAT). Follow these steps:

1. Right-click the ribbon and choose Customize Quick Access Toolbar.

2. In the Excel Options dialog, choose All Commands from the top-left drop-down.

3. Scroll down the left list box until you find an icon called AutoFilter. Click this icon and click the Add button in the center of the screen.

4. Click OK to return to the Excel grid.

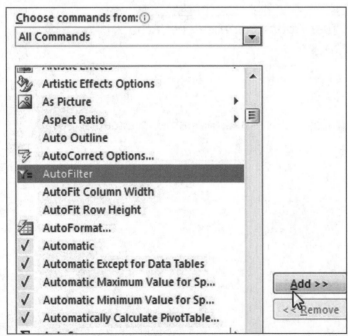

Figure 16.1 - *Filter by Selection is still mislabeled as AutoFilter.*

Suppose you have a dataset with headings in row 1, as shown in Figure 16.2. You would like to find the total sales for one particular customer in the East region.

1. Select one cell that contains the specific customer.

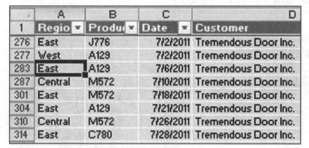

	A	B	C	D	E
1	Region	Product	Date	Customer	Quantity
275	East	C780	7/1/2011	Persuasive Meter Corporation	400
276	East	J776	7/2/2011	Tremendous Door Inc.	900
277	West	A129	7/2/2011	Tremendous Door Inc.	900
278	East	J776	7/2/2011	Best Bicycle Inc.	200
279	Central	A129	7/2/2011	Hip Bobsled Company	300
280	East	C780	7/3/2011	Best Bicycle Inc.	900
281	West	A129	7/4/2011	Steadfast Instrument Corporation	300
282	Central	J776	7/4/2011	Appealing Shoe Company	700

Figure 16.2 - *Choose any cell that contains the desired customer and click Filter by Selection.*

2. Click the Filter by Selection icon in the QAT. Excel will turn on the Filter drop-downs and filter the list to show only that customer.

3. Click a cell in the Region column that contains the desired region.

	A	B	C	D
1	Region	Product	Date	Customer
276	East	J776	7/2/2011	Tremendous Door Inc.
277	West	A129	7/2/2011	Tremendous Door Inc.
283	East	A129	7/6/2011	Tremendous Door Inc.
287	Central	M572	7/10/2011	Tremendous Door Inc.
301	East	M572	7/18/2011	Tremendous Door Inc.
304	East	A129	7/21/2011	Tremendous Door Inc.
310	Central	M572	7/26/2011	Tremendous Door Inc.
314	East	C780	7/28/2011	Tremendous Door Inc.

Figure 16.3 - *Choose a cell containing East and click Filter by Selection again.*

4. Click the Filter by Selection icon. Excel will further filter the list to only East region records.

5. Select the cells in the first blank row below the numeric columns, as shown in Figure 16.4.

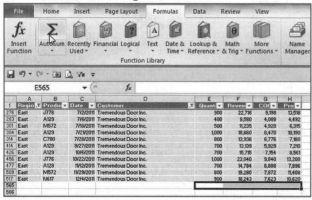

Figure 16.4 - *Choose the first blank cells under the numeric columns and click AutoSum to add ad hoc totals.*

6. Click the AutoSum icon or press Alt and the equals sign. Instead of filling in SUM functions, Excel uses the version of the SUBTOTAL function that totals only the visible rows. As shown in Figure 16.5, the total revenue for the East region is $313,454.

	E565			f_x	=SUBTOTAL(9,E2:E564)			
	A	B	C	D	E	F	G	H
1	Regio	Produ	Date	Customer	Quanti	Reven	COC	Pro
276	East	J776	7/2/2011	Tremendous Door Inc.	900	22,716	9,198	13,518
283	East	A129	7/6/2011	Tremendous Door Inc.	400	8,580	4,088	4,492
301	East	M572	7/18/2011	Tremendous Door Inc.	500	11,235	4,920	6,315
304	East	A129	7/21/2011	Tremendous Door Inc.	1,000	18,660	8,470	10,190
314	East	C780	7/28/2011	Tremendous Door Inc.	800	13,936	6,776	7,160
414	East	A129	9/27/2011	Tremendous Door Inc.	700	13,139	5,929	7,210
426	East	A129	10/6/2011	Tremendous Door Inc.	700	15,715	7,154	8,561
456	East	J776	10/22/2011	Tremendous Door Inc.	1,000	23,040	9,840	13,200
477	East	A129	11/12/2011	Tremendous Door Inc.	700	14,784	6,888	7,896
509	East	M572	11/29/2011	Tremendous Door Inc.	800	19,280	7,872	11,408
517	East	N617	12/4/2011	Tremendous Door Inc.	900	18,243	7,623	10,620
565					14500	313454	138043	175411
566								

Figure 16.5 - *The worksheet shows the total of the filtered cells.*

If you use the drop-down in A1 to change to the West region, the total automatically updates to $228,042.

	E565			f_x	=SUBTOTAL(9,E2:E564)			
	A	B	C	D	E	F	G	H
1	Regio	Produ	Date	Customer	Quanti	Reven	COC	Pro
277	West	A129	7/2/2011	Tremendous Door Inc.	900	18,099	8,856	9,243
328	West	S179	8/4/2011	Tremendous Door Inc.	200	3,418	1,694	1,724
365	West	C780	8/27/2011	Tremendous Door Inc.	300	5,859	2,541	3,318
415	West	M572	9/27/2011	Tremendous Door Inc.	800	13,552	6,776	6,776
421	West	A129	10/2/2011	Tremendous Door Inc.	500	12,760	5,110	7,650
423	West	J776	10/4/2011	Tremendous Door Inc.	1,000	24,070	10,220	13,850
490	West	J776	11/19/2011	Tremendous Door Inc.	400	6,880	3,388	3,492
545	West	C780	12/19/2011	Tremendous Door Inc.	800	18,560	8,176	10,384
557	West	N617	12/26/2011	Tremendous Door Inc.	700	14,560	6,888	7,672
565					10900	228042	101881	126161
566								

Figure 16.6 - *Change to a different filter and the total updates.*

Improved Date Filters

The filter drop-downs for date columns now automatically collapse the dates into years, months, and then dates. You can filter to a specific year or month. If you really need to filter by individual dates, expand the plus sign next to a month to reveal the days for that month.

New logical filters enable you to filter to Today, Next Week, Last Month, This Quarter, and so on. You can also choose All Dates in a particular quarter or month.

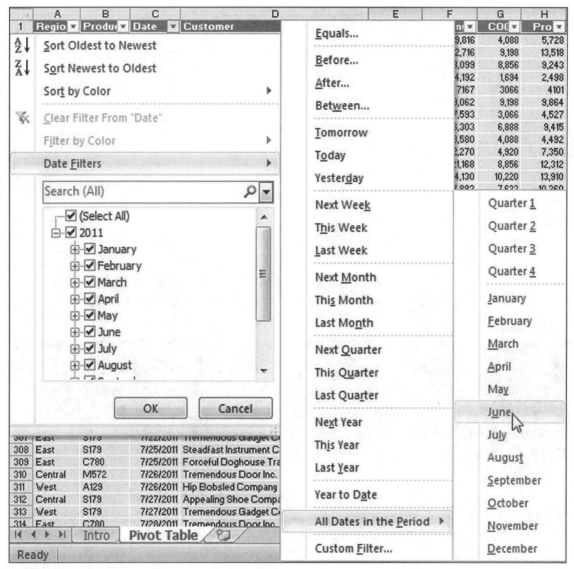

Figure 16.7 - *Date filters enable you to select a particular year or month.*

Depending on the type of data in the column, the Date Filter might be replaced with Value Filter or Text Filter menus. Each menu allows you to filter to a variety of new filter criteria.

Applying a Filter by Searching

The filter drop-downs offer a Search box. Type a word in the search box and all matching items appear in the Filter drop-down as checked. By default, Select

All Search Results is chosen, but you could opt to add the search results to the current filter.

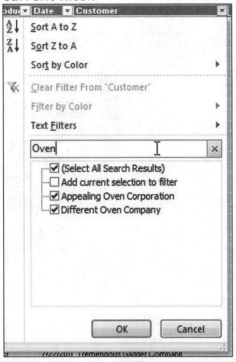

Figure 16.8 - *The Search box makes it easy to select all values that match a pattern.*

Caution: The multiselect nature of the Excel 2010 filter is a great improvement. However, if you were used to filtering to a single value in two clicks, you will now have the added step of unchecking the Select All entry before clicking the desired filter.

Filtering by Color or Icon

You can now filter cells by color or even by the conditional formatting icon applied to the cell. Although a list of icons, font colors, and fill colors will appear in a flyout menu in the filter drop-down, the easiest method is to right-click a cell with the desired icon or color, and then use Filter, Filter by Selected Cell's Icon.

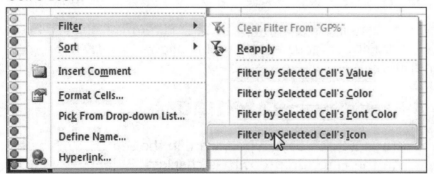

Figure 16.9 - *Filter to a certain color or icon.*

Improved Filter Tricks

In Figure 16.10, the dataset is filtered to show items in the top third of revenue but in the bottom third of gross profit percent.

D		E	F	G	H	I
Customer	▾	Quanti ▾	Reven ☕	CO(▾	Pro ▾	GF ☕
Fascinating Camera Company		1,000 ●	20,940	10,220	10,720 ●	51.2%
Tremendous Gadget Company		1,000 ●	20,490	10,220	10,270 ●	50.1%
Best Edger Company		900 ●	18,783	9,198	9,585 ●	51.0%
Steadfast Instrument Corporation		1,000 ●	20,090	9,840	10,250 ●	51.0%
Persuasive Meter Corporation		900 ●	19,539	9,198	10,341 ●	52.9%
Tremendous Gadget Company		1,000 ●	21,880	10,220	11,660 ●	53.3%
Steadfast Instrument Corporation		1000 ●	20670	10220	10450 ●	50.6%
Modular Eggbeater Supply		1,000 ●	20,950	9,840	11,110 ●	53.0%
Functional Shingle Supply		900 ●	17,757	8,856	8,901 ●	50.1%
Fascinating Camera Company		900 ●	18,918	9,198	9,720 ●	51.4%
Persuasive Meter Corporation		1,000 ●	20,480	9,840	10,640 ●	52.0%
Best Bicycle Inc.		1,000 ●	20,020	9,840	10,180 ●	50.8%
Tremendous Door Inc.		900 ●	18,099	8,856	9,243 ●	51.1%
Best Bicycle Inc.		900 ●	19,062	9,198	9,864 ●	51.7%
Inventive Wax Company		1,000 ●	17,840	8,470	9,370 ●	52.5%
Steadfast Instrument Corporation		900 ●	19,584	9,198	10,386 ●	53.0%
Supreme Yardstick Inc.		900 ●	18,684	9,198	9,486 ●	50.8%
Forceful Doghouse Traders		900 ●	19,593	9,198	10,395 ●	53.1%
Best Edger Company		900 ●	19,368	9,198	10,170 ●	52.5%
Steadfast Instrument Corporation		900 ●	18,486	8,856	9,630 ●	52.1%
Persuasive Meter Corporation		1,000 ●	20,190	9,840	10,350 ●	51.3%
Tremendous Gadget Company		900 ●	19,161	9,198	9,963 ●	52.0%
Best Edger Company		1,000 ●	20,540	9,840	10,700 ●	52.1%
Appealing Shoe Company		1000 ●	20840	9840	11000 ●	52.8%
Supreme Yardstick Inc.		900 ●	18,756	9,198	9,558 ●	51.0%
Tremendous Gadget Company		900 ●	18,666	9,198	9,468 ●	50.7%
		24600	509386	245976	263410	51.7%

Figure 16.10 - *The dataset after filtering Revenue to green icons and GP% to red icons.*

Next Steps

Chapter 17 covers the new Remove Duplicates command.

17

Remove Duplicates

For many tasks in Excel, you need to remove duplicates from a dataset.

> **Tip**: The Remove Duplicates feature can also be used to find the unique list of values in a dataset.

Suppose you want to find the unique list of customers in this range.

▲	A	B	C
1	Date ▼	Customer ▼	Sales ▼
2	6/27/2010	Inventive Eggbeater Inc.	184
3	6/14/2010	Amazing Yogurt Corporation	169
4	6/12/2010	Tasty Belt Corporation	106
5	6/23/2010	Modular Thermostat Company	181
6	6/6/2010	Tasty Belt Corporation	168
7	6/9/2010	Magnificent Tripod Inc.	153
8	6/9/2010	Hip Raft Corporation	135
9	6/25/2010	Tasty Belt Corporation	105
10	6/6/2010	Inventive Eggbeater Inc.	117
11	6/27/2010	Modular Thermostat Company	143
12	6/29/2010	Succulent Paint Supply	171
13	6/18/2010	Inventive Eggbeater Inc.	153
14	6/27/2010	Best Adhesive Inc.	124
15	6/10/2010	Best Adhesive Inc.	117
16	6/15/2010	Hip Raft Corporation	184
17	6/27/2010	Alluring Shingle Inc.	190
18	6/8/2010	Inventive Eggbeater Inc.	95
19	6/5/2010	Hip Raft Corporation	143
20	6/30/2010	Modular Thermostat Company	183

Figure 17.1 - *Who are the unique customers in the list?*

Caution: Remove Duplicates is a destructive function. It is best to make a copy of your data before you use the feature!

In Figure 17.2, a copy of the Customer column appears in column F. From the Data tab, choose Remove Duplicates.

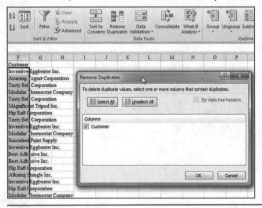

Figure 17.2 - *If your dataset has multiple columns, you can tell Excel to base the duplicates on a subset of the columns.*

Click OK and Excel will delete any duplicated values. The remaining dataset is the unique list of customers.

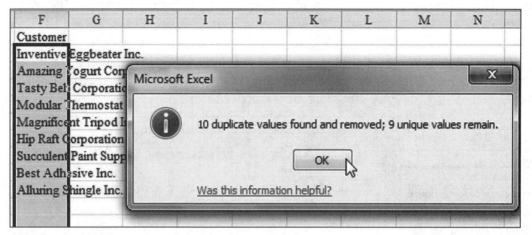

Figure 17.3 - *The duplicates are actually removed.*

Marking Duplicates

Although the Remove Duplicates button is amazing, it is also potentially destructive. Perhaps you want to identify the duplicates so that you can decide how to combine information from the duplicates.

Select the range of values. On the Home tab, choose Conditional Formatting, Highlight Cells Rules, Duplicate Values. Excel will highlight the duplicates in red.

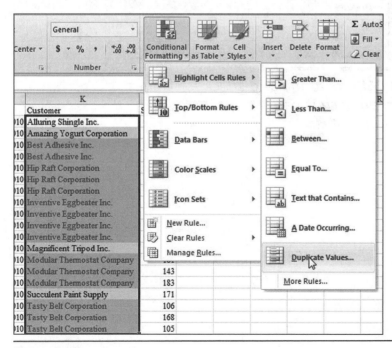

Figure 17.4 - *Marking the duplicates with conditional formatting is less destructive and gives you time to figure out how to combine duplicates.*

Note: Note that Excel marks all the duplicate values. I don't consider this to be extremely useful. I would rather have Excel leave the first occurrence of each duplicated value unhighlighted. This way, the highlighted cells could be deleted after review. If you would select Home, Conditional Formatting, Choose a Formula to Specify Which Cells to Highlight, and then you could set up a formula like the one shown in Figure 17.5 to mark only the true duplicate values.

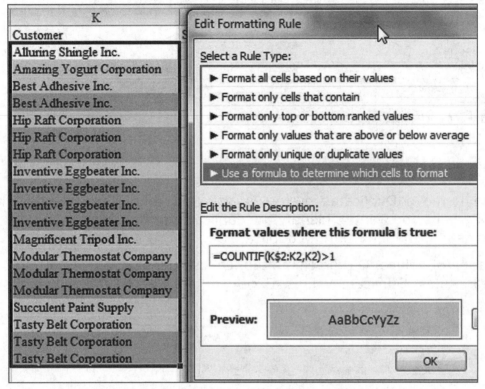

Figure 17.5 - *Using the COUNTIF formula to check for values that have occurred more than once is better than the built-in conditional formatting for duplicates.*

Next Steps

Chapter 18 discusses the Subtotals command.

18

Add Subtotals Automatically

Subtotals are not a new feature. They've been around since Excel 97. However, if you have never used them, they will seem miraculous to you. Even if you have used the Subtotal command, read through this chapter, as there are some tricks available after you have subtotaled the worksheet.

In Figure 18.1, you have a large dataset. You want to add a total for each customer that will total quantity, revenue, COGS, and profit.

	A	B	C	D	E	F	G	H
1	Region	Product	Date	Customer	Quantity	Revenue	COGS	Profit
2	Central	N617	1/1/2011	Tremendous Gadget Company	100	2,257	984	1,273
3	East	A129	1/1/2011	Forceful Doghouse Traders	1,000	22,810	10,220	12,590
4	East	C780	1/1/2011	Tremendous Gadget Company	500	10,245	4,235	6,010
5	Central	J776	1/2/2011	Fascinating Camera Company	500	11,240	5,110	6,130
6	Central	M572	1/3/2011	Fascinating Camera Company	400	9,204	4,088	5,116
7	East	C780	1/3/2011	Fine Faucet Inc.	800	18,552	7,872	10,680

Figure 18.1 - *Your manager wants this data summarized by customer.*

Follow these steps to add subtotals:

1. The data should be sorted by customer. Select a single cell in the Customer column. On the Data tab, click the AZ sort button. Excel sorts the data by customer.

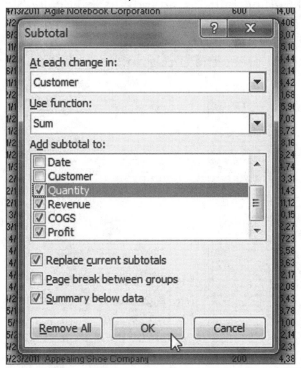

Figure 18.2 - *If your rightmost field contains text, be sure to change the Use Function dropdown from Count to Sum.*

2. On the Data tab, click the Subtotal icon.

3. The Subtotal dialog always assumes that you want to subtotal by the leftmost field and that the subtotal will be applied to the rightmost field. Change Region to Customer, ensure the function is the Sum function, and add checkmarks to Quantity, Revenue, and COGS, as shown in Figure 18.2. If you want each customer on a new page, click Page Break Between Groups.

4. Click the OK button. Excel quickly inserts new rows at every change in customer and adds new Subtotal functions as shown in row 6 and row 11 of Figure 18.3.

	E6			f_x	=SUBTOTAL(9,E2:E5)			

1 2 3		A	B	C	D	E	F	G	H
	1	Region	Product	Date	Customer	Quantity	Revenue	COGS	Profit
	2	East	C780	4/13/2011	Agile Notebook Corporation	600	14,004	5,904	8,100
	3	Central	A129	6/24/2011	Agile Notebook Corporation	200	4060	1968	2092
	4	West	J776	8/31/2011	Agile Notebook Corporation	800	18,072	8,176	9,896
	5	West	M572	11/4/2011	Agile Notebook Corporation	800	15,104	6,776	8,328
	6				Agile Notebook Corporation T	2,400	51,240	22,824	28,416
	7	East	M572	1/20/2011	Appealing Oven Corporation	800	14,440	6,776	7,664
	8	Central	S179	6/18/2011	Appealing Oven Corporation	1,000	22,140	9,840	12,300
	9	East	S179	11/19/2011	Appealing Oven Corporation	1,000	24,420	10,220	14,200
	10	West	N617	12/26/2011	Appealing Oven Corporation	500	11,680	5,110	6,570
	11				Appealing Oven Corporation T	3,300	72,680	31,946	40,734
	12	East	J776	1/16/2011	Appealing Shoe Company	300	5,961	2,952	3,009
	13	West	J776	1/20/2011	Appealing Shoe Company	300	7,032	2,952	4,080

Figure 18.3 - *Excel quickly adds the subtotals.*

5. Notice that to the left of column A, you have new buttons labeled 1, 2, and 3. These are group and outline buttons added automatically by the Subtotal command. Click the 2 button to see a summary of the customer totals as shown in Figure 18.4. If you press the 1 button, you will see just the grand total. If you press the 3 button, you will see all the detail rows again.

1 2 3		C	D	E	F	G	H
	1	Date	Customer	Quantity	Revenue	COGS	Profit
	6		Agile Notebook Corporation Total	2,400	51,240	22,824	28,416
	11		Appealing Oven Corporation Total	3,300	72,680	31,946	40,734
	78		Appealing Shoe Company Total	33,400	704,359	311,381	392,978
	119		Best Bicycle Inc. Total	23,100	498,937	219,978	278,959
	168		Best Edger Company Total	29,100	613,514	275,105	338,409
	173		Different Oven Company Total	1,700	34,710	16,423	18,287
	226		Fascinating Camera Company Total	26,600	568,851	252,522	316,329
	231		Fine Faucet Inc. Total	1,900	42,316	18,764	23,552
	236		First-Rate Hairpin Company Total	2,700	57,516	26,765	30,751
	293		Forceful Doghouse Traders Total	28,900	622,794	274,978	347,816
	298		Functional Shingle Supply Total	2,800	60,299	27,049	33,250
	303		Hip Bobsled Company Total	3,000	62,744	28,644	34,100
	308		Inventive Opener Corporation Total	2,000	46,717	19,961	26,756
	313		Inventive Wax Company Total	2,600	55,251	24,632	30,619
	318		Magnificent Vegetable Inc. Total	2,600	54,048	23,780	30,268
	323		Modular Chopstick Company Total	2,300	50,030	21,612	28,418
	328		Modular Eggbeater Supply Total	3,300	71,651	32,471	39,180
	333		New Lawn Inc. Total	2,700	59,881	25,913	33,968
	338		Paramount Saddle Corporation Total	1,600	34,384	15,576	18,788
	383		Persuasive Meter Corporation Total	19,700	427,349	189,331	238,018
	388		Persuasive Meter Inc. Total	1400	31369	13730	17639
	393		Secure Jewelry Inc. Total	1,400	31,021	13,745	17,276
	454		Steadfast Instrument Corporation T	35,700	750,163	334,614	415,549
	483		Supreme Yardstick Inc. Total	18,700	406,326	178,585	227,741
	549		Tremendous Door Inc. Total	40,400	869,454	382,170	487,284
	586		Tremendous Gadget Company Total	18,600	390,978	177,281	213,697
	591		Vibrant Juicer Company Total	2,000	39,250	18,614	20,636
	592		Grand Total	313,900	6,707,812	2,978,394	3,729,418

Figure 18.4 - *Pressing the 2 group and outline button provides an excellent view of just the customer totals.*

Removing Subtotals

To remove automatic subtotals, select one cell in the dataset. Click the Subtotal button in the Data tab. In the Subtotal dialog, click the Remove All button.

Copying Only the Subtotal Rows

After you have data in the 2 summarized view like in Figure 18.4, a natural reaction is to copy the subtotal rows and paste them to a new worksheet. Unfortunately, this also brings along the detail rows.

It is easy to copy only the subtotal rows, yet it is an incredibly obscure trick:

1. Add subtotals to a dataset and collapse the dataset using the 2 group and Outline button.

2. Select from the final grand total row up to the first heading.

3. Press Alt+; (that is, hold down the Alt key while pressing the semicolon).

4. Click Ctrl+C to copy. You will see that Excel is selecting just the visible rows. You can now paste to another worksheet.

The key step is the Alt+; to select only the visible rows. Alt+; is the shortcut key that replaces Home, Find & Select, Go to Special, Visible Cells Only, OK. The Go To Special dialog is a powerful dialog. Figure 18.5 shows the Go To Special dialog. This dialog is useful for selecting only the blanks, or only the errors, or only the formulas in a selection.

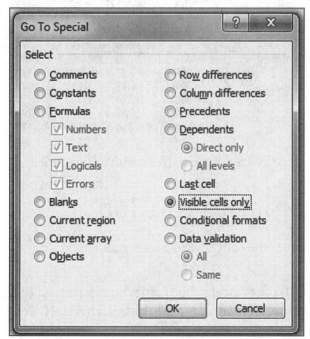

Figure 18.5 - *There are many useful options in the Go To Special dialog. Find it by selecting Home, Find & Select, Go To Special*

The Alt+; trick also works when you want to format the subtotal rows, as described in the next section.

Formatting the Subtotal Rows

The ability to select only the visible cells within a selection allows you to format the subtotal rows. Suppose in Figure 18.4 you want the customer totals to be in green. Follow these steps:

1. Add subtotals by customer.
2. Click the 2 Group and Outline button to see the customer totals.
3. Select from the last customer total row up to the first customer subtotal row.
4. Press Alt+; to select the visible cells within the selection.
5. From the Home tab, choose Cell Styles, Accent 3, 40%.
6. Click the 3 group and Outline button. You will see that each subtotal row has been formatted.

	B	C	D	E	F	G	H
1	Product	Date	Customer	Quantity	Revenue	COGS	Profit
286	M572	11/13/2011	Forceful Doghouse Traders	1,000	21,740	9,840	11,900
287	N617	11/14/2011	Forceful Doghouse Traders	900	19,674	8,856	10,818
288	A129	12/4/2011	Forceful Doghouse Traders	800	17,496	8,176	9,320
289	C780	12/5/2011	Forceful Doghouse Traders	800	16,856	6,776	10,080
290	M572	12/14/2011	Forceful Doghouse Traders	500	10,380	5,110	5,270
291	M572	12/17/2011	Forceful Doghouse Traders	700	13,552	5,929	7,623
292	J776	12/19/2011	Forceful Doghouse Traders	800	14,408	6,776	7,632
293			Forceful Doghouse Traders Total	28,900	622,794	274,978	347,816
294	A129	3/5/2011	Functional Shingle Supply	700	12,474	5,929	6,545
295	M572	4/3/2011	Functional Shingle Supply	800	20,408	8,176	12,232
296	N617	5/18/2011	Functional Shingle Supply	900	17,757	8,856	8,901
297	C780	12/8/2011	Functional Shingle Supply	400	9,660	4,088	5,572
298			Functional Shingle Supply Total	2,800	60,299	27,049	33,250
299	A129	7/2/2011	Hip Bobsled Company	300	7167	3066	4101
300	C780	7/14/2011	Hip Bobsled Company	700	14,497	6,888	7,609
301	A129	7/26/2011	Hip Bobsled Company	1,000	23,890	10,220	13,670
302	J776	10/13/2011	Hip Bobsled Company	1,000	17,190	8,470	8,720
303			Hip Bobsled Company Total	3,000	62,744	28,644	34,100
304	J776	4/30/2011	Inventive Opener Corporation	800	19,520	7,872	11,648

Figure 18.6 - *When you display the detail lines again, the subtotals appear in an offsetting color.*

Sorting Largest Customer to the Top

This is counterintuitive, but you can sort the data while it is collapsed. Excel will sort groups of records.

In Figure 18.4, you can see that the Tremendous Door Inc customer is the largest customer, with $869K of revenue and about 60+ detail rows. If you would choose a value in the Revenue column of Figure 18.4 and click the ZA

Add Subtotals Automatically

button, the total for Tremendous Door would sort to the top of the worksheet.

However, notice that the customer does not sort to row 2. It sorts to row 67. Rows 2 through 66 are the detail rows for Tremendous Door and were sorted along with the Total row!

1	Product	Date	Customer	Quantity	Revenue	COGS	Profit
67			Tremendous Door Inc. Total	40,400	869,454	382,170	487,284
128			Steadfast Instrument Corporation Total	35,700	750,163	334,614	415,549
195			Appealing Shoe Company Total	33,400	704,359	311,381	392,978
252			Forceful Doghouse Traders Total	28,900	622,794	274,978	347,816
301			Best Edger Company Total	29,100	613,514	275,105	338,409
354			Fascinating Camera Company Total	26,600	568,851	252,522	316,329
395			Best Bicycle Inc. Total	23,100	498,937	219,978	278,959
440			Persuasive Meter Corporation Total	19,700	427,349	189,331	238,018

F67 = =SUBTOTAL(9,F2:F66)

Figure 18.7 - *Sort the data while it is collapsed and the hidden detail rows move along with their subtotal row.*

Next Steps

Chapter 19 covers the Easy-XL software for Excel.

19

Using the Easy-XL Program

The Easy-XL program is a new tool for people who have to perform complex data analysis tasks in Excel. As the owner of this book, you can try out Easy-XL for 45 days, more than enough time to get through your next big data project.

If VLOOKUPs make your head hurt, the commands in Easy-XL will let you merge, compare, query, combine, and slice and dice data like an Excel pro. If you already are the Excel pro, you will appreciate that Easy-XL lets you do tasks faster than ever before.

If you find that Easy-XL is for you, you can buy a full license at 25% off the normal price.

Downloading and Installing Easy-XL

Easy-XL works with all 32-bit versions of Excel for Windows, from Excel 2000 up through Excel 2010. (A 64-bit version will be out in late 2010.) Easy-XL runs under Windows XP, Vista, or Windows 7. It does not run on the Macintosh platform.

To get started, visit this secret URL to download the software: www.easy-xl.com/upgbook.

You will download Easy-XL.msi. Make sure that Excel is closed. Double-click the installation file to install Easy-XL. When you load Excel, you should see a new Easy-XL tab in the Excel 2010 ribbon (Figure 19.1).

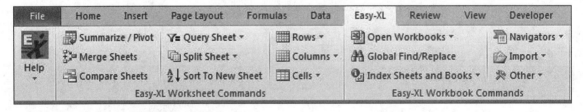

Figure 19.1 - *After installing Easy-XL, you should have this ribbon tab.*

Use Easy-XL with Tabular Data

Many of Easy-XL's powerful data analytics commands are looking for tabular data. This means field headings in row 1, no blank rows, and no blank columns. This probably describes most of your worksheets.

To test out Easy-XL, you can load up the sample workbook that ships with Easy-XL. Select Easy-XL, Other, Open Easy-XL Sample Workbook. You will get a workbook with six data worksheets. The sample file included in the download for this book is the same data, with some color formats applied. The data worksheets contain databases for invoices, products, customers, and salespeople.

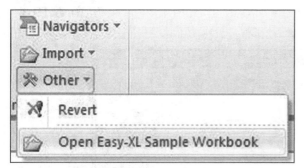

Figure 19.2 - *Easy-XL includes this sample dataset that you can use for learning the powerful Easy-XL features.*

Joining Two Tables Without VLOOKUP

The Invoices 2011 worksheet in the sample dataset includes a customer ID, but no useful information, such as customer name, state, and so on.

The sample workbook has a worksheet called Customer. This worksheet shows the customer name, address, city, and state for each customer ID.

	A	B	C	D	E	F	G	U
1	InvoiceNo	InvoiceDat	PaymentD	Custom	SalesP	Product	Quantity	U
2	20000	1/1/2011	3/6/2011	10220	8	8	4	
3	20001	1/1/2011	2/9/2011	10491	4	4	4	
4	20002	1/1/2011	2/22/2011	10704	3	1	3	
5	20003	1/1/2011	2/9/2011	10430	5	54	4	
6	20004	1/1/2011	2/28/2011	10841	17	11	2	
7	20005	1/1/2011	2/24/2011	10777	1	5	4	
8	20006	1/1/2011	2/5/2011	10653	19	58	2	
9	20007	1/1/2011	2/27/2011	10413	12	61	3	
10	20008	1/1/2011	1/23/2011	10654	12	4	3	
11	20009	1/1/2011	1/26/2011	10300	1	10	2	
12	20010	1/2/2011	2/6/2011	10439	99	38	4	
13	20010	1/1/2011	2/21/2011	10439	19	38	4	

Invoices2011 / Invoices2010 / Pro

	A	B	C
1	CustomerNo	ContactName	Address
2	10000	Kennedy Merrill	4773 Hanover Driv
3	10001	Kevon Cote De Neig	4615 Almeria Stre
4	10002	Annette Shields	4306 Covell Blvd.
5	10003	Peter Sellers	7219 Canoe Place
6	10004	Yessenia Holcomb	6734 Van Gogh S
7	10005	Richard Greer	8327 Matisse Stre
8	10006	Ronnie John Howell	5048 Jerome Stre
9	10007	Devan Larson	4432 Pomona Driv
10	10008	Bryant Singleton	4229 Coolidge Str
11	10009	Gonzalo Montgomer	2742 Washoe Str
12	10010	Eleanor Rigby	1226 Banyan Plac
13	10011	Priscilla Presley	3199 Galileo Cour

Products | **Customers** / SalesPeople2011

Figure 19.3 - *You want to match up data from these two worksheets.*

You want to merge data on these two sheets so that the customer name and state is included on the Invoices 2011 worksheet.

Follow these steps:

1. Start on the Invoices 2011 worksheet. Choose Easy-XL, Merge Sheets. Excel displays a Select a Sheet to Merge with Invoices 2011 dialog.

2. Select Customers and click Select. Excel displays the Merge Sheets dialog.

3. In the Merge Sheets dialog, indicate that you want to group by the Customer Number field. In the right list box, choose Contact Name and State. In the Merge Options section, choose that you want Rows in Sheet1 that match a row in Sheet2 and also Rows in Sheet1 that don't match a row in Sheet2. The Merge dialog should look like Figure 19.4. Click OK

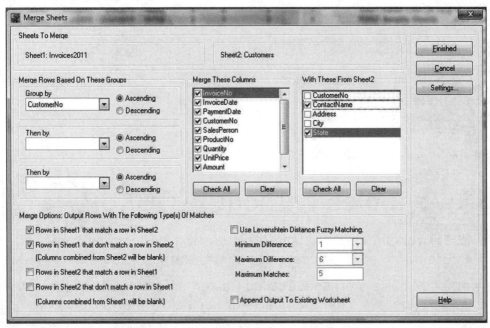

Figure 19.4 - *Combine two fields from the Customer worksheet into the Invoices worksheet.*

Easy-XL takes the data from the Invoices 2011 worksheet and the data from the Customer worksheet and creates a brand new worksheet called MergedInvoices2011.A comment in cell A1 indicates the date, time, and options used to create the worksheet. The formulas are converted to values.

	A	I	J	K	L
1	InvoiceNo	A	Bill Jelen:	Customers.ContactName	Customers.State
2	21369		3/13/2010 9:31:00 AM Star	Kennedy Merrill	NS
3	21893		Easy-XL Merge Sheets	Kennedy Merrill	NS
4	21966		Sheet1: Invoices2011 Pack	Kennedy Merrill	NS
5	23663		Sheet2: Customers	Kennedy Merrill	NS
6	20207		GroupBy CustomerNo /Ascending	Kevon Cote De Neige	ON
7	20231		# Rows: 5000	Kevon Cote De Neige	ON
8	22112	20	//	on 2 Kevon Cote De Neige	ON
9	22956	5,745.00	Microsoft ESP SDK	Kevon Cote De Neige	ON
10	23845	916.00	PowerPoint for Mac 2008	Kevon Cote De Neige	ON
11	20069	499.90	Easy-SQL From MrExcel	Annette Shields	MB

Invoices2011 **Merged Invoices2011** Invoices2010 Products Customers SalesPeople20

Figure 19.5 - *The new columns appear on the right side of the worksheet.*

> **Caution**: Check the final rows in the dataset. If any customers did not have a match in the customer worksheet, those records will appear with blank customer names at the end of the worksheet.

Splitting a Worksheet into Multiple Worksheets

You often have a large database of information. You need to split that data into multiple worksheets, one for each region or for each sales rep. Easy-XL makes this a snap.

Choose Easy-XL, Split Sheet, Split Sheet by Group.

Figure 19.6 - *Break the sheet into new sheets based on a field.*

In this example, the worksheet is being split into separate worksheets. However, you could split them into groups of nn rows, with shorter groups being padded so that each group is the same size.

Figure 19.7 - *Break the sheet into new sheets based on a field.*

In a few seconds, you have several new worksheets, one for each value found in the column. The worksheet contains records of only that state or province. An optional hyperlink at the right side of the worksheet will navigate back to the row in the original dataset.

	J	K	L	M
1	Description	Customers.ContactName	Customers.State	OriginalRow
2	Office for Mac 2008	Kevon Cote De Neige	ON	6
3	PowerPoint for Mac 2008	Kevon Cote De Neige	ON	7
4	Commerce Server Standard Edition 2	Kevon Cote De Neige	ON	8
5	Microsoft ESP SDK	Kevon Cote De Neige	ON	9
6	PowerPoint for Mac 2008	Kevon Cote De Neige	ON	10
7	Easy-SQL From MrExcel	Bella Callahan	ON	68
8	Office OneNote 2007	Bella Callahan	ON	69
9	Word for Mac 2008	Bella Callahan	ON	70
10	MapPoint® 2010 for Windows	Bella Callahan	ON	71
11	Customer Care Framework 2009 Ext	Bella Callahan	ON	72
12	Commerce Server Enterprise Edition	Edward Fulton	ON	105

ᴵ⁴ ◄ ► ►ᴵ / AB / BC / MB / NB / NL / NS / NT / NU | **ON** / PE / OC / SK / YT / blank / Merged Invoices

Figure 19.8 - *The worksheet is split to multiple worksheets.*

Getting Quick Statistics

Select any range of cells. Right-click and choose Easy-XL Quick Stats. A flyout menu appears that shows the total, min, max, median, number of positive values, number of negative values, number of errors, and so on.

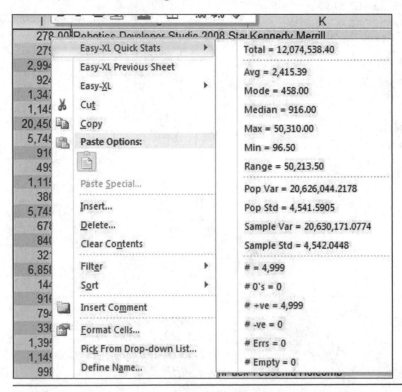

Figure 19.9 - *Quick statistics are a right-click away for any selection.*

Navigators

Easy-XL includes a number of floating navigator panels. These can help you navigate through workbooks, worksheets, or cells. In Figure 19.10, the cells navigator can be used to expand the current selection or to nudge the selection in any direction. For example, when you nudge the selection in Figure 19.10 down, the same size range is selected, but one row farther down.

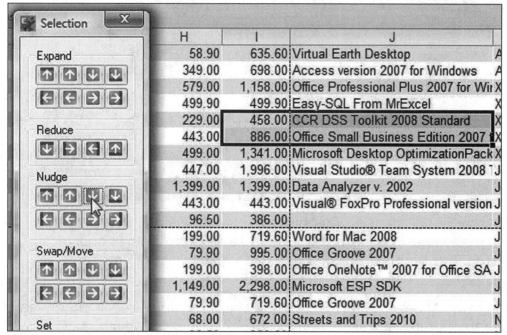

Figure 19.10 - *Expand, reduce, or nudge the selection.*

Figure 19.11 shows what it looks like after you nudge the selection.

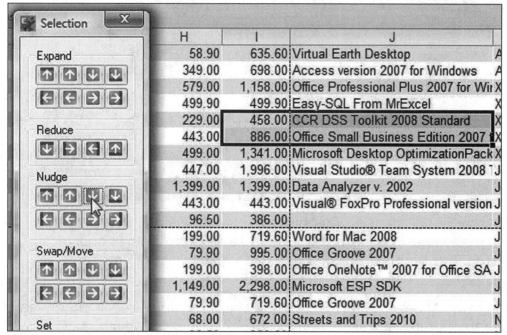

Figure 19.11 - *After nudging, the selection moves down one row.*

Comparing Two Worksheets

The Compare Worksheets command will summarize two worksheets. In Figure 19.12, the dialog is set up to compare Invoices 2011 to Invoices 2010. The result will show total amount sold by salesperson.

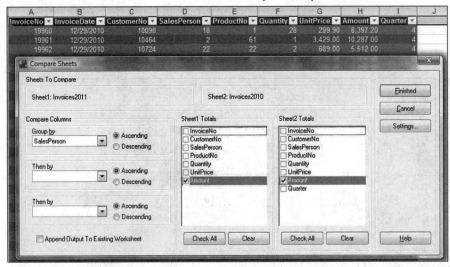

Figure 19.12
- *Compare two sheets, summarizing by sales rep.*

Tip: Do you notice the Settings button in every dialog? If you have a particularly complex dialog box, you can save your settings and recall them later. The Settings button leads to a dialog where you can save settings for future use or load previous settings.

The resulting worksheet shows you each sales rep who appeared in either year. You can see the number of records and the total amount for each.

	SalesPerson	Count.Invoices2011	Count.Invoices2010	Count.Difference	Amount.Total.Invoices2011	Amount.Total.Invoices2010	Tags
1	SalesPerson	Count.Invoices2011	Count.Invoices2010	Count.Difference	Amount.Total.Invoices2011	Amount.Total.Invoices2010	Tags
2	1	100	95	5	189,493.36	159,894.78	
3	2	202	195	7	432,967.59	309,746.51	
4	3	203	200	3	419,241.81	396,192.69	
5	4	180	181	-1	468,563.73	320,541.15	
6	5	195	195	0	378,014.07	316,565.02	
7	6	217	202	15	448,933.24	341,791.95	
8	7	189	189	0	353,037.03	333,180.60	
9	8	171	197	-26	300,969.86	348,638.64	
10	9	201	206	-5	398,553.49	347,886.38	
11	10	196	178	18	401,475.48	266,570.49	
12	11	206	187	19	431,883.95	348,365.72	
13	12	225	205	20	430,065.03	409,209.19	
14	13	217	165	52	399,084.55	296,022.45	
15	14	210	164	46	524,024.52	276,039.53	
16	15	179	173	6	334,878.83	296,522.72	
17	16	204	193	11	460,860.85	397,758.23	
18	17	184	218	-34	346,677.18	346,872.37	
19	18	223	187	36	534,510.10	286,704.71	
20	19	209	195	14	389,831.35	302,493.80	
21	20	218	182	36	587,328.83	335,089.56	
22	21	212	182	30	914,789.73	299,923.54	
23	22	186	176	10	579,574.62	276,174.50	
24	23	189	112	77	581,837.85	167,391.82	
25	24	185	0	185	627,891.19		+
26	25	204	0	204	900,783.51		+
27	26	92	0	92	235,648.65		+
28	27	1	0	1	2,546.00		+
29	28	0	85	-85		130,395.00	+
30	99	1	0	1	1,072.00		+

Figure 19.13 - *In these 30 lines, 10,000 records are summarized.*

Adding a Calculated Column

Easy-XL offers dialog boxes that help you add calculated columns. If you need to figure out the number of days difference between an invoice date and a payment date, this is just one of the many calculations available.

Choose Easy-XL, Columns, Calculated Column.

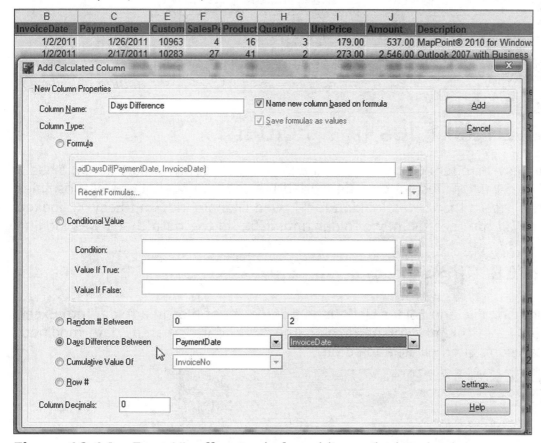

Figure 19.14 - *Easy-XL offers tools for adding calculated columns.*

The result is added as values rather than formulas.

B	C	D
InvoiceDate	PaymentDate	Days Difference
1/2/2011	1/26/2011	25
1/2/2011	2/17/2011	47
1/2/2011	3/9/2011	66
1/2/2011	2/3/2011	32
1/2/2011	2/11/2011	40
1/2/2011	3/10/2011	68
1/2/2011	2/5/2011	35
1/2/2011	2/10/2011	40
1/3/2011	3/3/2011	59

Figure 19.15 - *Easy-XL offers tools for adding calculated columns.*

Easy-XL even adds new functions to Excel. If you need to figure out fiscal quarters, the adFiscalQuarter function lets you do that. Even the time intelligence functions in the PowerPivot DAX language can't do this.

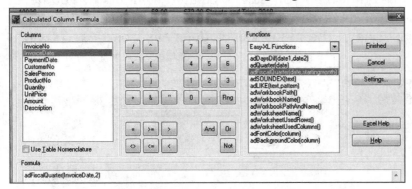

Figure 19.16 - *Easy-XL offers tools for adding calculated columns.*

Search All Files in a Folder

When Easy-XL offers Global Find and Replace, they really mean *global*. I had a series of 81 Excel files out on a network drive and I knew that one of those files had the record that I was looking for. I used Global Find, and Easy-XL looked through all the records in the folder until it found the data that I was looking for.

List All Files in a Folder

Use Import, File and Folder Listings to bring a list of files in a folder into Excel. You will have columns for path, filename, size, date created, date modified. You can sort, filter, print, and so on.

	A	B	C	D	E
1	Path	Name	Size	SizeMB	DateCreated
2	M:\aaProductFolders\2010Miracles\SampleFiles\	03-ThisFileHasLinks.xlsx	11,757	0.01	2010/03/13 08:39:02 AM
3	M:\aaProductFolders\2010Miracles\SampleFiles\	03-WithMacros.xlsm	15,440	0.01	2010/03/13 08:39:02 AM
4	M:\aaProductFolders\2010Miracles\SampleFiles\	05-BigGrid.xlsm	41,521	0.04	2010/03/13 08:39:04 AM
5	M:\aaProductFolders\2010Miracles\SampleFiles\	05-Tax97.xlsx	9,881	0.01	2010/03/13 08:39:05 AM
6	M:\aaProductFolders\2010Miracles\SampleFiles\	07-PageLayoutPreview.xlsm	3,660,754	3.49	2010/03/13 08:39:05 AM
7	M:\aaProductFolders\2010Miracles\SampleFiles\	08-KeyboardShortcuts.xlsm	50,715	0.05	2010/03/13 08:39:06 AM
8	M:\aaProductFolders\2010Miracles\SampleFiles\	08-Visualizations.xlsm	47,104	0.04	2010/03/13 08:39:06 AM
9	M:\aaProductFolders\2010Miracles\SampleFiles\	09-FillHandle.xlsx	40,471	0.04	2010/03/13 08:39:06 AM
10	M:\aaProductFolders\2010Miracles\SampleFiles\	09-FormulaBar.xlsm	1,022,571	0.98	2010/03/13 08:39:06 AM
11	M:\aaProductFolders\2010Miracles\SampleFiles\	09-SortByColor.xlsm	41,311	0.04	2010/03/13 08:39:06 AM
12	M:\aaProductFolders\2010Miracles\SampleFiles\	1-Ribbon.xlsx	10,584	0.01	2010/03/13 08:39:01 AM
13	M:\aaProductFolders\2010Miracles\SampleFiles\	11-StatusBar.xlsm	259,852	0.25	2010/03/13 08:39:06 AM
14	M:\aaProductFolders\2010Miracles\SampleFiles\	12-Functions.xlsm	87,176	0.08	2010/03/13 08:39:06 AM
15	M:\aaProductFolders\2010Miracles\SampleFiles\	13-Tables.xlsx	49,910	0.05	2010/03/13 08:39:06 AM
16	M:\aaProductFolders\2010Miracles\SampleFiles\	15-SortByColor.xlsx	41,355	0.04	2010/03/13 08:39:07 AM
17	M:\aaProductFolders\2010Miracles\SampleFiles\	16-Filtering.xlsx	83,518	0.08	2010/03/13 08:39:07 AM
18	M:\aaProductFolders\2010Miracles\SampleFiles\	16-Pictures.xlsm	7,537,194	7.19	2010/03/13 08:39:07 AM
19	M:\aaProductFolders\2010Miracles\SampleFiles\	18-Subtotals.xlsm	78,225	0.07	2010/03/13 08:39:08 AM

Figure 19.17 - *Get a list of files in a folder.*

These are just a few of the 50 new commands added to Excel by the Easy-XL program. Download a free trial from www.easy-xl.com/upgbook to try it out yourself.

Next Steps

Chapter 20 covers the most powerful feature in Excel: pivot tables.

20

Pivot Tables

A pivot table report enables you to analyze and summarize a million rows of data in Excel 2010 without entering a single formula.

Pivot tables are incredibly flexible, and you can create hundreds of different styles of reports. This chapter shows you how to create a basic pivot table in Excel 2010, and then shows off some of the new features available in Excel 2010. Note that a complete book on pivot tables would be larger than this volume. If you want to learn about pivot tables, the best-selling pivot table book is *Pivot Table Data Crunching* by Michael Alexander and me.

Creating a Pivot Table

Start with a transactional dataset. You should have unique headings in the first row, and then no blank rows or blank columns in the data. For best results, keep your numeric columns filled with numeric data and replace any blank cells with a 0. A typical dataset will look like Figure 20.1.

	A	B	C	D	E	F	G	H
1	Customer	Region	Product	Date	Quantity	Revenue	COGS	Profit
83503	Fascinating Utensil Inc.	Midwest	F175	31-Dec-11	60	1860	900	960
83504	Agile Umbrella Inc.	Southeast	H897	31-Dec-11	36	1476	720	756
83505	Functional Ink Corporatic	SoCal	L117	31-Dec-11	132	9372	4620	4752
83506	Guaranteed Camera Cor	SoCal	J832	31-Dec-11	60	3060	1500	1560
83507	Supreme Raft Traders	Southeast	F175	31-Dec-11	36	1116	540	576
83508	Bright Tackle Corporatio	Northwest	R554	31-Dec-11	12	1092	540	552
83509	Ideal Yardstick Inc.	Southeast	J832	31-Dec-11	72	3672	1800	1872
83510	Succulent Oven Traders	Northwest	A681	31-Dec-11	144	1584	720	864
83511	Ideal Yardstick Inc	Southeast	H897	31-Dec-11	84	3444	1680	1764

Figure 20.1 - *This dataset is appropriate for summarizing with a pivot table.*

Select one cell in the dataset.

From the Insert tab, choose the top half of the PivotTable icon.

Excel will predict that your data includes the current region around your selected cell. Make sure this is okay, and then click OK.

In Excel 2010, pivot tables are built in the PivotTable Field List. A blank pivot table appears in cell A3, and the PivotTable Field List appears on your screen.

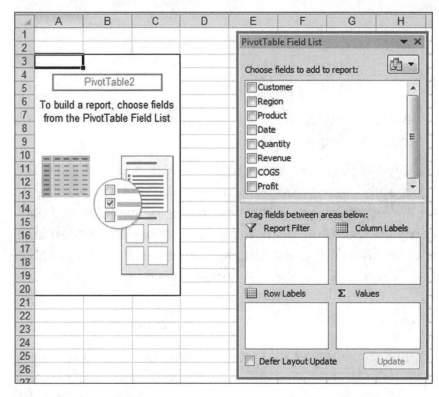

Figure 20.2 -
Initially, a blank pivot table has no fields.

To include a field in the pivot table summary, simply checkmark the field in the PivotTable Field List.

To create the report shown in Figure 20.3, click the Region field, the Customer field, and then the Revenue field.

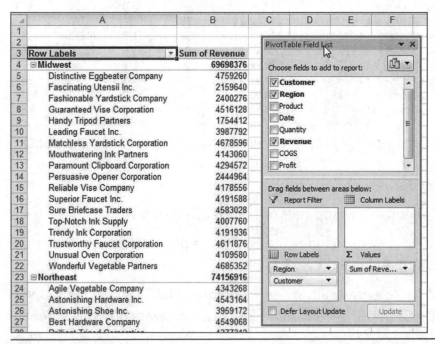

Figure 20.3 -
Excel uses the field types to determine where to display the fields.

When a pivot table has multiple fields in the Row Labels area, you can use the Collapse or Expand buttons to produce summaries of the data.

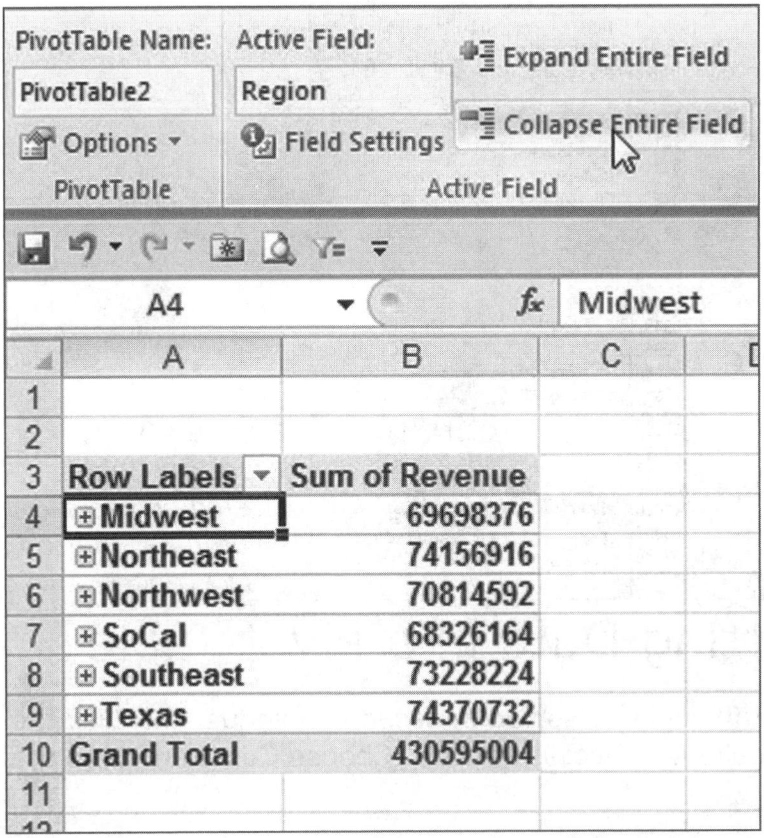

Figure 20.4 - *After you collapse a table, the customer information is temporarily hidden.*

Rearranging a Pivot Table Report

It is easy to change a pivot table report. Just check or uncheck fields in the top half of the PivotTable Field List. You can always rearrange the order of fields by dragging the fields around the bottom half of the PivotTable Field List.

Suppose you want to add Product to the summary report. If you click the Product check box, the report will grow vertically. The Product field might be a good field to add to the Column Labels area to produce a crosstab analysis.

Grab the Product field from the top half of the PivotTable Field List, drag it, and drop it in the Column Labels section at the bottom of the PivotTable Field List. Excel creates a summary with Region and Customer down the side and Product fields across the top.

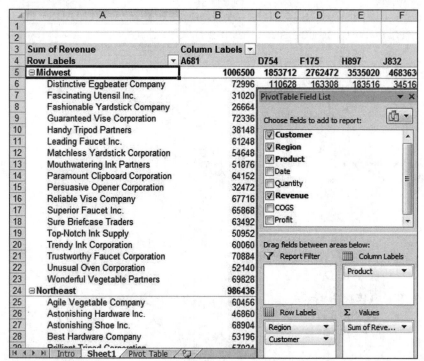

Figure 20.5
- *Product fields stretch across the columns at the top of the report.*

Filtering or Sorting Data in a Pivot Table

Initially, values in a pivot table will be sorted in ascending sequence. Click the Row Labels drop-down in cell A4 to access a menu. Choose Customer from the Select Field drop-down.

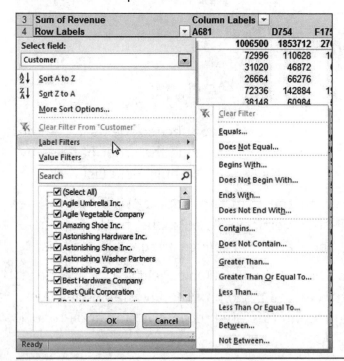

Figure 20.6 - *Open the Row Labels dropdown. A variety of value, date, and label filters are available.*

> **Note**: You can hover over the Customer field in the top half of the field list to access a similar menu. This saves the extra step of choosing Customer from the Select Field drop-down.

The menu offers choices where you can sort or filter the field. Figure 20.6 shows the various options available in the Label filters for the Customer field.

Suppose you want to sequence the customers in high-to-low sequence and show only the top 12 customers. Follow these steps:

1. Click the Customer field in the top half of the PivotTable Field List. Use the drop-down arrow to open a menu.

2. Choose More Sort Options.

3. In the Sort (Customer) dialog, choose to sort descending by Sum of Revenue.

Figure 20.7 - *You are sorting one field (Customer) by the results in another field (Revenue).*

4. Repeat step 1 to access the menu again.

5. Choose Value Filters, Top 10.

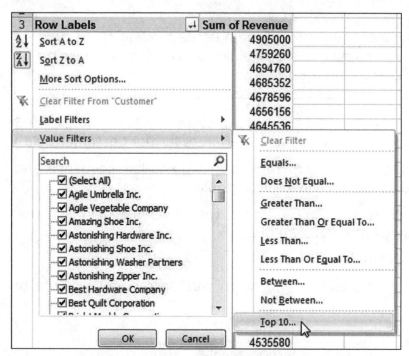

3	Row Labels ↲	Sum of Revenue
2↓	Sort A to Z	4905000
Z↓	Sort Z to A	4759260
	More Sort Options...	4694760
		4685352
🍸	Clear Filter From "Customer"	4678596
	Label Filters ▸	4656156
	Value Filters ▸	4645536

Value Filters submenu:
- 🍸 Clear Filter
- Equals...
- Does Not Equal...
- Greater Than...
- Greater Than Or Equal To...
- Less Than...
- Less Than Or Equal To...
- Between...
- Not Between...
- Top 10...

Search box list:
- ☑ (Select All)
- ☑ Agile Umbrella Inc.
- ☑ Agile Vegetable Company
- ☑ Amazing Shoe Inc.
- ☑ Astonishing Hardware Inc.
- ☑ Astonishing Shoe Inc.
- ☑ Astonishing Washer Partners
- ☑ Astonishing Zipper Inc.
- ☑ Best Hardware Company
- ☑ Best Quilt Corporation

OK   Cancel   4535580

Figure 20.8 - *The Top 10 filter will let you choose any number, not just 10.*

6. In the Top 10 Filter dialog, choose to show the top 12 items by Sum of Revenue.

Top 10 Filter (Customer)

Show

Top | 12 | Items | by | Sum of Revenue

OK   Cancel

Figure 20.9 - *The filter can also show the Bottom n customers.*

The result is a report of the top 12 customers.

	A	B
1		
2		
3	**Row Labels** 🍸	**Sum of Revenue**
4	Hip Ink Supply	4905000
5	Distinctive Eggbeater Company	4759260
6	Unique Notebook Company	4694760
7	Wonderful Vegetable Partners	4685352
8	Matchless Yardstick Corporation	4678596
9	Special Scooter Company	4656156
10	Fascinating Washer Company	4645536
11	Guaranteed Vegetable Company	4643592
12	Well-Suited Shovel Inc.	4621308
13	Different Meter Inc.	4618632
14	Effortless Adhesive Company	4614432
15	Trustworthy Faucet Corporation	4611876
16	**Grand Total**	**56134500**

Figure 20.10 - *Note that the grand total excludes the hidden customers.*

Grouping Daily Dates into Months or Years

In Figure 20.11, the pivot table shows daily dates in the Row Labels area. Select one of the cells with a date and choose Group Field from the PivotTable Tools Options tab.

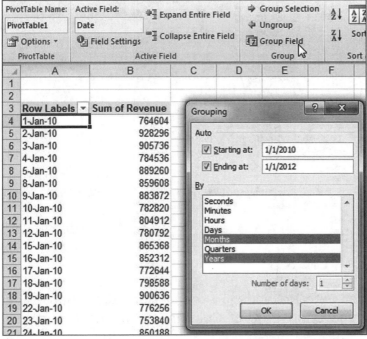

Figure 20.11 - *Select a cell containing a date, choose the Group Field icon and then choose how to group the field.*

Never group a field only by month. Always include Months and Years in the Grouping dialog. (Otherwise, Excel will add January of 2011 and January of 2010 into a single value called January!)

The result is a summary by month and year.

	A	B
1		
2		
3	Row Labels ▼	Sum of Revenue
4	⊟2010	
5	Jan	19026348
6	Feb	16301508
7	Mar	18148164
8	Apr	17378844
9	May	18719760
10	Jun	17187084
11	Jul	18311520
12	Aug	19169940
13	Sep	16522584
14	Oct	19429164
15	Nov	18229224
16	Dec	16929696
17	⊟2011	
18	Jan	18967380
19	Feb	16571844
20	Mar	17207724

Figure 20.12 - *Excel replaces the daily dates with monthly dates.*

Grouping the Date field actually adds a new virtual field to the PivotTable Field List. Move Years from Row Labels to Column Labels to produce a report showing year-to-year comparisons.

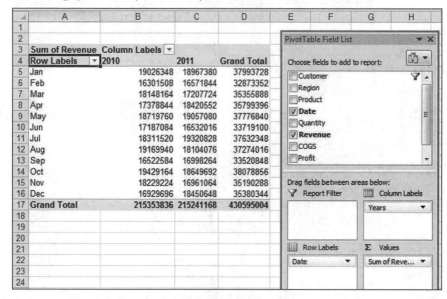

Figure 20.13 - *December 2011 is up over December 2010.*

More Pivot Table Tricks

In Figure 20.14, select any cell with Revenue. In the Options tab, choose the Show Values As drop-down and choose % of Column Total. The report will change to show % of Total.

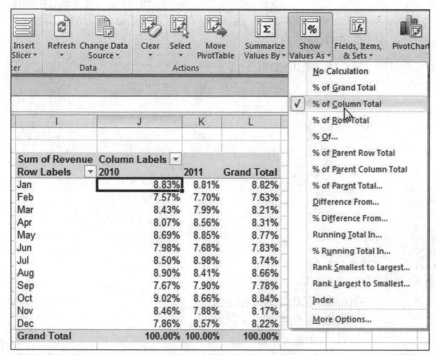

Figure 20.14 - *The percentages will total to 100% down the column.*

New in Excel 2010, the Show Values As drop-down offers a setting for % of Parent Row. When you have two fields in the row area, you can use this setting to show nested totals.

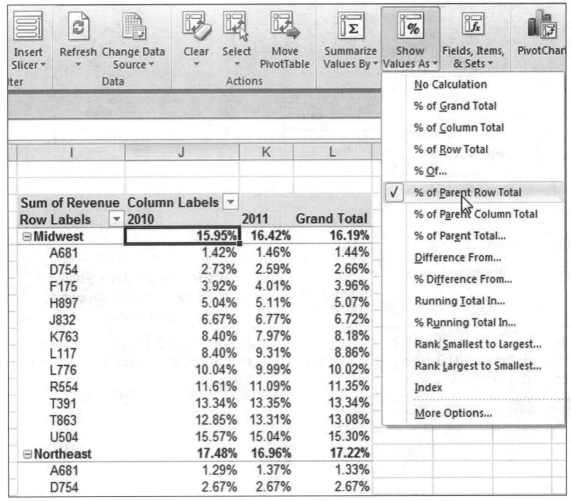

Figure 20.15 - *Rank and % of Parent are new in Excel 2010.*

Killing the Compact View

Microsoft is in love with this new compact layout. This means that all the row fields will be jammed into the left column of the data. Any good data analyst knows that putting two different fields in the same column is a horrible practice.

On the Design tab, choose Report Layout, Show in Tabular Form to move each row field into its own column.

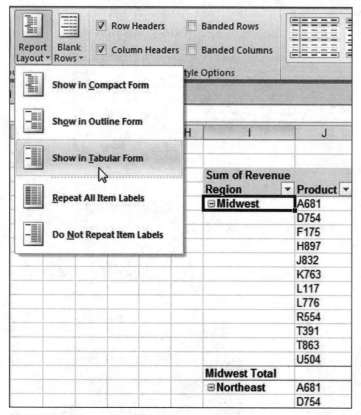

Figure 20.16 - *Switch from Compact layout to Tabular layout.*

Tabular layout includes blank cells in the outer row fields. You can finally fix this in Excel 2010 using the Repeat All Item Labels selection in the Report Layout drop-down.

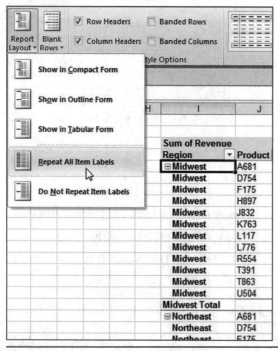

Figure 20.17 - *Finally, an easy fix for this common problem.*

Formatting a Pivot Table

The Design tab offers a gallery where you can quickly apply a format to the pivot table.

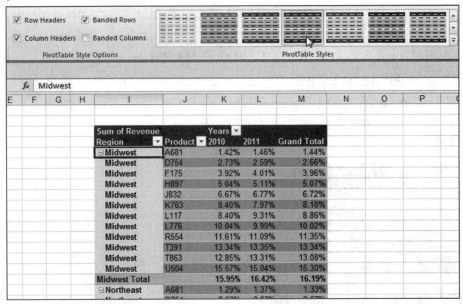

Figure 20.18 - *The galleries offer different styles based on the currently selected theme.*

Creating a Report for Every Month

Drag a field such as Date to the Report Filter section of the PivotTable Field List. You now have a drop-down in cell B1 where you can choose to filter the report to a particular month.

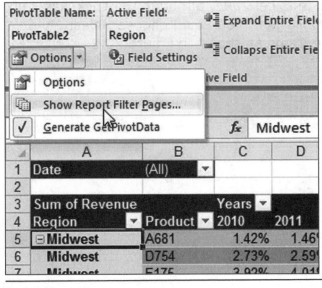

Figure 20.19 - *Create a report with one field in the Filter area.*

After you have a field in the Report Filter section, you can quickly replicate the report for every value in the filter field. Follow these steps:

1. Add at least one field to the filter area of the report.

2. On the PivotTable Tools Options tab, look for the Options icon on the left side of the tab. Do not press the Options button, but click the drop-down arrow to the right of the button.

3. From the drop-down, choose Show Report Filter Pages.

4. Choose to Show All Report Filter Pages of Date and click OK.

Excel quickly adds new worksheets for each value in the Date drop-down.

	A	B	C	D	E	F
1	Date	Jan				
2						
3	Sum of Re		Years			
4	Region	Product	2010	2011	Grand Total	
5	Midwes	A681	1.27%	1.00%	1.14%	
6	Midwes	D754	2.82%	2.68%	2.75%	
7	Midwes	F175	2.84%	4.48%	3.63%	
8	Midwes	H897	6.52%	5.94%	6.24%	
9	Midwes	J832	5.72%	8.81%	7.20%	
10	Midwes	K763	10.69%	7.64%	9.23%	
11	Midwes	L117	8.71%	9.91%	9.28%	
12	Midwes	L776	8.05%	6.77%	7.44%	
13	Midwes	R554	11.58%	10.98%	11.29%	
14	Midwes	T391	13.80%	13.67%	13.73%	
15	Midwes	T863	10.01%	12.50%	11.20%	
16	Midwes	U504	17.98%	15.61%	16.84%	
17	Midwest Total		16.30%	15.05%	15.68%	

Intro / **Jan** / Feb / Mar / Apr / May / Jun / Jul / Aug

Figure 20.20 - *Excel added 12 copies of the pivot table in less than a second.*

Creating Visual Filters with Slicers

Report filters picked up a new trick in Excel 2007, although the trick was half-baked. When a field was in the report filter, you could choose Select Multiple Items, and then select two or more items as shown in Figure 20.21.

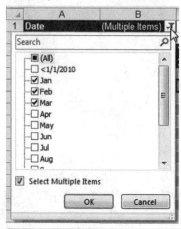

Figure 20.21 - *New in Excel 2007, choose multiple items.*

However, the problem was that the report heading in cell B1 would then show the completely baffling (Multiple Items). If you printed this report, no one would have any idea which multiple items were selected.

I now see that the Excel 2007 feature was only a stepping stone on the way to the Excel 2010 slicer feature. Slicers are visual filters.

From the PivotTable Tools Options tab, choose Insert Slicers. You can choose multiple fields to serve as slicers from the Insert Slicers dialog.

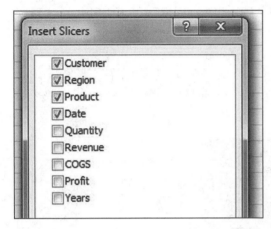

Figure 20.22 - *Select fields for the slicers.*

Excel 2010 then tiles the slicers in the middle of the screen. Every slicer has one column. It is a unimaginative presentation of the slicers. For a cool presentation, read about PowerPivot in Chapter 21.

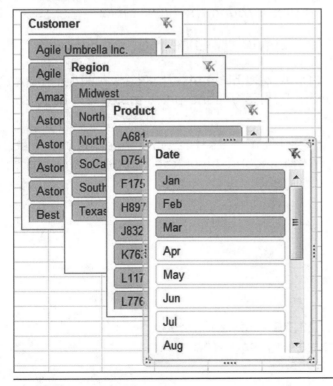

Figure 20.23 - *Excel stacks the slicers in the middle of the screen.*

Rearrange the slicers around your pivot table. Use the Slicer Tools tab to change the color of each slicer and the number of columns in each slicer. Slicers with many values make great tall vertical slicers. Slicers with short values can handle multiple columns and fit well above the pivot table.

Figure 20.24 shows one possible arrangement of the slicers.

The slicers provide a visual filter. You can instantly see which items are included and not included. To select multiple items from the slicer, you can either hold down the Ctrl key or click and drag to select multiple adjacent items.

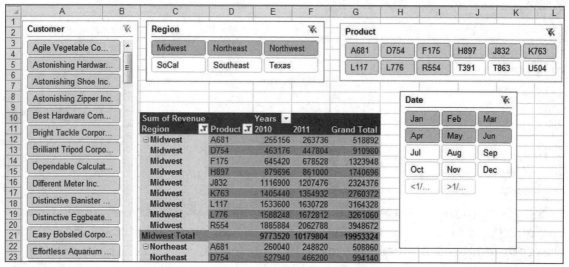

Figure 20.24 - *Rearrange the slicers to fit around the pivot table.*

Controlling Multiple Pivot Tables with One Set of Slicers

Suppose you have created one pivot table and have insert slicers for that pivot table. If you want to have those slicers filter a second pivot table, it is easy to do.

Define the second pivot table and place it on the same worksheet as the first pivot table. With the cell pointer in the second pivot table, open the Insert Slicer drop-down and choose Slicer Connections.

Figure 20.25 - *For additional pivot tables, manage the slicer connections.*

Excel will show you the Slicer Connections dialog. You can connect any or all existing slicers to the new pivot table.

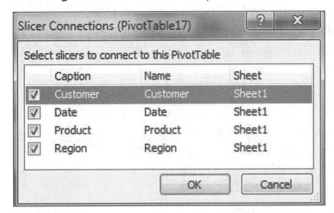

Figure 20.26 - *Connect the existing slicers to the new pivot table.*

In Figure 20.27, four slicers are filtering two different pivot tables. This would have been hard to do in earlier versions of Excel. You needed a macro to have one set of report filters drive multiple pivot tables.

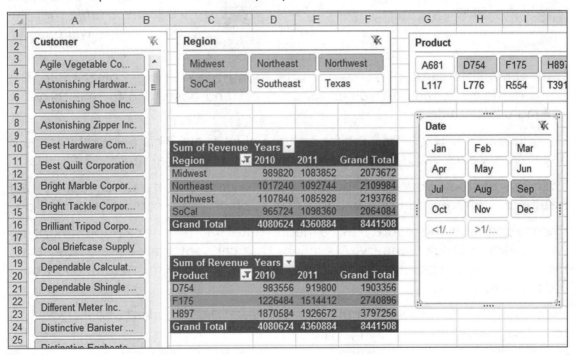

Figure 20.27 - *It is easy to drive multiple pivot tables from one set of slicers.*

Creating Perfectly Formatted Reports

If I have one remaining complaint about pivot tables, it is that they are ugly. Even with the new Formatting gallery, pivot tables generally lack the polish that makes them suitable for the boardroom.

Consider the ugly pivot table in Figure 20.28. You have January Actual, January Plan, and then the completely meaningless January Actual+Plan. In reality, you want to show actuals for January through the last completed month, and then plan for the remaining months. This is impossible with a regular pivot table. If you turn off Plan for January, it gets turned off for all months.

	A	B	C	D	E
3	Sum of Sales	Column Labels			
4		⊟Jan		Jan Total	⊟Feb
5	Row Labels	Actual	Plan		Actual
6	Lakeside	10723	11000	21723	15202
7	Ala Moana	11739	11100	22839	16105
8	Altamonte Mall	11421	11400	22821	14854
9	Annapolis Mall	11689	10800	22489	14675
10	Aventura Mall	13646	12900	26546	17473
11	Baybrook	12366	12100	24466	16625
12	Beachwood Place Mall	10833	11400	22233	16370
13	Bellevue Square	13684	14100	27784	17821
14	Bellmar	15356	14200	29556	19953
15	Branson Landing	14288	13300	27588	18395

Figure 20.28 - *Create an ugly pivot table that no one will have to look at.*

Frequently, I would do these steps every month: (a) Create a pivot table, (b) Convert the pivot table to values, and (c) cut and paste and format to get it looking presentable.

There is a better way. First, create an ugly pivot table. This pivot table should have every conceivable field that you will need in the final report.

Then, on another worksheet, build the framework of a beautiful report. Feel free to use different fonts, number formats, blank rows, subtotals, and so on.

Choose one cell in the report. Make a mental note that this one cell is summarizing values for Baybrook, January, Actual. In that cell, enter an equals sign. Click the pivot table worksheet, and then click the cell for January, Actual, Baybrook. Press Enter.

Excel builds the unusable formula of =GETPIVOTDATA("Sales",Sheet1!$A$3,"Store","Baybrook","Month","Jan","Type","Actual").

	E6			*fx*	=GETPIVOTDATA("Sales",Sheet1!$A$3,"Store","Baybrook","Month","Jan","Type","Actual")									
	A	B	C	D	E	F	G	H	I	J	K	L	M	N	O
1	XYZ Company Super Report													Actuals Through	
2															
3					Jan	Feb	Mar	Apr	May	Jun	Jul	Aug	Sep	Oct	No
4					Actual	Actual	Actual	Actual	Plan	Plan	Plan	Plan	Plan	Plan	Pla
5			Houston Area												
6				Baybrook	$12K										
7				Highland Village											
8				Willowbrook											
9				The Woodlands Mall											
10			Houston Total		$12K	$0K	$0K	$0K	$0K	$0K	$0K	$0K	$0K	$0K	$0
11															

Figure 20.29 - *The initial formula needs tweaking to make it copyable.*

You have probably seen GETPIVOTDATA formulas before, and you probably hate them. When you copy these formulas, they are essentially hard-coded to return the same value, and they do not copy well at all.

To make use of GETPIVOTDATA, you have to take that hard-coded GETPIVOTDATA formula and parameterize it. Instead of having the formula hard-coded for "Baybrook", change "Baybrook" to cell $D6. Change "Actual" to E$4. Change "Jan" to E$3.

The new formula is =GETPIVOTDATA("Sales",Sheet1!$A$3,"Store",$D6,"Month",E$3,"Type",E$4). You can then copy this formula and use Paste Special Formulas to paste the formula to all the other cells on the report.

The final result is a workbook where you will follow these steps each month: (a) Paste data below the original table on the data worksheet. (b) Visit the pivot table to Refresh the pivot table. (c) Print the nicely formatted report which is now getting fresh data from the pivot table.

E6				f_x =GETPIVOTDATA("Sales",Sheet1!$A$3,"Store",$D6,"Month",TEXT(E$3,"MMM"),"Type",E$4)												
	A	B	C	D	E	F	G	H	I	J	K	L	M	N	O	P	Q
1	XYZ Company Super Report													Actuals Through:		4/30	
2																	
3					Jan	Feb	Mar	Apr	May	Jun	Jul	Aug	Sep	Oct	Nov	Dec	
4					Actual	Actual	Actual	Actual	Plan	Plan	Plan	Plan	Plan	Plan	Plan	Plan	Total
5			Houston Area														
6				Baybrook	$12K	$17K	$22K	$25K	$24K	$32K	$28K	$24K	$20K	$32K	$49K	$121K	$407K
7				Highland Village	13K	17K	20K	24K	24K	33K	29K	24K	20K	33K	49K	122K	407K
8				Willowbrook	15K	19K	24K	30K	28K	37K	32K	28K	23K	37K	55K	138K	465K
9				The Woodlands Mall	14K	19K	24K	28K	27K	36K	32K	27K	23K	36K	54K	135K	453K
10			Houston Total		$54K	$71K	$90K	$106K	$103K	$138K	$120K	$103K	$86K	$138K	$207K	$516K	$1,732K
11																	
12			Dallas/Forth Worth Area														
13				Firewheel	$11K	$15K	$18K	$23K	$22K	$29K	$25K	$22K	$18K	$29K	$43K	$108K	$363K
14				Galleria	11K	15K	19K	25K	23K	30K	27K	23K	19K	30K	46K	114K	382K
15				Hulen Mall	13K	17K	23K	26K	26K	34K	30K	26K	21K	34K	51K	128K	429K
16				Northeast Mall	11K	15K	19K	23K	23K	31K	27K	23K	20K	31K	47K	117K	389K

Figure 20.30 - *This report is based on a pivot table.*

Although it will take a bit more time in month one to get the formulas in the report pointing to the pivot table, there will be tremendous time saving in all future months as you no longer have to rebuild the pivot table.

Next Steps

Chapter 21 discusses an amazing new add-in called PowerPivot.

21

PowerPivot

A new add-in for Excel 2010 adds many interesting tricks to your pivot tables. The add-in is free from the Microsoft SQL Server Analysis Services team. Using this add-in, you can do any of these tasks:

Import 100 million rows of data into your Excel workbook.

Define a relationship between two tables without using VLOOKUP.

Create a pivot table from multiple tables.

Define new measures using the DAX formula language, which offers time intelligence such as MTD from the parallel period last year.

Create named sets to allow asymmetric reporting in a pivot table.

Installing PowerPivot

PowerPivot does not ship on the Office 2010 CD. You have to download PowerPivot from www.PowerPivot.com. You want to download the client add-in. Be careful to get either the 32-bit or 64-bit version of the add-in to match your installation of Office 2010.

After you install the add-in, you will have a new PowerPivot tab in the Excel ribbon.

Getting Your Data into PowerPivot

There are many ways to get your data into PowerPivot. If your data is in Excel, creating a linked table is one easy way to proceed.

Using a Linked Table

First, convert your dataset to a table by selecting one cell and pressing Ctrl+T. Excel will ask you to confirm that your data has headers. Click OK. On the Table Tools Design tab, enter a new name for the table on the left side of the ribbon. This name will carry through to PowerPivot and be used in formulas later, so keep it short and easy to spell.

On the PowerPivot tab, choose Create Linked Table.

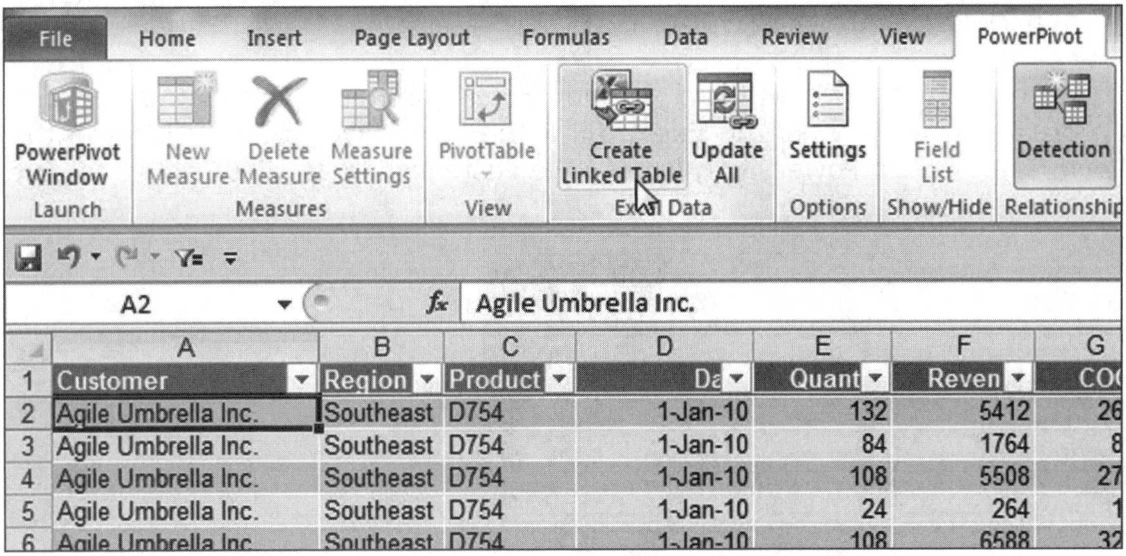

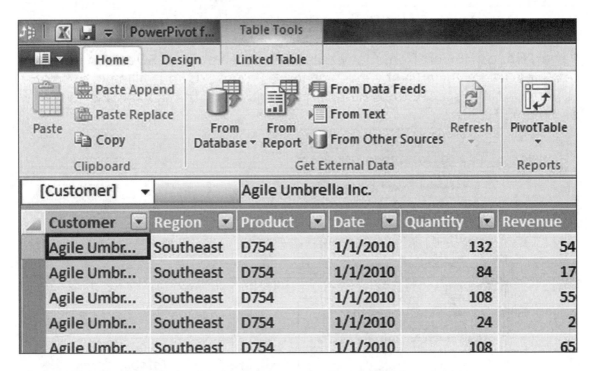

Figure 21.1 - *If you define your data as a table, you can simply link to the table.*

After a moment, you will see your data in the green grid of the PowerPivot window.

Figure 21.2 - *The linked table appears in PowerPivot.*

Pasting Data into PowerPivot

If you need to bring data from another Excel workbook, you can use a copy and paste. Copy the data in Excel. Click the PowerPivot Window icon on the PowerPivot tab. In PowerPivot, choose the Paste icon. You will be asked to give the pasted table a name.

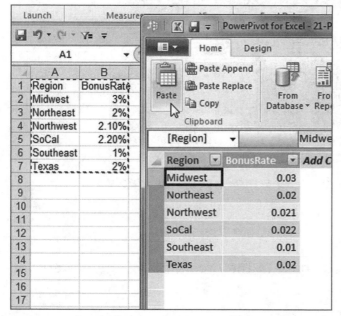

Figure 21.3 - *You can paste your data into PowerPivot.*

Importing Data into PowerPivot

PowerPivot can import from many databases, such as from SQL Server or even text files. In the PowerPivot window, choose From Text. You will have to browse to your text file, specify the field delimiter, and check the box for Use First Row as Column Headers.

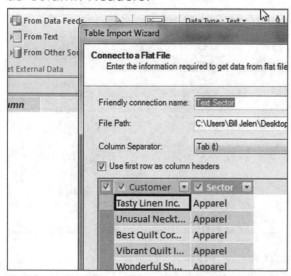

Figure 21.4 - *Import data from a text file.*

As you are importing data, you can choose to skip certain columns. If you are bringing in many million rows of data, skipping long text fields is a way to save space in the Excel file.

Defining Relationships Between Tables

PowerPivot has an automatic relationship detector. It works when you are linking from a base table to a lookup table and there is exactly one perfect matching column. It is cool when it works, but it works perhaps only 20% of the time, so I've given up on trying to have PowerPivot autodetect the relationships.

Besides, it is so incredibly trivial to define a relationship, there doesn't seem to be any reason not to manually define the relationships.

Your main Sales table has a Customer field. The Sector table also has a Customer field. Here is how to tell PowerPivot that these table should be linked:

1. Go to the Customer heading in the Sales table in the PowerPivot window. Right-click the heading and choose Create Relationship.

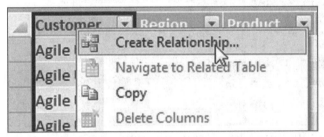

Figure 21.5 - *Start in the base table and right-click the key field for the lookup table.*

2. By taking the time to start from the proper column in the base table, the first half of the Create Relationship dialog will be filled in for you. The top Table and Column will show the table and column that you clicked on.

3. Open the drop-down for Related Lookup Table and choose Sector. If the Sector table has a field that is also called Customer, this will automatically be filled in for the Related Lookup Column. Literally, it takes one selection in this dialog to define the relationship. Click Create.

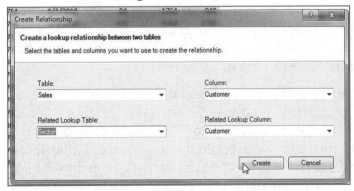

Figure 21.6 - *Define a relationship between the two tables.*

You would follow a similar process to link the Region field to the Bonus Rate table.

Adding Calculations in the PowerPivot Window

Microsoft introduces a new formula language called DAX (Data Analysis eXpressions). DAX is used to add new calculated fields to the table in PowerPivot and also for adding new measures to the pivot table. DAX shares 81 functions with Excel, so if you are proficient with Excel functions, you should have little problem working in DAX.

The first blank column in the PowerPivot window is called Add Column. Click in any cell in that column. Type an equals sign and enter your formula.

The Year field in Figure 21.7 is =Year(Sales[Date]). The Month field in Figure 21.7 is =FORMAT(Sales[Date],"MMM").

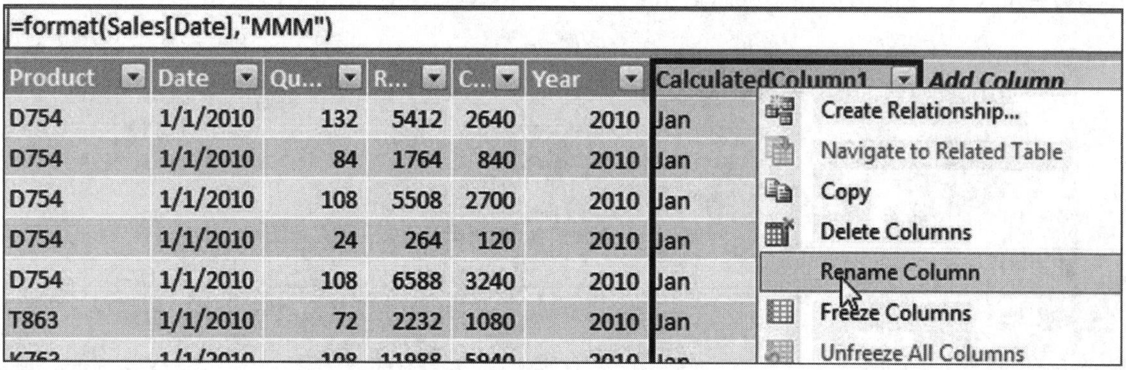

=format(Sales[Date],"MMM")								
Product	Date	Qu...	R...	C...	Year	CalculatedColumn1		Add Column
D754	1/1/2010	132	5412	2640	2010	Jan	Create Relationship...	
D754	1/1/2010	84	1764	840	2010	Jan	Navigate to Related Table	
D754	1/1/2010	108	5508	2700	2010	Jan	Copy	
D754	1/1/2010	24	264	120	2010	Jan	Delete Columns	
D754	1/1/2010	108	6588	3240	2010	Jan	Rename Column	
T863	1/1/2010	72	2232	1080	2010	Jan	Freeze Columns	
K763	1/1/2010	108	11988	5940	2010	Jan	Unfreeze All Columns	

Figure 21.7 - *Add new calculations in the PowerPivot window.*

After adding a calculation, the heading for that column will be called CalculatedColumn1. This is a bit frustrating to me. It seems like there should be a way to specify the proper heading before creating the calculation. Instead, you have to right-click the heading and choose Rename Column.

Each Column Can Have Only One Formula

Unlike Excel, every cell in a column has to have an identical formula. You cannot refer to cells in other rows. Therefore, the concept of cell addresses like A2 is not relevant in PowerPivot. You will always specify the formula using the table nomenclature that was introduced in Excel 2007.

As you are building your formula, you can click a field with the mouse to refer to that field. You cannot use the arrow keys to select a field. When you click a field, PowerPivot will build the syntax of TableName[FieldName]. If you were simply typing the formula, you could leave off the TableName and just type [FieldName]. However, if I am referring to a field in this table, I will be using the mouse to point to that field, so you will always see the full TableName[FieldName] nomenclature in this book.

Referring to a Column in Another Table

Because you have already defined the relationship, you would think that you could easily multiply Revenue in the Sales table by BonusRate in the Rates table. Although you can enter this formula, it will return an error.

The promise of PowerPivot is that you won't have to do VLOOKUPs anymore. When you are building a calculated field, you will have to use a simpler lookup function called RELATED. In the Sales table, you can enter the following:

=Sales[Revenue]*Related(Rates[BonusRate])

That is a simple one-argument lookup function. This function tells PowerPivot to follow the defined relationship and retrieve the value from the other table.

When building this formula, you can type the equals sign, click Revenue, and then type the asterisk. You then have to remember the name of the field in the other table. I start by typing the first letter of that other table. The Formula AutoComplete drop-down will then show you the list of available fields.

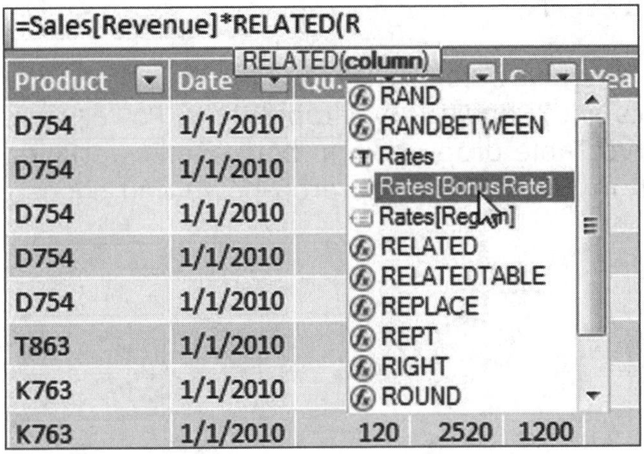

Figure 21.8 - *When referring to a field in another worksheet, use Formula AutoComplete.*

> **Tip**: When you define a calculated column in the PowerPivot window, that value is calculated for every row in the table. This can be a lot of overhead for a 100 million row dataset. In contrast, the DAX measures are calculated only once for each cell in the pivot table. Read more about DAX measures later in this chapter.

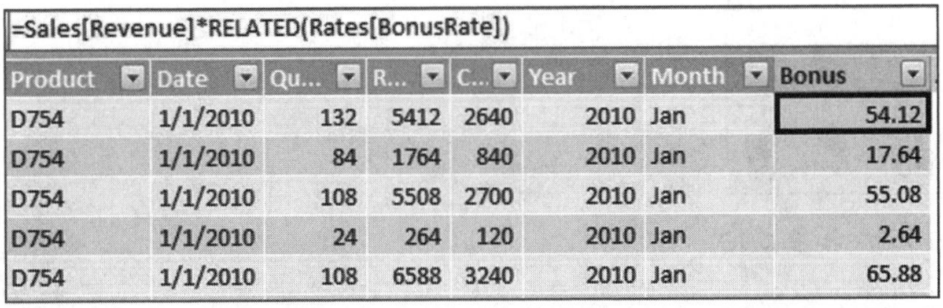

=Sales[Revenue]*RELATED(Rates[BonusRate])

Product	Date	Qu...	R...	C...	Year	Month	Bonus
D754	1/1/2010	132	5412	2640	2010	Jan	54.12
D754	1/1/2010	84	1764	840	2010	Jan	17.64
D754	1/1/2010	108	5508	2700	2010	Jan	55.08
D754	1/1/2010	24	264	120	2010	Jan	2.64
D754	1/1/2010	108	6588	3240	2010	Jan	65.88

Figure 21.9 - *Year, Month, and Bonus are calculated fields. They are calculated for every row in the source data.*

Other Tools in the PowerPivot Window

You can scroll through the data in the PowerPivot window. You can sort. You can filter. You can even format, which seems pointless. You cannot print. Although it might be mildly amusing to sort 100 million records in Excel, working in the PowerPivot windows is not what PowerPivot is about. You really need to move on to creating pivot tables.

Two other tools in the PowerPivot window are worth mentioning. If you have imported data from an external source, you can use the Refresh button on the Home tab to reload the data.

Also, there is a Hide and Unhide icon on the Design tab in the PowerPivot window. In the Hide and Unhide dialog, you can choose which fields to show in the PowerPivot Field List. If your SQL Server data has a bunch of meaningless ID fields, you can prevent those from appearing in the PowerPivot Field List.

Creating the Pivot Table

PowerPivot can create one, two, or four pivot tables that all work from the same slicers. It is easy enough to do this with regular pivot tables, but PowerPivot makes it a bit easier. There is a PivotTable drop-down in both the PowerPivot window and on the PowerPivot tab in Excel. Open the drop-down and choose to create a pivot table.

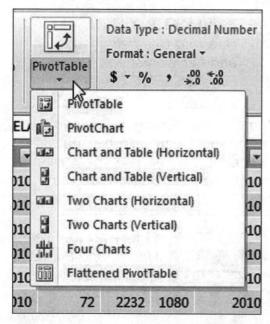

Figure 21.10 - *You can create one, two, or four pivot tables.*

The first thing you will notice is that the regular PivotTable Field List is replaced with a new PowerPivot Field List. This field list has extra zones for slicers. It also lists all the fields in all your tables in the same field list.

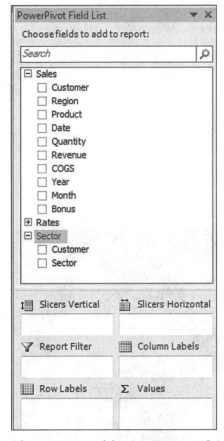

Figure 21.11 - *Having fields from multiple tables is new for pivot tables.*

The pivot table in Figure 21.12 mashes up data from the Sales table with information from the Sector table.

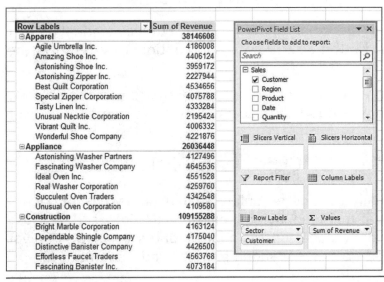

Figure 21.12 - *You just reported on data from two worksheets without doing a VLOOKUP.*

Slicer AutoLayout

Add fields to the Slicer drop zones and PowerPivot will take care of arranging the slicers. In Figure 21.13, PowerPivot decided that Sector would look good as a two-column slicer and that Product would work as a three-column slicer.

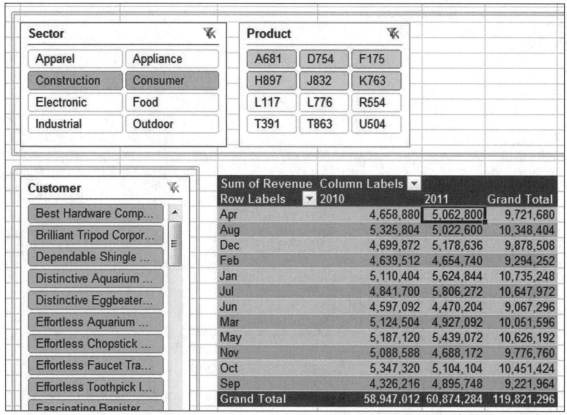

Figure 21.13 - *Slicers look better in PowerPivot.*

Note that you can change the color of the slicers, but you cannot adjust the number of columns or button size. PowerPivot continuously redraws the slicers.

If this drives you crazy, grab the slicer's title bar and drag the slicer completely outside of the bounding box around the slicers. You now have control over formatting the slicer.

PowerPivot Annoyances: Custom Lists

PowerPivot tables are actually considered online analytical processing (OLAP) pivot tables. This means that many annoying limitations are imposed on those tables. You cannot group daily dates up to monthly dates in an OLAP pivot table. This is why calculated fields were added for year and month.

In a regular pivot table, data is automatically sorted based on custom lists. This allows month names to appear as Jan, Feb, Mar rather than Apr, Aug, Dec. Look at the pivot table in Figure 21.13 and you will see that the month names do not automatically sort in a PowerPivot table.

It requires eight clicks to fix this problem and they are the most annoying eight clicks. I've come to take for granted the fact that months sort correctly. I can create a pivot table in six clicks. When I have to spend eight clicks to fix the month names over and over, it becomes annoying.

To fix the month names, follow these steps:

1. Open the Row Labels drop-down.

2. Choose More Sort Options.

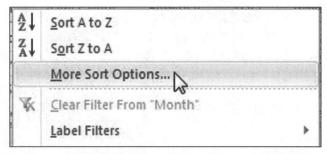

Figure 21.14 - *Choose More Sort Options.*

3. Choose Ascending. Click More Options.

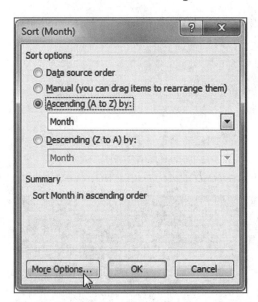

Figure 21.15 - *Choose Ascending, and then More Options.*

4. In the More Sort Options dialog, uncheck Sort Automatically Every Time the Report Is Updated.

5. You can now open the first Key Sort Order drop-down and choose Jan, Feb, Mar.

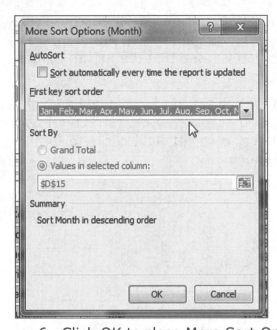

Figure 21.16 - *Uncheck Sort Automatically, and then choose the month custom list.*

6. Click OK to close More Sort Options. Click OK to close Sort Options.

The result after eight clicks is that months are sorted into the correct sequence.

Sum of Revenue	Column Labels		
Row Labels	2010	2011	Grand Total
Jan	5,110,404	5,624,844	10,735,248
Feb	4,639,512	4,654,740	9,294,252
Mar	5,124,504	4,927,092	10,051,596
Apr	4,658,880	5,062,800	9,721,680
May	5,187,120	5,439,072	10,626,192
Jun	4,597,092	4,470,204	9,067,296
Jul	4,841,700	5,806,272	10,647,972
Aug	5,325,804	5,022,600	10,348,404
Sep	4,326,216	4,895,748	9,221,964
Oct	5,347,320	5,104,104	10,451,424
Nov	5,088,588	4,688,172	9,776,760
Dec	4,699,872	5,178,636	9,878,508
Grand Total	58,947,012	60,874,284	119,821,296

Figure 21.17 - *You finally have month names sorted into the correct sequence.*

Caution: If you pick up a book by one of the SQL Server authors who are writing about PowerPivot tables, you will see that they suggest a formula of =Month([Date])&"-"&Format([Date],"MMM"). This produces values that do sort correctly (1-Jan, 2-Feb, 3-Mar). However, it is abundantly clear that those authors have never worked for *your* manager. Your manager would never accept a report with bizarre month names like 1-Jan, 2-Feb, 3-Mar. This is some crazy thing that an IT person would try to sneak into the board room. It just won't pass in a real reporting environment.

Changing the Calculation from Sum

It is relatively easy to change the calculation in regular pivot tables. It is impossible to change the calculation in OLAP pivot tables. There is a way to change the calculation in a PowerPivot pivot table, although it is hard to find:

1. Go to the Sum of Revenue field in the Values drop zone of the PowerPivot Field List. Click the drop-down arrow to open the flyout menu.

2. The third item from the bottom of the flyout menu is Summarize By. Open this flyout menu to choose between Sum, Count, Min, Max, and Average.

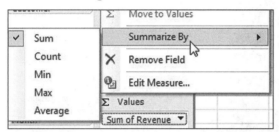

Figure 21.18 - *You can choose from these five calculations.*

Adding a New Calculated Measure in the Pivot Table

The DAX formula language really shines when you use it to create a new measure for your pivot table. DAX measures are in the same genre as calculated fields, but are infinitely more powerful.

To create a new measure, select New Measure from the PowerPivot tab in Excel.

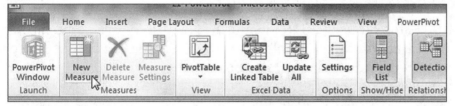

Figure 21.19 - *Define a new measure.*

Build the measure in the Measure Settings dialog. Use the Check Formula button to check the syntax.

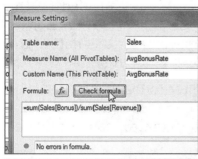

Figure 21.20 - *Define a new measure.*

Excel will calculate the measure once for every value cell in the pivot table. In Figure 21.21, this means that the calculation will happen 39 times. This is faster than adding the calculation to a million rows of source data.

AvgBonusRate			
	2010	2011	Grand Total
Jan	1.98%	1.97%	1.98%
Feb	1.99%	1.99%	1.99%
Mar	1.92%	1.97%	1.95%
Apr	1.98%	1.95%	1.96%
May	1.89%	1.94%	1.92%
Jun	1.96%	1.99%	1.97%
Jul	1.92%	1.95%	1.94%
Aug	1.96%	1.96%	1.96%
Sep	1.96%	1.94%	1.95%
Oct	1.93%	1.96%	1.94%
Nov	1.99%	1.98%	1.98%
Dec	2.02%	1.96%	1.99%
Grand Total	1.96%	1.96%	1.96%

Figure 21.21 - *Excel calculates the formula 39 times in this pivot table.*

I've written a complete DAX reference in my *PowerPivot for the Excel Data Analyst* book, and I won't attempt to replicate that guide here. However, there are two key concepts.

To calculate the 1.98% for January 2010 in Figure 21.21, there are some filters applied to that cell. In addition to any filters in the slicers, that one cell also has a filter applied where the Month is Jan and the year is 2010. By default, all DAX measures will respect all the filters that are applied to the cell being calculated. This takes a lot of work off of your hands. You don't need to worry about dealing with the filters. There are two instances when you do care:

In many ratios, you want to calculate the sales for this cell divided by the sales for all cells. In those cases, you will use the ALL() function to unfilter. When you use All([Months]), you are saying, for this part of the calculation, don't bother filtering by month, use all the months.

In many time calculations, you want to modify the filter to include all dates up to and including the current data point. There are 30 time intelligence functions that you can use to change the date filter, to, say, include all YTD dates up through July.

Converting the PowerPivot Pivot Table to Cube Formulas

At the end of Chapter 20, you learned how to use =GETPIVOTDATA to grab values from a pivot table. Because PowerPivot data is stored as an OLAP cube, you have access to the Convert to Formulas command for your PowerPivot pivot tables.

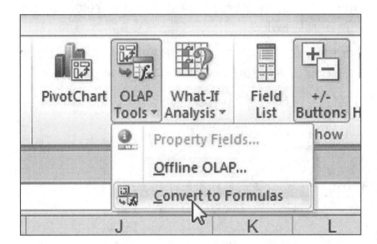

Figure 21.22 - *Change the pivot table to formulas.*

After invoking this command, the pivot table changes to formulas using the cube functions. Even though the pivot table no longer exists, the formulas continue to respond to the slicers!

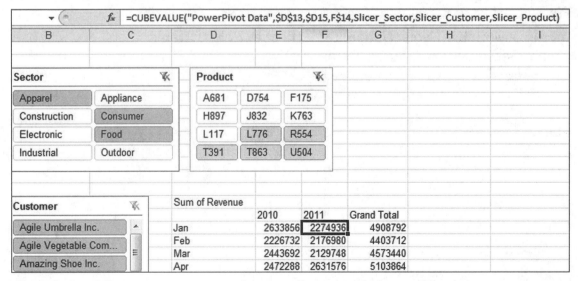

Figure 21.23 - *You can move these cells around, insert blank rows, and so on.*

Creating Asymmetric Reports with Named Sets

The example at the end of Chapter 20 used GetPivotData to show Actual for some months and plan for other months.

Good news: Excel 2010 offers a new feature called named sets that finally allows you to create asymmetric reports.

Bad news: Named sets work only with OLAP pivot tables for this release, so you cannot use them with regular pivot tables.

Good news: If you take your regular Excel data through PowerPivot, the data becomes an OLAP pivot table, and therefore you can use named sets.

To recap the problem, you want to show Actuals for January through April and Plan for the remaining months:

Sum of Sales	Column Labels			
	⊟Jan		⊟Feb	
Row Labels	Actual	Plan	Actual	Plan
Ala Moana	11739	11100	16105	14800
Altamonte Mall	11421	11400	14854	15100
Annapolis Mall	11689	10800	14675	14400
Aventura Mall	13646	12900	17473	17300
Baybrook	12366	12100	16625	16200
Beachwood Place Mall	10833	11400	16370	15200

Figure 21.24 - *You want to show Actuals for some months and Plan for other months.*

In the PivotTable Tools Option tab, choose Fields, Items, Sets and choose Create Set Based on Column Items.

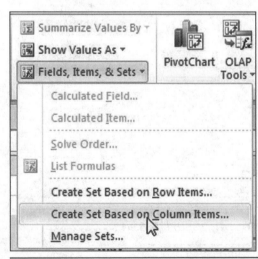

Figure 21.25 - *Create a named set.*

Excel shows you a dialog with a new row for every column in your pivot table. Highlight a column and click Delete Row to remove it from the pivot table.

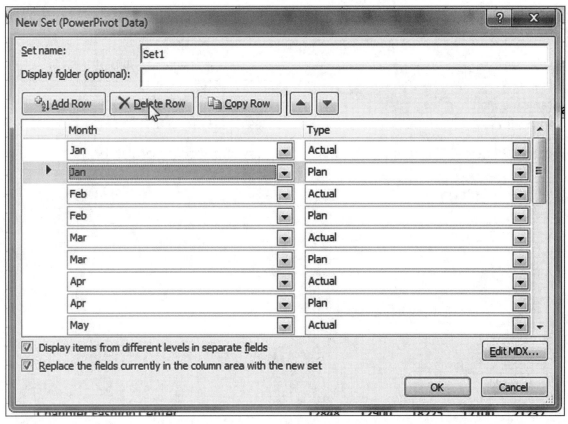

Figure 21.26 - *You can delete specific columns from the set.*

You eventually end up with a list of only the desired columns.

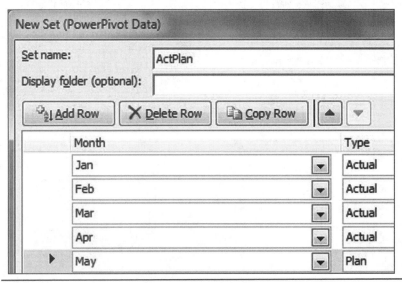

Figure 21.27 - *Keep deleting columns until only the desired items are left.*

The resulting pivot table is shown in Figure 21.28. It is amazing how hard this is in regular pivot tables, but certainly possible with PowerPivot datasets.

Sum of Sales	Column Labels				
	Jan	Feb	Mar	Apr	May
Row Labels	Actual	Actual	Actual	Actual	Plan
Ala Moana	11739	16105	19816	23727	22200
Altamonte Mall	11421	14854	20510	22918	22700
Annapolis Mall	11689	14675	17641	23134	21600

Figure 21.28 - *The named set leaves an asymmetric pivot table.*

Next Steps

Chapter 22 covers the new charting engine.

22

Charting

The Excel 2003 charting engine looked tired and old. Little had changed in 15 years in charting. The charting engine in Office 2007 was completely rewritten. The charting engine in Office 2010 is the same as in Excel 2007, with most of the 1,500 bugs wiped out.

Excel, Word, and PowerPoint all share the same charting engine. The process of creating a chart is streamlined, although you might have to look further to make changes to the default chart.

Creating a Chart in Excel 2010

Creating a chart involves four broad steps:

1. Prepare your data. Make sure that you have headings above and to the left of the data to be charted. If one of the headings has date or numeric fields, leave the top-left corner cell blank. Select the range of data to be charted.

◢	A	B	C	D
1		Jan-11	Feb-11	Mar-11
2	East	75748	90879	99540
3	Central	65897	72487	79736
4	West	82974	66379	73017

Figure 22.1 - *Leave the top left cell blank when your headings are dates.*

2. Choose one of the broad chart types from the gallery on the Insert tab. Although there are 70+ chart types, there are often 3 to 4 variations of each type.

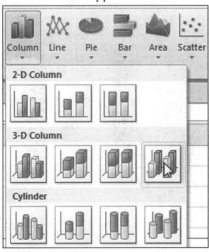

Figure 22.2 - *Choose a subtype from the drop-down menu.*

The thumbnails often use a light blue and dark blue element arranged to suggest one of these four chart types (see Figure 22.3).

➢ In a clustered column chart, each region will have its own column for each month. This allows you to compare each region to each other, and also to compare the growth of one region from month to month. (See the top left of Figure 22.3.)

➢ In a stacked column chart, the individual regions are stacked on top of each other. This allows you to compare the height of the Total column, but makes it hard to discern whether the West region increased from month 1 to month 2. (See the bottom left of Figure 22.3.)

➢ In a 100% stacked column chart, the regions are stacked, and every month's column is exactly the same height. This would enable you to see the relative contribution of each region from month to month. (See the lower-right chart of Figure 22.3.)

➢ The 3D chart actually stacks the columns behind each other. You often have to rotate this chart to see the smaller series. (See the top right of Figure 22.3.)

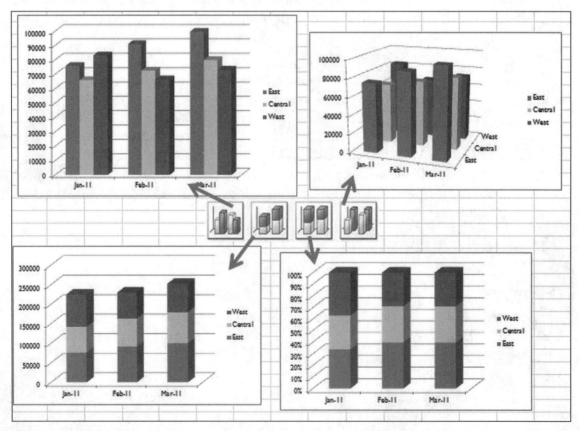

Figure 22.3 - *Most chart types come in variations where series are plotted side by side, stacked, or 100% stacked.*

3. Visit the Chart Tools Design tab to choose a Chart Layout and a Chart Style. Chart Layouts offer up to a dozen different views of the same chart. In Figure 22.4, the formerly difficult process of creating a histogram is now one click away.

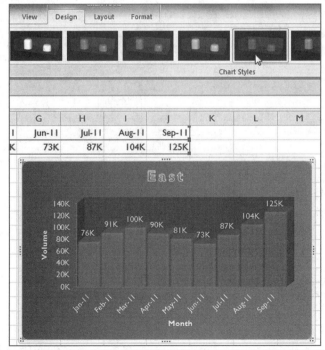

Figure 22.4 - *The layouts offer 4 to 12 built-in presets that vary from chart type to chart type.*

The Chart Styles gallery offers 48 color combinations built around the current theme. If you will be copying the chart to PowerPoint, you can use the new darker layouts to match the background of your slide.

Figure 22.5 - *It is easy to recolor the chart.*

4. If the built-in layout didn't perfectly provide axis titles, legends, and so on, visit the Layout tab to have easy editing choices for all chart elements.

For more granular control, visit the Format tab, where you can apply an effect to any particular element in the chart.

Using Other Chart Types

In a scatter chart, your data should contain pairs of numbers. Excel will find the first number along the horizontal access and the second number along the vertical axis and add plot a marker at the intersection of those values. This chart is good for seeing if two variables are related.

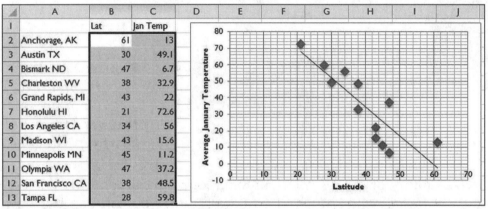

Figure 22.6 - *Each point represents the intersection of an X, Y pair.*

For the stock charts, your data must be in the exact order specified by the name of the chart type. In Figure 22.7, a high-low-close chart requires columns sequenced in high, low, close sequence.

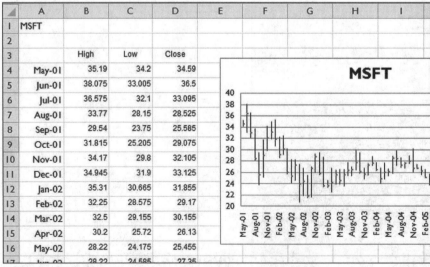

Figure 22.7 - *The high-low-close chart is one of four stock charts available.*

A bubble chart is like a scatter chart, but a third column of numbers controls the size of the data marker. In Figure 22.8, used car prices are plotted to show age, mileage, and price.

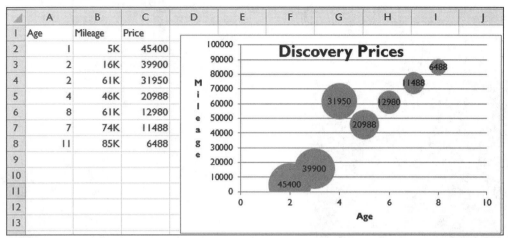

Figure 22.8 - *The third column is used to figure the relative size of each circle.*

Adding New Data to a Chart

Suppose you have produced a series of charts last month and now you need to update all of those charts to reflect a new month of data. Follow these steps:

1. Open the workbook from last month. Enter the new month's data adjacent to the old month in the workbook.

2. Click the plot area of the chart. You will see a blue rectangle appear around the range of data currently plotted on the chart. Notice that there are blue square handles in each corner of the range.

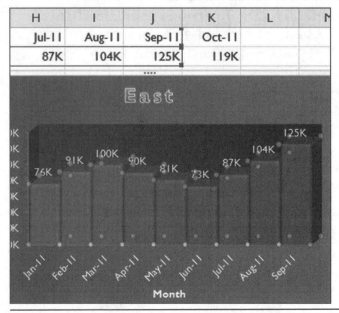

Figure 22.9 - *Drag the handle to the right to include the new October data.*

3. Grab the blue handle at the right edge of the data. Drag so that the blue box includes your new data. The chart will update to include the new data points.

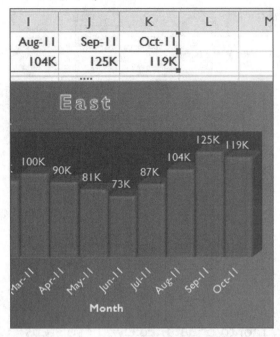

Figure 22.10 - *After you drag the handle, the chart updates to include the new month.*

Creating a Chart with One Keystroke

To create a chart with one keystroke, select your data to be charted and press Alt+F1 to embed a default chart on the current sheet. Or, use the F11 key to create a default chart on a new chart sheet.

> **Tip**: The keystroke creates a default chart. To change the default chart type, click Chart Tools Design, Change Chart Type. Select a chart type from the dialog, and click the Set as Default Chart button.

Keeping the Formatting Dialog Box Open

It is time for a bit of a reality check. The Layout gallery on the Design tab offers at most 12 chart choices. If you consider that there are 55,000 permutations of chart options, the odds that the exact combination of gridlines, titles, labels, and so on will be found in the Layouts gallery is slim.

Further, all those drop-downs in the Layout tab are notorious for showing the 20% of the options that will make 80% of the people happy, but they don't show all the options.

Sooner or later, you are going to have to visit the Format dialog box where you can reach all the options.

You can double-click any chart element to open the Format dialog box. In Figure 22.11, you see the options available for formatting Series 1.

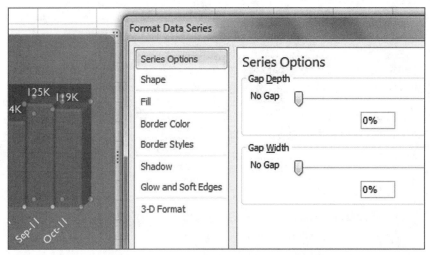

Figure 22.11 - *Double-click the columns to format the series.*

Suppose you realize you also want to format the vertical axis. Without closing the Format dialog box, reach behind the Format dialog box with the mouse and click the vertical axis. The choices in the Format dialog box will change to reflect things that you can change in the vertical axis.

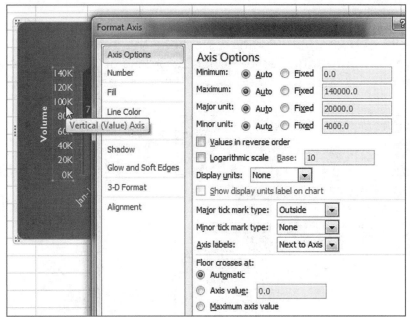

Figure 22.12 - *Click another chart element while the Format dialog is open to change see new settings.*

You can continue doing this, choosing other chart elements and formatting without ever closing the Format dialog box.

Next Steps

Chapter 23 covers sparklines, a new Excel 2010 feature that creates intense, tiny, word-sized charts.

Create Tiny Charts with Sparklines

Professor Edward Tufte introduced the concept of sparklines in his book *Beautiful Evidence*. Tufte described sparklines as intense word-sized charts.

Microsoft implemented Tufte's ideas in Excel 2010 with three types of tiny charts: line charts, column charts, and win/loss charts.

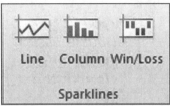

Figure 23.1 - *The entry point for creating sparklines is on the Insert tab.*

Creating sparklines is simple, although you might want to tweak the default sparklines. In Figure 23.2, there are 27 months of closing stock prices for 3 financial firms. Select the data that you want to plot in the sparklines.

From the Insert tab, choose the Line sparkline.

Excel displays the Create Sparklines dialog. Because you pre-selected the data, you need to specify only the output range. Because the input range is 3 rows by 27 columns, the output range has to either be 3 cells or 27 cells. The size of the output range will determine whether you want 3 sparklines or 27 sparklines.

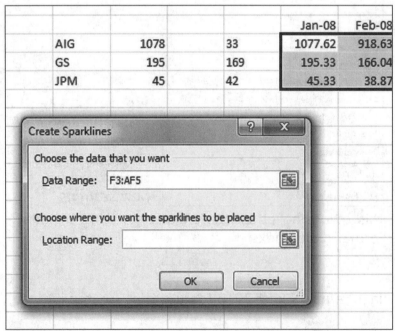

Figure 23.2 - *Specify an output range.*

Excel will draw in the line charts, one in each cell. Figure 27.3 shows default sparklines.

AIG	1078		33
GS	195		169
JPM	45		42

Figure 23.3 - *By default, sparklines are rather plain.*

Adding Markers to Sparklines

Excel will let you add markers to your sparklines. With a sparkline selected, the Sparkline Tools Design tab will be available in the ribbon. You can toggle on all points by choosing Markers, but a more interesting option is to choose High Point and Low Point, as shown in Figure 23.4.

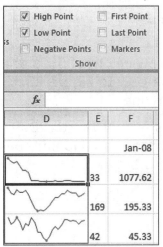

Figure 23.4 - *Choose which points to add to the line.*

After you've added the high and low point, use the Marker Color drop-down to choose a color for each type of point. For example mark the high point in green and the low point in red.

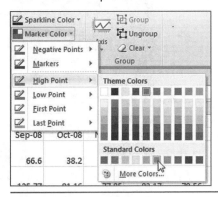

Figure 23.5 - *Change the color of the points.*

Bigger Is Sometimes Better, Adding Labels

Tufte's sparklines include some features that are a bit difficult to do in Excel. Tufte would usually label the last point in the chart to give some idea of scale. Tufte would sometimes add shading to show the normal range of values so that it became apparent when the sparkline deviated from normal.

In Figure 23.6, the row height is set to 30. The beginning value to the left of the sparkline and the ending value to the right of the sparkline is in 8 point font. With this arrangement, you can manually set the vertical alignment for each label to top, middle, or bottom in an effort to make the label roughly appear next to the beginning or end of the sparkline.

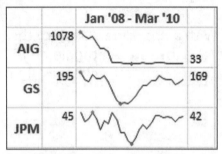

Figure 23.6 - *By increasing the row height, you can position the labels roughly at the same point as the line.*

Another strategy is to set the row height to 55 or 110. A row height of 55 is tall enough to allow five lines of 8 point font to appear in the cell. In Figure 23.7, the range of the sparkline is added to the left of the sparkline.

The first cell contains the prices for a pound of bananas from 1980 to 2009. The range is 34 cents to 61 cents. To create this cell manually, you would type 0.61 and then press Alt+Enter four times, and then type 0.34.

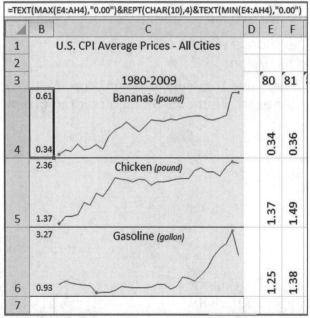

Figure 23.7 - *A formula in column B shows the high and low range for each sparkline. Text in the cell provides the title.*

    Create Tiny Charts with Sparklines

Instead of having to manually type the high and the low, a formula calculates the high and the low and concatenates it together with linefeed characters:

=TEXT(MAX(E4:AH4),"0.00")&REPT(CHAR(10),4)& TEXT(MIN(E4: AH4),"0.00")

The background for sparklines are transparent so that any text in the cell will appear behind the sparkline. The title for each sparkline is just text typed in the cell, vertically aligned to the top of the cell.

Another trick is to use the row under the sparklines to provide labels for the horizontal axis. If you have a sparkline that spanned 12 months, you can enter a label of JFMAMJJASOND below the sparkline. Change the font in this label cell to be a monospace font such as Courier New. Adjust the column width until the label is as wide as the sparkline. It takes a bit of tweaking, but you can eventually get the items to line up.

In the next section, a sparkline column chart shows hourly readings from 7AM to 2PM. Because the label for 12 would be twice as wide as the label for 7AM, a bit of trickery is employed. The label is 7 followed by Alt+Enter, 8 followed by Alt+Enter, 9 followed by Alt+Enter, and so on through 2. Use the Alignment tab of the Format Cells dialog to turn the values sideways, vertical align top, horizontal align center. Back in the Home tab, keep reducing the font and/or adjusting the column widths until all the values show in the cell. See Figure 23.8 for an example of labels along the horizontal axis.

Forcing All Sparklines to Have the Same Scale

By default, each individual sparkline will have an unseen vertical scale that strives to fill the height of the cell with the sparkline.

This might be fine when you are trying to show how separate measures have a causal relationship.

However, this is not always the best setting.

In Figure 23.8, reject ranges for five manufacturing lines are plotted as spark columns. Excel defaults to filling up the height of each cell with the largest value. This makes all five lines appear as if they had high reject rates.

Reject Rates by Hour and Line

	Line 1	Line 2	Line 3	Line 4	Line 5
7AM	0.000075	0.0106965	0.0066195	0.0012	0.00105
8AM	0.00045	0.0066195	0.003675	0.000675	0.00165
9AM	0.000225	0.002175	0.0088845	0.0015	0.001275
10AM	0.000525	0.0070725	0.01047	0.0018	0.00075
11AM	0.0006	0.0061665	0.01047	0.001425	0.001575
12PM	0.0006	0.001425	0.005487	0.001725	0.000825
1PM	0.000675	0.00315	0.008658	0.00165	0.0015
2PM	0.00135	0.00315	0.011376	0.002325	0.0033

Reject Rates by Hour and Manufacturing Line

Figure 23.8 - *By default, you never really know the vertical scale.*

When one sparkline cell is selected, open the Axis drop-down on the Sparkline Tools Design tab. There are three settings for the minimum and maximum scale.

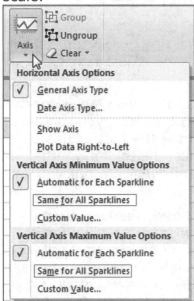

Figure 23.9 - *You will frequently be changing the axis scaling options.*

If you choose Same for All Sparklines for both the minimum and maximum value, you will force all the sparklines to have the same vertical range. This is the setting I used in Figure 23.10. You can now see that Line 2 and Line 3 had the highest reject rates for the day. You still don't know whether the rates were in the acceptable range or not.

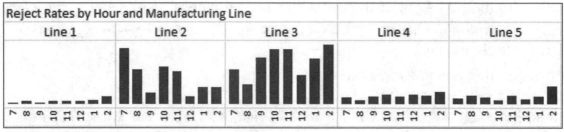

Figure 23.10 - *Set all sparklines to have the same minimum and maximum scale to get a true picture of relative rates.*

Highlighting the Normal Range

The examples in Tufte's book would often draw a rectangular box to show the expected normal range for a sparkline. This allowed you to see when the sparkline deviated from normal.

This functionality is not built in to Excel sparklines, but you can use drawing tools to create a fairly good normal range.

These guidelines provide a rough set of steps for adding the shading:

    1. Use the Axis Scaling settings in Figure 23.9 and use a custom value

Create Tiny Charts with Sparklines

for both the minimum and maximum value. This allows you to actually know that the sparklines range from exactly 0% to 1.5%.

2. Copy the real values for one or two sparklines and paste them outside of the data range. You are going to be temporarily changing those values and you want to paste the real values back into the dataset when you are done.

3. Suppose you want to draw a box for the caution range of 0.5% to 1%. Fill the values for one sparkline with 0.005. Fill the values for the next sparkline with 0.01.

4. Using Insert, Shapes, Rectangle and draw a rectangle over the sparklines. Make the bottom of the rectangle line up with the 0.005 sparklines and make the top of the rectangle line up with the 0.01 sparklines.

5. On the Drawing Tools Format tab, choose Shape Outline, None.

6. Choose Shape Fill, and choose a color for the highlighted area.

7. Press Ctrl+1 or use the dialog launcher in the Shape Styles group to get to the Format Shape dialog box. There is a Transparency slider in the Fill category of the dialog box. Change the slider up to 75% transparent. Click Close to close the dialog box.

8. Adjust the top and bottom of the shape one last time so that they line up with the 0.005 and 0.01 guides in the two temporary sparklines.

9. Click away from the rectangle shape.

10. Copy the real values from the temporary area back to the sparkline data.

In Figure 23.11, you can see that Line 3 spent most of the day in the caution range.

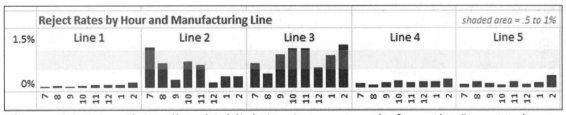

Figure 23.11 - *The yellow highlighting is a rectangle from the Insert tab.*

Win/Loss Sparklines

The Win/Loss chart shows positive numbers as an upward rectangle and negative numbers as a downward rectangle.

The classic example that I won't repeat here is showing winning streaks in sports teams. Win/loss can also be good for showing which bids were accepted. It can be used to show whether the price of a security rose or fell each day.

The example in Figure 23.12 is a year-by-year analysis showing whether a particular artist had a single on the Hot 100 chart. This analysis doesn't show how many singles were on the chart or even where the single peaked. It simply shows the years when the artist had at least one single on the chart.

You can look at this example and see that Elton John was on the chart every year from 1970 through 2001 with the exception of 1977. James Brown was popular from 1959 through 1977, and managed to chart again in 1986 (with the theme song from *Rocky IV*).

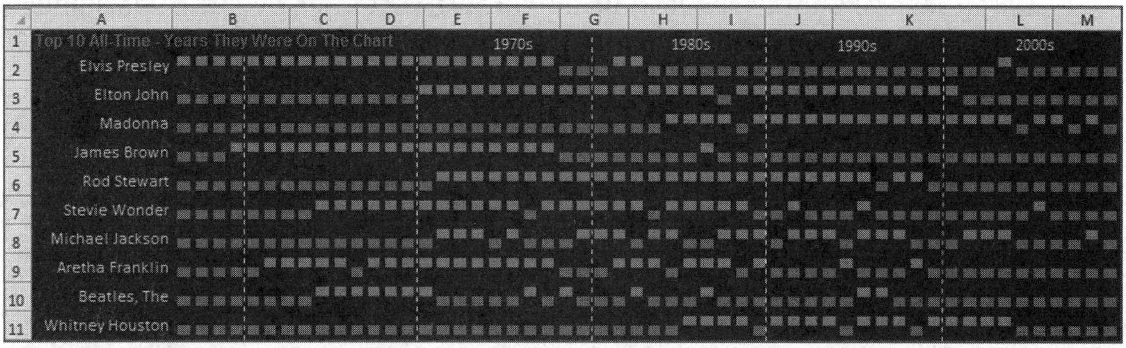

Figure 23.12 - *This win/loss sparkline shows 54 years of data.*

The data for the win/loss sparkline has to have any positive number for a win and any negative number for a loss. Zeros do not appear on the chart; a blank space appears instead of that marker.

Requiring a negative for a loss might require a bit of tweaking on your part. Because the data for Figure 23.12 came from a pivot table, the years with no singles on the chart were appearing as 0. A calculation of 2 times the result minus 1 transformed the chart data into something that could be shown as a win/loss. Artists with a single song on the chart would still have a positive number. (1 times 2 minus 1 is 1.) Artists with 0 songs would show as a negative number (0 times 2 minus 1 is -1.) If someone had 5 songs on the chart, the calculation would yield 9, which is meaningless, but it does not matter because I simply needed any positive number to generate the win marker.

The labels for the decades are text boxes. The white dotted lines were drawn in using Insert Shapes. To make the sparkline span the range from column B through column M, I merged cells B2:M2 into a single cell. This is the first time that I can ever recall suggesting that anyone merge a cell. Generally, merging cells causes so many nightmares. But, it works in this case.

Next Steps

Chapter 24 covers data visualizations such as icon sets, data bars, and color scales.

Data Visualizations

In addition to sparklines, Excel 2010 offers three new data visualization tools. These tools are ideal for the nonfinancial manager. If you can see their eyes glaze over when they see a page full of numbers, you can use the data visualization tools to show patterns in the data.

Although these visualizations are easy to set up, there are additional settings buried in the Excel interface that enable you to create interesting variations.

In-Cell Data Bar Charts

Select a range of numbers. Choose Home, Conditional Formatting, Data Bars, Orange. Excel will add a tiny in-cell data bar to every number in the selection. The largest numbers get the longest swath of color and the smallest numbers get the shortest swath of color. This makes it easy to quickly focus on the largest or smallest numbers in the dataset.

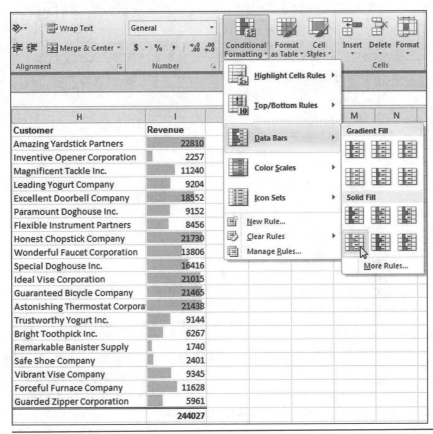

Figure 24.1 - *The longer bars enable you to quickly see the top cells.*

> **Tip**: Do not include the total cell in your selection. If you included the $244K total in the range, that one cell would be the only cell to have a large data bar. All the other cells would appear small.

Data bars in Excel 2010 can appear in either solid or gradient-filled styles. If you use the gradient-filled style, you should always include a solid border so that people can tell the actual extent of the data bar.

> **Tip**: After setting up any conditional formatting, you can choose Home, Conditional Formatting, Manage Rules, Edit Rule to go to a dialog with more settings.

Negative Data Bars

New in Excel 2010, the data bar can show negative values. You can show the negative bar in a contrasting color, and control the location and color of the central axis.

After applying the data bar, use Home, Conditional Formatting, Manage Rules, Edit Rule to access the dialog shown later in Figure 24.3. From that dialog, click the Negative Value and Axis button to get to the dialog shown in Figure 24.2.

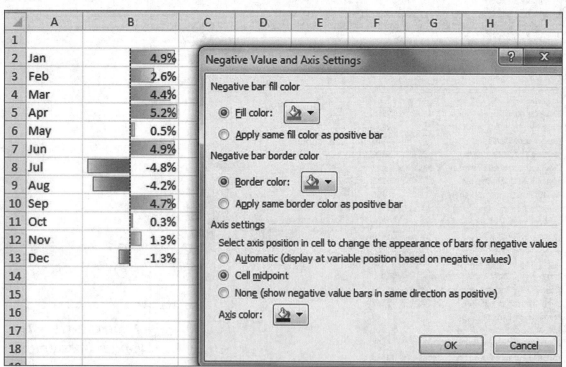

Figure 24.2 - *New in Excel 2010, data bars can be negative.*

Personally, I prefer the axis to be at the cell midpoint or automatic. The choice of None will show the negative bars in the same direction as positive. This setting will shift the virtual axis leftward, so that the left edge of the cell is -5% and the right edge of the cell is +5.2%. To me, it is difficult to figure out what is going on when a value of 0% is filled in to about half the cell.

Comparative Histograms with Right-to-Left Data Bars

New in Excel 2010 is the ability to have a data bar run from right to left. This allows for comparative histograms using data bars. In Figure 24.3, the blue data bars in column H are regular data bars. The red data bars in column F have been modified to run right to left and also have their Maximum setting set to a number of 0.29 so that the size of the red data bars matches the size of the blue data bars.

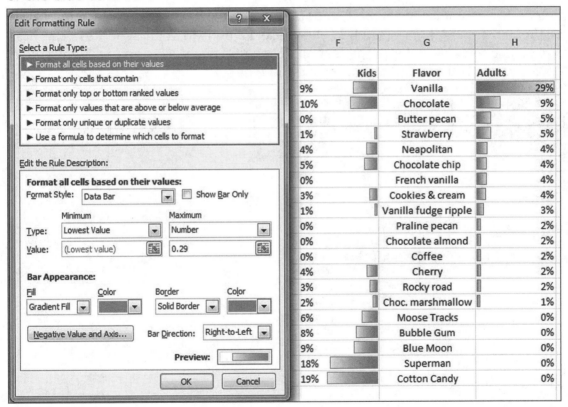

Figure 24.3 - *The red data bars are positive, but set to run right to left.*

Applying a Gradient Using Color Scales

Figure 24.4 shows a table of reject rates by hour by manufacturing line. With all the decimal places, it is hard to spot trends in this data.

	Line 1	Line 2	Line 3	Line 4	Line 5
Reject Rates by Hour and Line					
7AM	0.0000750	0.0106965	0.0066195	0.0012000	0.0010500
8AM	0.0004500	0.0066195	0.0036750	0.0006750	0.0016500
9AM	0.0002250	0.0021750	0.0088845	0.0015000	0.0012750
10AM	0.0005250	0.0070725	0.0104700	0.0018000	0.0007500
11AM	0.0006000	0.0061665	0.0104700	0.0014250	0.0015750
12PM	0.0006000	0.0014250	0.0054870	0.0017250	0.0008250
1PM	0.0006750	0.0031500	0.0086580	0.0016500	0.0015000
2PM	0.0013500	0.0031500	0.0113760	0.0023250	0.0033000

Figure 24.4 - *It is tough to spot trends in this sea of decimal places.*

Select the numeric cells and choose Home, Conditional Formatting, Color Scales, as shown in Figure 24.5. There are 12 built-in color schemes. The first six icons use three colors. The last six icons use two colors and will look much better when you are printing in black and white.

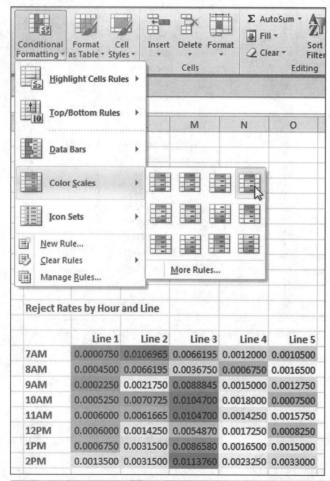

Figure 24.5 - *Line 3 had the most problems today, although quality declined throughout the day for all lines.*

Figure 24.6 shows five of the built-in color scales and a custom color scale using red for large values, yellow for small values, and orange for the middle values.

	A	B	C	D	E	F	G	H	I	J	K
1	Green-Yellow-Red						Green-Yellow				
2		Q1	Q2	Q3	Q4			Q1	Q2	Q3	Q4
3	Baseball	121	2145	816	57		Baseball	121	2145	816	57
4	Football	68	82	2050	980		Football	68	82	2050	980
5	Running	125	892	790	167		Running	125	892	790	167
6	Skiing	1907	12	15	1485		Skiing	1907	12	15	1485
7	Tennis	214	654	121	62		Tennis	214	654	121	62
8											
9	Green-White-Red						Red-White				
10		Q1	Q2	Q3	Q4			Q1	Q2	Q3	Q4
11	Baseball	121	2145	816	57		Baseball	121	2145	816	57
12	Football	68	82	2050	980		Football	68	82	2050	980
13	Running	125	892	790	167		Running	125	892	790	167
14	Skiing	1907	12	15	1485		Skiing	1907	12	15	1485
15	Tennis	214	654	121	62		Tennis	214	654	121	62
16											
17	Blue-White-Red						Red-Orange-Yellow (custom colors)				
18		Q1	Q2	Q3	Q4			Q1	Q2	Q3	Q4
19	Baseball	121	2145	816	57		Baseball	121	2145	816	57
20	Football	68	82	2050	980		Football	68	82	2050	980
21	Running	125	892	790	167		Running	125	892	790	167
22	Skiing	1907	12	15	1485		Skiing	1907	12	15	1485
23	Tennis	214	654	121	62		Tennis	214	654	121	62

Figure 24.6 - *Color scales can use a variety of colors.*

To specify other colors, you can either use the More Rules menu item in Figure 24.5 or choose Home, Conditional Formatting, Manage Rules, Edit Rule to access the dialog shown in Figure 24.7. First, choose either a 3-Color Scale or a 2-Color Scale from the drop-down. You can then choose any colors for the scale. By default, the colors are distributed throughout the range of data. You can use the drop-downs to change the minimum, midpoint, and maximum values in this drop-down.

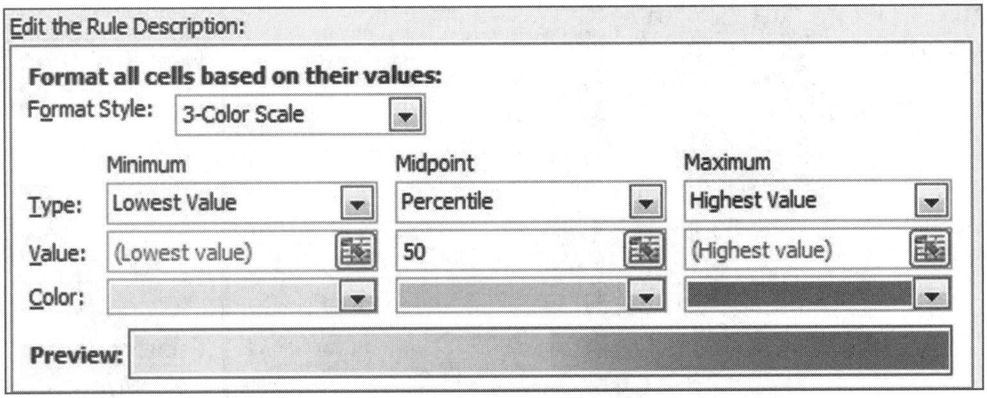

Edit the Rule Description:

Format all cells based on their values:
Format Style: 3-Color Scale

	Minimum	Midpoint	Maximum
Type:	Lowest Value	Percentile	Highest Value
Value:	(Lowest value)	50	(Highest value)
Color:			

Preview:

Figure 24.7 - *Adjust the colors used in the color scale.*

The Type drop-downs in Figure 24.7 enable you to specify lowest value, highest value, a specific number, a percent, a percentile, or even write a formula to determine where the colors break. The formula could use Excel functions such as average and standard deviation to calculate a specific point for the colors to change.

Icon Sets

Icon sets let you apply an icon to each cell based on its value. Icon sets come in three-, four-, and five-icon varieties.

Excel will calculate the max and min of the cells in the range. It will divide that number span into uniform size ranges and assign icons based on those ranges.

As an example, suppose that you have 100 cells with values from 1 to 100. There are 50 cells below 25, 40 cells between 40 and 60, and a rare 10 cells above 80. Excel will calculate the range as running from 1 to 100. Anything from 1 to 33 will get the red circle. Anything from 34 to 66 will get the yellow circle. Anything from 67 to 100 will get the green circle. Using the default settings, you will have 50 red icons, 40 yellow icons, and 10 green icons.

If you edit the icon set and change the Type from Percent to Percentile, you will always have 33 or 34 icons of each color. The Percentile setting might be better when you have a few outlier cells which dramatically skew the range.

As shown in Figure 24.8, there are 20 different icon sets. Some of the icons require color to be differentiated. If you are going to be printing in black and white, use icon sets that have different shapes, such as the cell phone power bars or the circle-triangle-diamond sets.

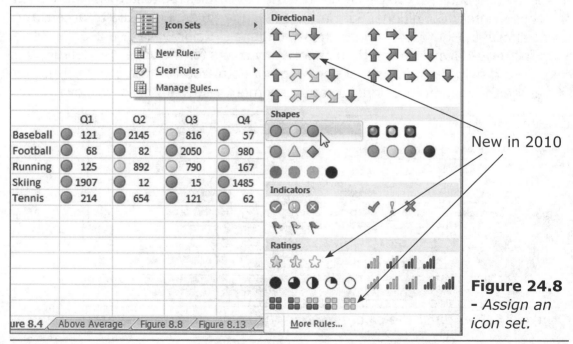

New in 2010

Figure 24.8 - *Assign an icon set.*

> **Caution**: Three icon sets are new in Excel 2010 and will not appear when opened in Excel 2007. If you distribute your workbook to people with Excel 2007, do not use the 3-Stars, 5-Boxes, or the 3-Triangles icon sets. (Although the official name is 3-Triangles, this is the set with a red triangle pointing down, a yellow dash, and a green triangle pointing up.)

Moving the Numbers Closer to the Icons

The icons always appear along the left edge of the cell. Because numbers are usually right-aligned, you often have the icon appearing closer to the number in the column to the left.

At first, I started centering numbers, but this looks really bad. Instead, I now use the Alignment tab of the Format Cells dialog to choose Right (Indent) for the Horizontal Alignment, and then use the Indent spin button to move the numbers closer to the icon. To get to the Format Cells dialog, use one of the dialog launchers on the Home tab or press Ctrl+1.

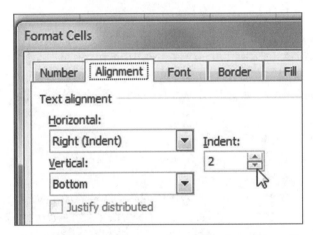

Figure 24.9 - *Increase the right indent to move numbers closer to the icons.*

Showing Icons for Only the Best Cells

Suppose you want to add a star icon to any cells that are above 90. If you choose the 3-Stars icon set, you will see something like Figure 24.10.

		Q1		Q2		Q3		Q4
Andy	☆	88	☆	87	☆	94	☆	85
Bob	☆	87	☆	94	☆	89	☆	94
Charlie	☆	93	☆	99	☆	100	☆	91
Dale	☆	83	☆	82	☆	89	☆	85
Eddy	☆	80	☆	83	☆	82	☆	91

Figure 24.10 - *Default icons.*

Select one of those cells and choose Home, Conditional Formatting, Manage Rules, Edit Rule. You will see the default settings that divide the icons based on a percentage of the range.

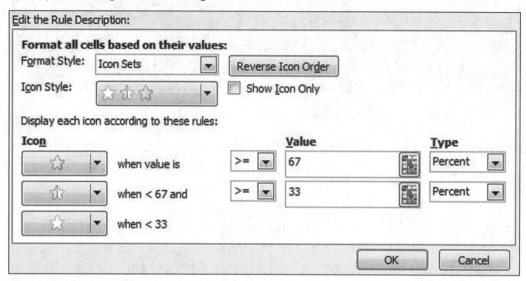

Figure 24.11 - *By default, icons are distributed based on the high and low of the range.*

Change the Type for the gold star to a number and enter 90 as the value. There is really nothing you can do in this dialog to get the lower values to show with nothing. If you change the half star so that it is >=89.9, you can effectively remove the half stars, but you will still have a lot of white stars, as shown in Figure 24.12.

	Q1	Q2	Q3	Q4
Andy	☆ 88	☆ 87	☆ 94	☆ 85
Bob	☆ 87	☆ 94	☆ 89	☆ 94
Charlie	☆ 93	☆ 99	☆ 100	☆ 91
Dale	☆ 83	☆ 82	☆ 89	☆ 85
Eddy	☆ 80	☆ 83	☆ 82	☆ 91

Figure 24.12 - *You can eliminate one of the three stars.*

Go back to the Manage Rules dialog and choose New Rule.

Figure 24.13 - *Choose New Rule.*

As shown in Figure 24.14, set the new rule to Format Only Cells That Contain. Use Cell Value less than 90. Do not apply any format to those cells.

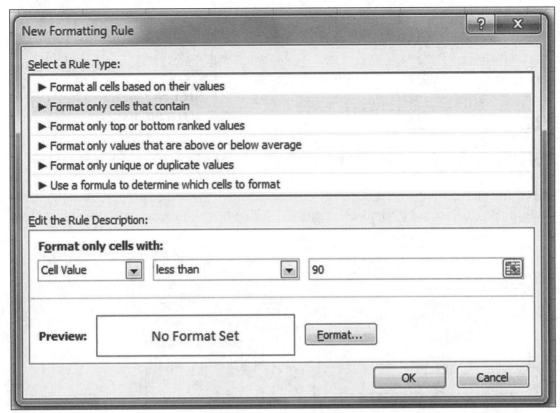

Figure 24.14 - *Choose New Rule.*

Click OK to finish the new rule.

Now, back in the Rules Manager, check the box for Stop If True for the Cell Value < 90 rule! Because the rules are applied in order, any cells with values less than 90 will be formatted with no special formatting and the cell will never have a chance to get an icon. Only values greater than or equal to 90 will get icons.

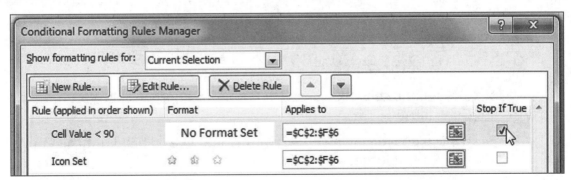

Figure 24.15 - *Choose Stop If True for the first rule.*

The final result, shown in Figure 24.16, is stars appearing only on values of 90 or higher.

	Q1	Q2	Q3	Q4
Andy	88	87	☆ 94	85
Bob	87	☆ 94	89	☆ 94
Charlie	☆ 93	☆ 99	☆ 100	☆ 91
Dale	83	82	89	85
Eddy	80	83	82	☆ 91

Figure 24.16 - *Only gold stars appear.*

Using Other Conditional Formatting Rules

Excel 2007 introduced a new set of conditional formatting rules such as Above Average, Bottom n %, and so on. Figure 24.17 shows a range where everything above average is highlighted.

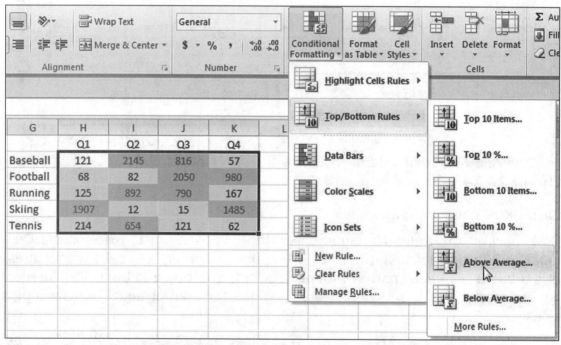

Figure 24.17 - *Highlight cells above average.*

Using a Formula as a Rule

If you want to highlight cells based on the value in another cell, you have to use a formula-based rule.

In Figure 24.18, the active cell in cell A2. You would like to highlight the entire row of the item with the largest value in column B.

You have to right the formula as if it applied to the active cell of A2 but then would be evaluated for each cell in the range. This often requires judicious use of the absolute-reference dollar signs.

The formula would be =$B2=MAX($B$2:$B$21).

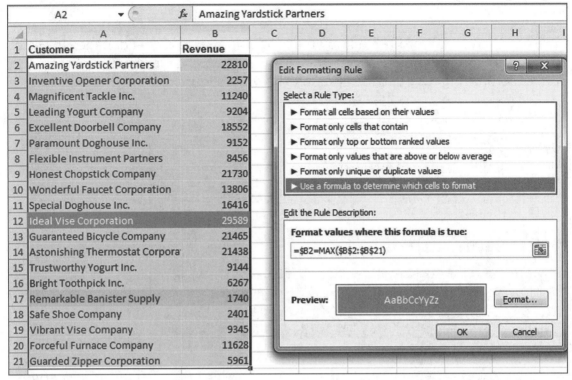

Figure 24.18 - *Use a formula to identify which row has the largest value.*

In Figure 24.19, a second rule has been added to highlight the smallest row in yellow.

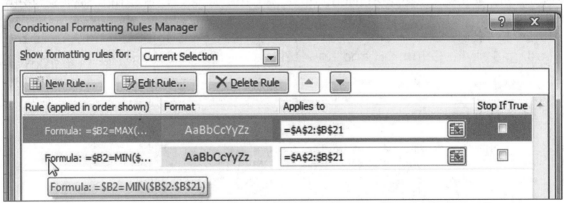

Figure 24.19 - *A similar formula highlights the smallest row in yellow.*

Next Steps

Chapter 25 covers the Cell Styles gallery on the Home tab.

---

2 5

Cell Styles

Gurus of Microsoft Word have known about using styles for a decade. In Excel 2010, Microsoft promotes styles in Excel, adding a drop-down right on the Home tab offering 42 built-in styles as shown in Figure 25.1.

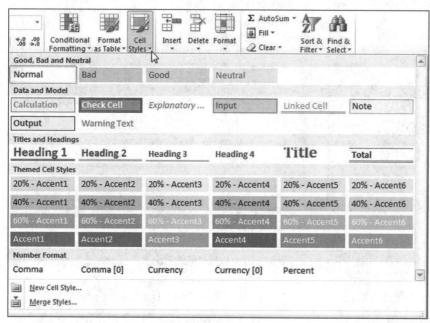

Figure 25.1 -
Excel offers 42 built-in cell styles on the Home tab.

You can choose which styles you think are appropriate and which are not. Personally, I use Title and Heading 4 all the time. The other styles seem arbitrary. Why should calculated cells have an orange font? It makes no sense to me. In Figure 25.2, cell A1 has a Title style. Row 3 and column A uses the Heading 4 style. Column H and Row 12 use the Calculation style.

⊿	A	B	C	D	E	F	G	H
1	**This is the Title**							
2								
3		**Headings**	**Headings**	**Headings**	**Headings**	**Headings**	**Headings**	**Total**
4	Labels	18750	10287	12054	19738	2959	15927	79715
5	Labels	8635	1240	14715	16042	7985	4003	52620
6	Labels	7768	10600	11238	14132	5635	15347	64720
7	Labels	7726	19501	12781	16170	9286	19351	84815
8	Labels	5108	8494	18558	14340	12908	19311	78719
9	Labels	7948	19227	19226	16281	11506	18377	92565
10	Labels	18480	7075	7536	4230	3065	8461	48847
11	Labels	4938	14170	1277	6396	10598	5190	42569
12	Total	79353	90594	97385	107329	63942	105967	544570

Figure 25.2 -
Some styles look good. Others do not.

Adding New Styles

Most of my worksheets deal with positive numbers. Thus, I prefer to use a number format of "#,##0" instead of the accounting format. When you use the Comma style, Excel uses the accounting format. This format allows for the possibility of negative numbers in parentheses, and therefore all the positive numbers are not quite right-aligned with the cell as shown in Figure 25.3.

18,750	10,287	12,054
8,635	1,240	14,715
7,768	10,600	11,238

Figure 25.3 - *The built-in comma style uses leaves space after positive numbers.*

You can add your own new style to a workbook. First, format a cell with the correct formatting. It might be easiest to go to a blank cell that had not previously been formatted. Type a number and format that cell. To reach the full Format Cells dialog, use the Ctrl+1 shortcut key. On the Number tab, choose the Number category. Specify 0 decimal places and a thousands separator, as shown in Figure 25.4. On the Alignment tab, specify right-aligned and top-aligned.

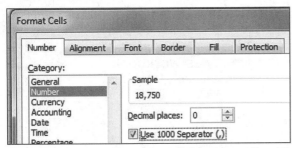

Figure 25.4 - *Use Ctrl+1 to access all the Format options.*

To create a new style, select the cell with the formatting for that style. Open the Cell Styles drop-down and choose New Style from the bottom of the menu.

Give the style a name such as CommaGood.

Because this a numeric style, you want to apply the settings from the Number and Alignment tab, but you do not want to change the existing font, color, fill, or borders. Uncheck the boxes for Font, Border, Fill, and Protection.

Figure 25.5 - *This style will change only the number format and alignment.*

Click OK to create the style.

Your custom styles now appear at the top of the Cell Styles menu.

When you apply the CommaGood style, you get the thousands separator without the extra space after the number.

18,750	10,287	12,054
8,635	1,240	14,715
7,768	10,600	11,238

Figure 25.6 - *Commas but no extra space to the right of the number.*

Sharing Styles with Other Workbooks

Styles that you create are available only in the current workbook. It would be better if you could globally make the style available to all workbooks.

There are two approaches that you can use.

In the first approach, you create a sample workbook that contains all your favorite custom styles. You can copy those styles to any workbook by following these steps:

1. Open the new workbook and the sample styles workbook.

2. Make the new workbook the active workbook.

3. Open the Cell Styles menu and choose Merge.

4. In the Merge Styles dialog, choose to merge from the sample styles workbook.

Excel will copy the styles to the new workbook.

This approach is admittedly a hassle because you would have to apply the styles to every workbook you ever create.

The second approach is more difficult at first, but then will be easier as you create new workbooks. This approach uses a new book template. Follow these steps to define a book template:

1. Open a blank workbook with a single worksheet.

2. Create new styles as described earlier.

3. Clear the cells that you used to create the styles.

4. Optionally, if you have favorite Page Setup settings, apply any custom margins, headers, footers, or scaling settings.

5. In Windows Explorer, create a new folder. You might call this folder c:\ XLDefault.

6. In Excel, go to File, Options. In the left navigation, choose Advanced. Scroll to the bottom and look for a section called General. There is a setting for At Startup, Open All Files In. Enter the name of the folder from step 5 in that box. Click OK.

7. Use File, Save As. In the Save as Type drop-down, choose Excel Template. Annoyingly, Excel navigates to a different path. Browse back to C:\XLDefault.

8. Save the file with a name of Book.

9. Perform a second Save As to save as a template with the name of Sheet.

Whenever you want to create a new workbook, use the Ctrl+N shortcut. This will load the Book.xltx file as the new blank workbook. All your favorite cell styles will be available. When you click the new worksheet icon, Excel will insert Sheet.xltx as the new sheet. This will ensure that your page setup settings apply to the new worksheet.

Next Steps

Chapter 26 looks at using themes in Excel.

26

Document Themes Across Microsoft Office

Three components of Microsoft Office 2010 enable you to easily create documents that look like they belong together. If you are preparing a presentation in PowerPoint 2010, an introduction in Word 2010, and some tables in Excel 2010, all of these documents can look similar if you use document themes.

Document Themes, Borrowed from PowerPoint

If you dabble in PowerPoint, you know that you can change the slide background. You may or may not have noticed that when the slide background changes, the fonts, colors, font sizes, and effects also change. As I create a PowerPoint document, I try to choose a background that matches my message.

In PowerPoint 2010, Microsoft offers 44 themes. With each theme, you get new colors, fonts, effects, and a choice of backgrounds. Microsoft added these same 44 themes to Excel 2010 and Word 2010. If you choose a certain theme in PowerPoint, choose an identical theme in Word and Excel to make your entire report look like it came from the same application. You can staple together pages that came from Excel, Word, and PowerPoint. Provided you used the same theme in all the applications, the documents should look similar.

Choosing a New Theme

So far, most of the images in this book have been created using the Office theme. This is the default theme in Excel 2010. Figure 26.1 shows a worksheet with several elements: shapes, SmartArt graphics, a photograph, a chart, WordArt, and cells formatted with various cell styles.

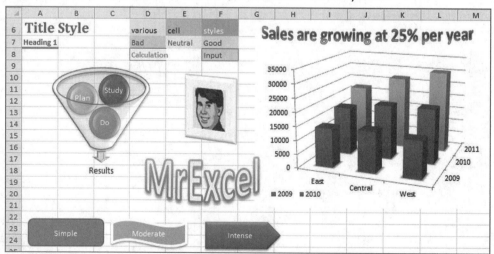

Figure 26.1 - *This document is in the Office theme.*

To change the look and feel of your document, choose a new theme from the Themes drop-down on the Page Layout ribbon. Figure 26.2 shows the document in the Grid theme.

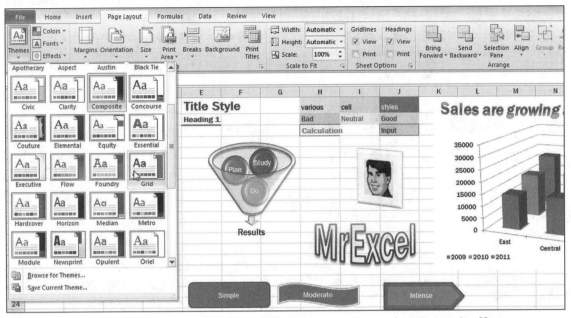

Figure 26.2 - *Change to Grid theme for new colors, fonts, and effects.*

Themes range from subdued, such as Paper, to gaudy (take your pick from Metro, Opulent, or Verve).

When you change a theme, you inherit new fonts, colors, and effects. The Colors drop-down shows the palette for many of the built-in themes (see Figure 26.3).

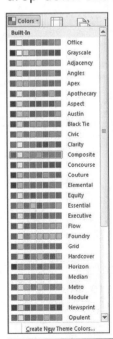

Figure 26.3 - *Colors available in the built-in themes.*

Although colors are fairly easy to understand, the Effects drop-down seems confusing.

Throughout Excel 2010, galleries typically offer styles from plain to moderate to intense. For example, the Shape Styles gallery ranges from plain styles at the top, to moderate styles in row 3 and 4 to intense styles in row 6 (see Figure 26.4).

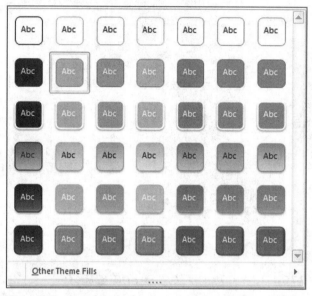

Figure 26.4 - *Many galleries in Excel 2010 range from simple to moderate to intense.*

The Effects drop-down shows three shapes for each theme. The circle is meant to indicate the effects when you choose simple styles. The arrow is meant to indicate effects when you choose moderate styles. The rectangle is meant to indicate effects when you choose intense styles (see Figure 26.5)

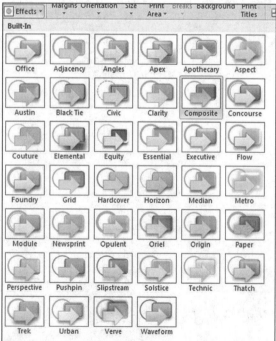

Figure 26.5 - *The Effects drop-down gives a clue to the effects in each theme, if you understand the code.*

Document Themes Across Microsoft Office

If you study Figure 26.5, you can guess that Metro is going to apply a jeweled effect to intense styles and Paper will apply a texture to moderate styles. Technic offers a glow around the moderate styles. Module uses a double-line for simple styles. You are certainly wondering why you should care. This becomes important when you want to design your own theme.

Designing a Theme to Match Your Company Colors

Microsoft allows you to create new themes. You can share these themes with others in your company. Thus, you could create a company theme with your company colors. Or, you could simply mix and match fonts from one theme, colors from another theme, and styles from a third theme.

Creating a Theme by Mixing and Matching

On the Page Layout tab, use the Colors, Fonts, and Effects drop-down to define a new theme. Choose Colors from the Verve theme, Fonts from the Apex theme, Effects from the Opulent theme.

On the Themes drop-down, choose Save Current Theme. Save the themes as MyTheme. A theme gets saved as a file with a .thmx extension. Excel will automatically save the file in the appropriate folder, usually %appdata%\ Microsoft\Templates\Document Themes.

The next time you start Excel 2010, your theme will be in a built-in section of the Themes drop-down.

Sharing Your Theme with Others

Open Windows Explorer. In the address bar, type %AppData% and press Enter. Excel will find the application data folder for your operating system. From there, browse to Microsoft, Templates, Document Themes. You will see the theme that you saved, stored as a THMX file.

You can copy this THMX file and save it in the similar folder of every computer in your department, and everyone will have access to the same theme.

Creating a Theme to Match Your Company Colors

Although you are allowed to customize colors and fonts in your theme, you must start with one of the 40 built-in effects.

Open the Effects drop-down in the Page Layout tab. Choose one of the 40 built-in effects themes. Read the paragraph after Figure 26.4 to understand how the thumbnails work.

Your theme will need a title font and a body font. If your company has a font that is used to render your logo, this is appropriate for the title font. (Visit www. Chank.com if you need a custom font designed to match an existing logo.) For the body font, you should choose something simple such as Cambria, Arial, or Times.

To specify the fonts for your theme, use Page Layout, Fonts, Create New Theme Fonts. Specify the font to be used for titles and body copy.

Choosing colors for the theme is more difficult. You need to specify a color for text and titles (black works great), a color for text and titles on a dark background (white?), a color for hyperlinks and followed hyperlinks, and then six accent colors. The accent colors are the colors that will come up again and again in charts, SmartArt, shapes, WordArt, and so forth. Use your company logo colors for the first accent colors. Unless your company has six accent colors, you will need to find complementary colors for your logo colors. There are free tools on the Web for finding complementary colors. Go to Google and search for "Complementary Color Tool."

On the Page Layout tab, choose Colors, Create New Theme Colors to display the dialog in Figure 26.6. For each color, choose the drop-down, and then More Colors. You can specify the Red, Green, Blue components for the selected color.

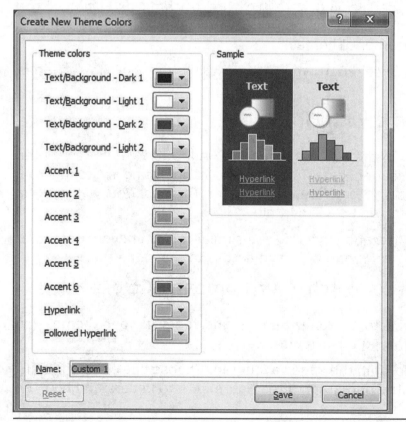

Figure 26.6 - *Specify company colors in the Theme Color dialog.*

Finally, use Page Layout, Themes, Save Current Theme. Specify a name for the theme (perhaps your company name).

When you restart Excel, you will be able to choose your custom theme from the drop-down. The document, charts, graphics will all use colors from your company logo.

Themes are a great tool for branding documents from Word, PowerPoint, and Excel into a single cohesive document.

Next Steps

Chapter 27 covers the picture tools and the new Background Removal tool.

27

Using Picture Tools and Background Removal

Excel 2010 has a new set of picture tools. Use the Picture icon on the Insert tab to add a picture to your worksheet. One of the best picture tools in Excel 2010 is the Background Removal tool.

Removing the Picture Background

New in Excel 2010, you can easily remove the background from a picture. I can imagine this will lead to a variety of Excel cover sheets with decorative pictures with the backgrounds removed.

In Figure 27.1, you see two versions of a lighthouse picture. The picture on the right shows the original picture. The picture on the left is in the beginning stages of background removal.

Figure 27.1 - *Initially, the Background Removal tool guesses wrong.*

The most important part of using the Background Removal tool is to drag the resize handles so that the box surrounds the subject of the photograph. In Figure 27.1, the tool incorrectly guessed the extent of the lighthouse and ended up cropping out a large chunk of the bottom of the lighthouse.

In Figure 27.2, the bounding box is extended to include all the lighthouse. Given the correct bounding box, the Picture Removal tool does a good job of predicting what to remove.

Figure 27.2 - *You can improve the results simply by resizing the bounding box.*

The Background Removal tab of the ribbon includes icons where you can mark areas to keep or remove. Some of the trees along the left side of the lighthouse were getting included, so you can use the Mark Areas to Remove icon to remove those areas.

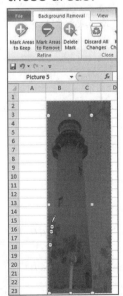

Figure 27.3 - *If necessary, mark additional areas to remove.*

When you click the Keep Changes icon, the background will be removed.

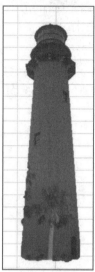

Figure 27.4 - *The background is removed.*

Using Other Picture Tools in Excel 2010

To insert a picture in a worksheet, use the Picture icon on the Insert tab.

When the picture is selected, you can access the Picture Tools Format tab.

With today's digital cameras, it is likely that your picture will appear too large. Use the Size group to resize your image. Click the down spin button for Height several times. Excel will reduce both the height and width of the picture.

To cut out unnecessary background, click the Crop button. Eight crop handles will appear on the edge of the picture. Drag any handle inward to crop out portions of the photo. Click the Crop icon again to complete the operation.

Figure 27.5 - *Use the Crop icon, and then drag the handles inward to crop.*

The Crop drop-down now enables you to crop the image to a particular shape or a particular aspect ratio.

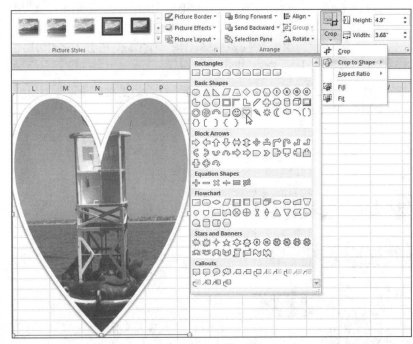

Figure 27.6 - *You can now crop the picture to a shape.*

The Adjust group offers several clever improvements in Excel 2010. There have previously been places to adjust color, brightness, and contrast. But people using Excel are numbers people. We aren't artsy Photoshop people.

In Excel 2010, the various adjustment drop-downs now feature thumbnails of your picture with various corrections applied. Instead of using a pair of spin buttons to choose brightness and contrast, you can simply click the thumbnail with the best-looking combination of brightness and contrast. The gallery shown in Figure 27.7 gives you several combinations of brightness and contrast. This seems much easier than the Excel 2007 controls where you separately applied brightness and contrast.

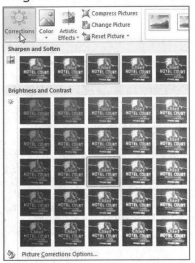

Figure 27.7 - *Choose the thumbnail with the best combination of brightness and contrast.*

In reality, brightness and contrast can be set from -100% to +100% in 1% increments. There are thus 201x201 or 40,401 combinations, and the Corrections drop-down is only showing you 25 possible combinations out of the 40,401 combinations. However, you can always use the Picture Corrections Options choice at the bottom of the flyout to access the Format Picture dialog where you can dial up any of the 40,401 possibilities.

The Color drop-down enables you to set saturation, tone, and recolor. Again, thumbnails show you how your picture will appear.

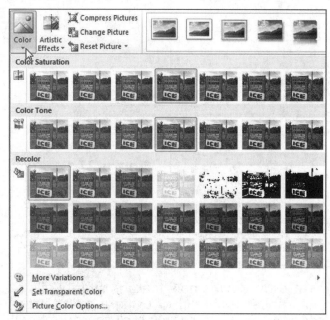

Figure 27.8 - *You can change the color to one of several presets or access the menus at the bottom for more options.*

The new Artistic Effects drop-down offers ways to convert a photograph to a graphic. Figure 27.9 shows the drop-down, and Figure 27.10 shows five effects applied to the original picture in the top left.

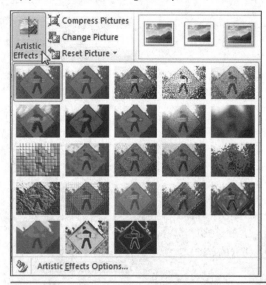

Figure 27.9 - *Excel 2010 offers 23 new artistic effects.*

Figure 27.10 - *Convert the photo to an illustration using the various Artistic Effects filters.*

The Picture Styles gallery offers 28 different built-in style effects for your picture.

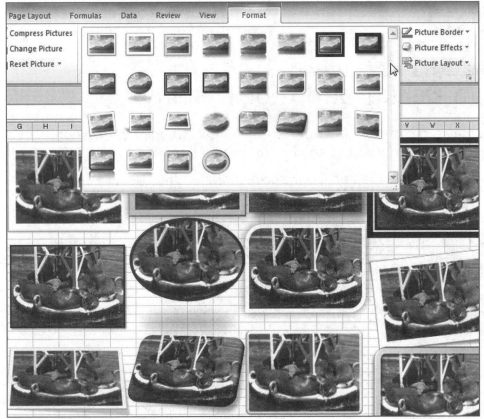

Figure 27.11 - *The built-in styles change the frame, bevel, tilt, and so on.*

If you don't like the built-in styles, use the Picture Shape, Picture Border, or Picture Effects drop-downs to apply a wide variety of effects to your pictures.

Compressing Pictures

If you are not planning on printing the spreadsheet in a glossy magazine, you can save file size by using the Compress Pictures icon.

As you can see, by default, the cropped areas of a picture remain in the workbook. Someone could use the Crop tool to later see what you cropped out. So to prevent a Cat Schwartz-type problem, always make sure to visit the Compress Pictures dialog to permanently remove the cropped portions of the photograph.

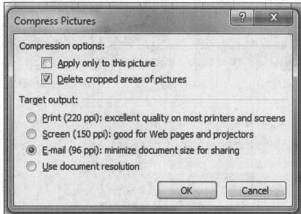

Figure 27.12 - *Remove the cropped portions of pictures and reduce resolution to save file size.*

Adding a Background for Display

Excel can display a picture behind your spreadsheet. Choose Background from the Page Layout tab. Browse and select any picture.

Excel will tile that picture behind your spreadsheet cells. Be sure to choose a contrasting color for the text in the spreadsheet.

Figure 27.13 - *Excel will tile the picture behind your spreadsheet.*

Adding a Picture Background for Printing

Unfortunately, the background as described earlier does not print! To create a printable picture background, follow these steps:

1. On the Insert tab, choose Shapes, and then a rectangle shape.

2. Click and drag in your worksheet to draw a solid background of the proper size.

3. With the shape selected, choose Drawing Tools Format, Shape Fill, From Picture.

4. Browse and select a picture. The picture will fill the shape and will cover the worksheet cells.

5. Press Ctrl+1 to format the picture. Choose the Fill category from the left side of the Format Picture dialog. Drag the Transparency slider so that you can still see the picture but the text in the cells shows through. In Figure 27.14, a 71% transparency offers a good balance.

6. Choose the Line Color category from the left side of the Format Picture dialog. Choose No Line to remove the border from around the picture.

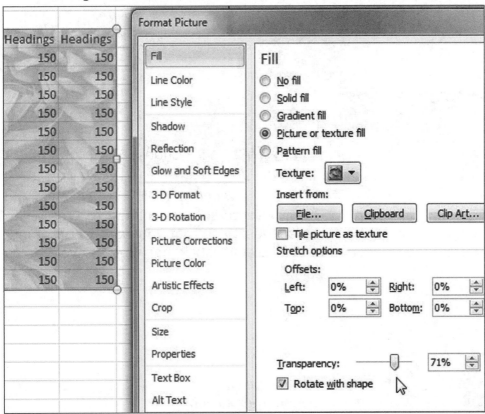

Figure 27.14 - *By adjusting the transparency, you can see the cells behind the picture. Unlike the background picture, this one will print.*

Inserting a Screen Shot

Excel 2010 offers a new Screenshot icon on the Insert tab. If you open this drop-down, you will see a list of available windows that you can paste as a picture into the worksheet. Excel always pastes the entire window, including the title bar. You will then be using the Crop tool to remove all but the relevant portions of the window.

Instead, I prefer to use Screen Clipping tool. This tool requires a bit more set up, but then it requires no post-screen-shot work.

You might have several different applications open. You want to grab a picture from a web page. From Excel, switch to the browser session where you can see the image.

The Screen Clipping command works on the window that was active immediately before you switched to Excel. It is important that you switch directly from the browser back to Excel. If you use Alt+Tab to switch applications and you accidentally stop on the wrong application, that application will appear in the screen clipping.

When you are back in Excel, open the Screenshot drop-down on the Insert tab and choose the Screen Clipping item from the bottom of the drop-down.

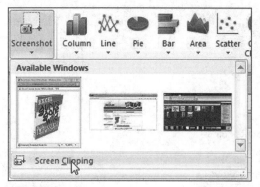

Figure 27.15 - *Choose Screen Clipping.*

Excel will show you a picture of the browser window. Wait a few seconds and the picture will be grayed out. The mouse cursor will change to crosshairs. Drag a rectangle around the portion of the screen that you want to paste into Excel. As you drag, that portion of the screen will change from grayed out to full color.

Figure 27.16 - *Draw a rectangle around the portion of the window that you want to paste into Excel.*

When you finish the box, a picture of that screen will be pasted into the worksheet.

Note that you cannot use the Screen Clipping tool to paste a picture of an Excel worksheet. You can, however, use the Paste Picture icon or the Paste Picture Link icon on the Paste drop-down to paste a picture of a range that you've copied.

Next Steps

Chapter 28 shows you the new business diagram tool that Microsoft calls SmartArt.

Create Business Diagrams with SmartArt

Office 2010 adds support for 150+ different types of business diagrams. These diagrams include list charts, process charts, cycle charts, hierarchy and org charts, relationship charts, matrix charts, and pyramid charts.

Figure 28.1 shows a selection of SmartArt diagrams.

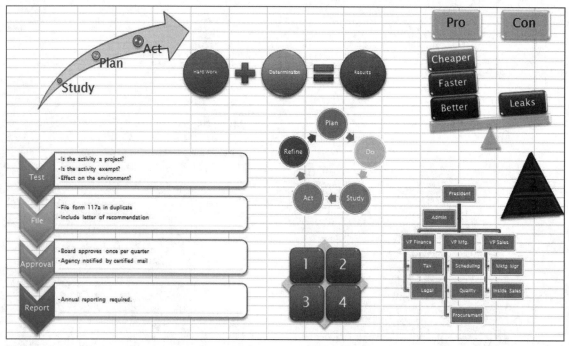

Figure 28.1 - *Communicate ideas using SmartArt diagrams.*

Creating SmartArt Diagrams

To create a SmartArt diagram, choose the basic layout, and then type the text to build the shape. In most cases, the diagram will support Level 1 and Level 2 text. Each Level 1 bullet point translates to a new shape in the diagram. Each Level 2 bullet point appears near the Level 1 shape.

> **Note**: This is not a hard-and-fast rule. Some layouts support only Level 1 text, and some layouts add shapes for Level 2 text. Certain layouts, such as the org chart or hierarchy, can support Level 3, Level 4, and Level 5 text.

1. From the Insert tab, choose SmartArt.

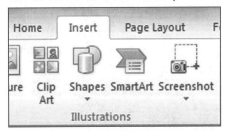

Figure 28.2 - *Access the SmartArt icon on the Insert tab.*

2. Choose a layout from the dialog.

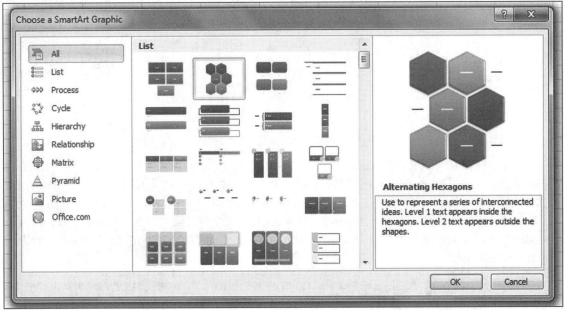

Figure 28.3 - *Click a layout thumbnail in the center to see a description on the right.*

Excel displays a default diagram, usually with three placeholders for text in the Text pane.

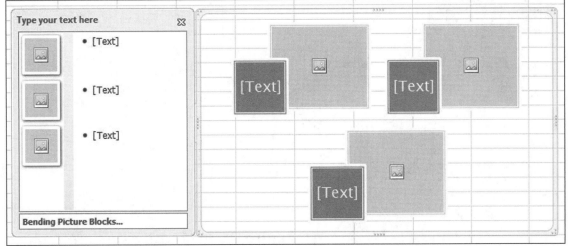

Figure 28.4 - *The [Text] entries are placeholders, waiting for you to add your own text.*

3. Type your text in the text pane. Pressing Tab will demote the current entry from Level 1 to Level 2. Pressing Shift+Tab will promote Level 2 text to Level 1 text. Pressing Enter will add a new entry at the current level. Adding a new Level 1 entry will add a shape to the diagram. As you add text, Excel automatically resizes the fonts in the diagram (see Figure 28.5).

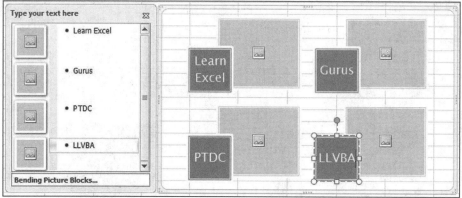

Figure 28.5 - *New Level 1 entries add shapes to the diagram.*

4. If your layout includes picture placeholders, click each picture placeholder and browse for a picture. The picture will usually be too large. Right-click the picture and choose Size and Properties. You can then use Size or Crop categories to resize the picture. If you use the Offset Y setting in the Crop category, you can move the shape so that the top of the picture is visible in the shape.

5. On the SmartArt Tools Design tab, choose the Change Colors drop-down to choose from 32 different color variations for the graphic.

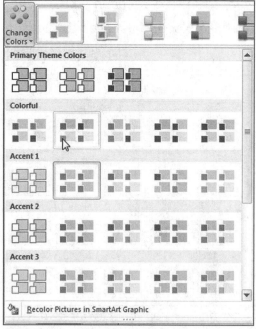

Figure 28.6 - *These colors are based on the current theme.*

Create Business Diagrams with SmartArt

6. Choose the SmartArt Styles gallery to add 1 of 14 built-in styles to the diagram. There are five 2D styles and nine 3D styles. The styles go from fairly plain, to stylish, to impossible to read. Something from the middle of this list, such as Polished or Inset, adds sufficient effect while still making the diagram easy to read. If you go with the final choices, either Sunset or Bird's Eye, it will be difficult to read the diagram.

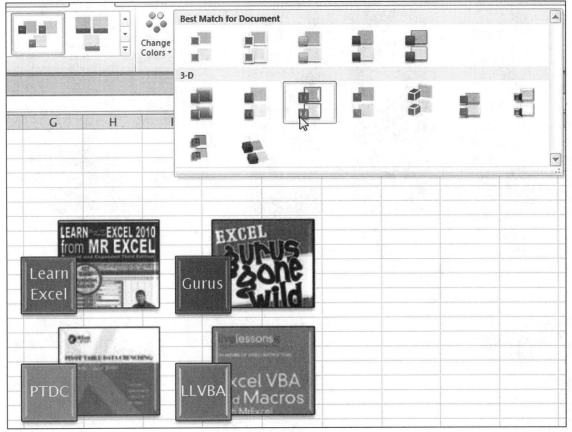

Figure 28.7 - *Fourteen different styles change the diagram from 2D to 3D.*

Changing to a New Layout

After you have built your diagram, you can easily change it to any of the other layouts. From the SmartArt Tools Design tab, open the Layout gallery and choose a different layout.

Micromanaging Settings

In general, Excel will try to keep your SmartArt diagram looking consistent. If you add a lot of text to one shape, Excel will make the text smaller in all shapes so that the diagram has identical fonts in all shapes.

You can micromanage these settings using the SmartArt Tools Format tab. Select an individual shape and use the tools on the Format tab to add effects. As you can see in Figure 28.8, you can make horrible looking SmartArt diagrams using the tools on the Format tab.

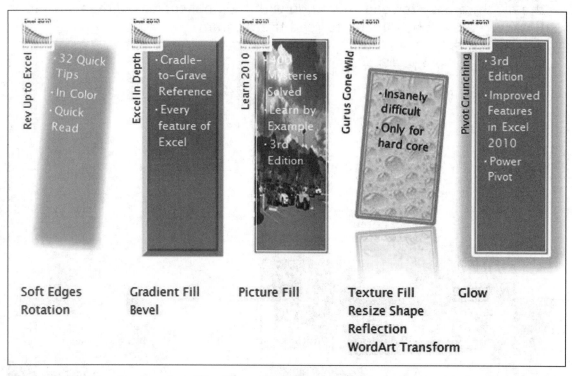

Figure 28.8 - *Customize the fill, reflection, and so on for a single shape using the Format tab.*

Tip: Get your SmartArt diagram as close to finished as possible before venturing over to the Format tab.

Adding Formulas to Shapes

For Excel fans, the biggest disappointment with SmartArt diagrams is that their text is static. You cannot have the text for a SmartArt diagram dynamically calculated by Excel. Also, Microsoft did not expose the SmartArt object model to VBA, so you cannot use macros to dynamically build SmartArt.

Excel has been able to apply a formula to a shape for more than decade. It is disappointing that the Excel team could not hook up this 10-year-old feature for the shiny new SmartArt diagrams.

The only workaround is to use the SmartArt tools to build a diagram, and then convert the diagram to shapes. You can then apply formulas to the shapes.

Create Business Diagrams with SmartArt

In Figure 28.9, a database query feeds individual sales figures in columns A:C. SUMIF formulas in G4:G6 show the current sales for each rep. RANK formulas in E4:E6 figure out which rep is in the lead. VLOOKUP formulas in F8:H10 combine the associate name and their sales total. This report is functional, but it lacks visual interest.

	A	B	C	D	E	F	G	H	I	J
G8						fx	=VLOOKUP($E8,$E$4:$G$6,COLUMN(C1),FALSE)			
1	Sales Log					Summary by Associate				
2										
3	Associate	Ticket	Revenue							
4	Ted	1891	33.6		1	Ted	772.7			
5	Bob	1892	63.77		2	Mary	718.22			
6	Mary	1893	105.2		3	Bob	559.6			
7	Ted	1894	10.76							
8	Mary	1895	210.47		1	Ted	772.7	1. Ted is the daily star with $773		
9	Ted	1896	13.84		2	Mary	718.22	2. Mary has sales of $718		
10	Bob	1897	95.85		3	Bob	559.6	3. Bob has sales of $560		

Figure 28.9 - *My eyes glaze over just trying to write the caption.*

1. Build a SmartArt diagram with three shapes. Use dummy text of about the right length. Use the SmartArt tools to format the diagram. In this example, use the Format tab to resize the individual shapes.

2. With the SmartArt selected, click Convert to Shapes. This will convert the SmartArt diagram from being SmartArt (which is limited to static text) to Shapes (which allows the text to come from worksheet cells).

3. Click the text in the first shape. Drag to select the text in the shape. Click in the formula bar and type =H8 and press Enter. The text in the selected shape changes to reflect the result of the formula in H8.

4. Repeat step 6 to assign =H9 to the second shape and =H10 to the third shape.

You now have something that looks like a SmartArt diagram, but the text for the shapes comes dynamically from the worksheet.

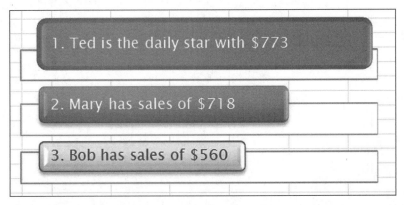

Figure 28.10 - *Now the text in the diagram is a live result from the data.*

> **Tip**: The case study above was adapted from ideas in Ron Martin's *Retail Selling Made Easy*. If you manage a retail store and want to motivate your sales staff, Ron's book is invaluable. Order it from http://www.ronmartin.net/sdi/books_dvds/bks_rsme.htm.

Next Steps

Chapter 29 shows you how to use WordArt to create interesting headlines.

29

Using WordArt

WordArt changed after Excel 2003. It actually seems a bit less intuitive to use. Follow these steps to create some WordArt.

1. From the Insert tab, open the WordArt drop-down. Choose from 30 different styles. These styles will differ depending on your selected theme.

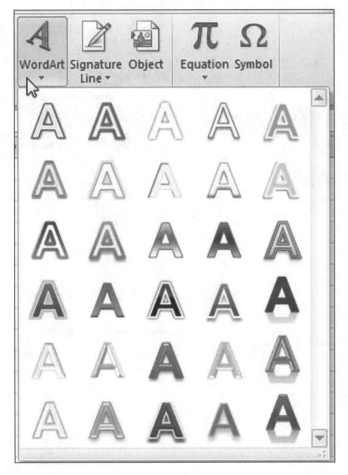

Figure 29.1 - *Don't worry that these choices aren't as interesting as previous renditions of WordArt.*

2. WordArt appears as *Your Text Here*. Type new text to replace *Your Text Here*.

3. Click the border of the WordArt so that the border appears as a solid box rather than dotted lines.

4. If desired, choose a different font from the Font drop-down on the Home tab. Meatier fonts can work better for WordArt.

5. On the Drawing Tools Format tab, use the Text Fill, Text Outline, and Text Effects drop-downs to change the WordArt. In Figure 29.2, the familiar WordArt shapes are on the Transform menu.

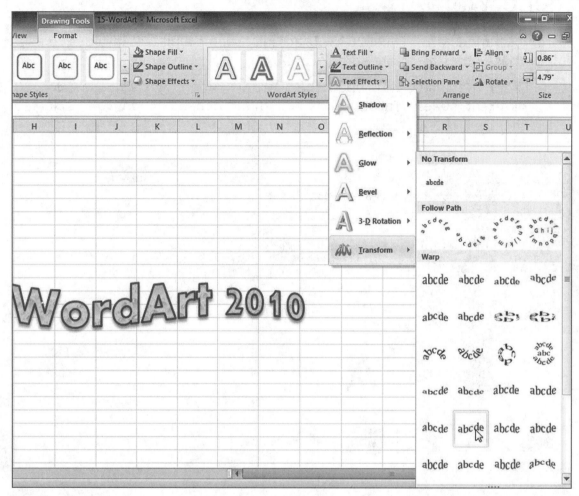

Figure 29.2 - *You can find the familiar shapes under Transform.*

Note that you can also apply most WordArt effects (except Transform) to chart titles. Choose the chart title and use the WordArt Styles gallery on the Format tab.

After applying a transform, look for two handles on the WordArt. The green circular handle will enable you to rotate the WordArt. A pink diamond handle will enable you to tweak the angle of inflection used in the transform. In Figure 29.3, the pink diamond handle is near the left edge of the *W*.

If you use a font with thick letters, you can use the Text Fill to fill the letters with a photograph or gradient.

Figure 29.3 - *A picture fill.*

Next Steps

In Chapter 30, you learn how to use the new text box tools in Excel 2010.

Handling Large Blocks of Text

Excel is great with numbers, but also has some tricks for dealing with text.

Suppose you have typed some text at the bottom of a worksheet and you want to wrap the text to fit a rectangular range from columns B through I.

	A	B	C	D	E	F	G	H	I	J	K	
29		Costs in year 1			1176120	0	0	0	0			
30		Bottom Line			3693144	4869264	4869264	4869264	4869264	23170200		
31												
32			Final Result	3980883.2								
33												
34												
35		Lorem ipsum dolor sit amet, consectetuer adipiscing elit. Aenean congue blandit velit. Sed scelerisque blandit sem.										
36		Sed tincidunt tincidunt felis.										
37		Morbi vel eros vel felis consectetuer accumsan. Donec a arcu eu urna lacinia dictum. Proin consectetuer elit sed nisi.										
38		Donec eleifend arcu porta tellus. Nunc feugiat lacus et nunc.										
39		Mauris scelerisque magna ac diam.										
40		Maecenas eget ipsum in augue hendrerit suscipit.										
41		Nunc tempor tortor et est. Morbi egestas neque eu nisl. Sed sit amet quam in augue pellentesque ultrices.										
42		Aenean dapibus arcu ut neque. Vestibulum interdum mattis magna. Phasellus euismod ante nec massa.										
43		Cras mattis sagittis ipsum. Praesent dignissim massa id erat. Nam facilisis diam vel nisl.										
44		Duis nonummy elit rhoncus pede.										
45												
46												
47												

Figure 30.1 - *You would like to word wrap this text to fill columns B:I.*

Select a rectangular range that includes all the text in B and is wide enough to fill the range that you want to fill. It is a good idea to include a few extra blank rows at the bottom in case the wrapped text needs to extend that far.

From the Home tab, select Fill, Justify.

Figure 30.2 - *Select the Justify command.*

Excel will wrap the text to fill the selected area.

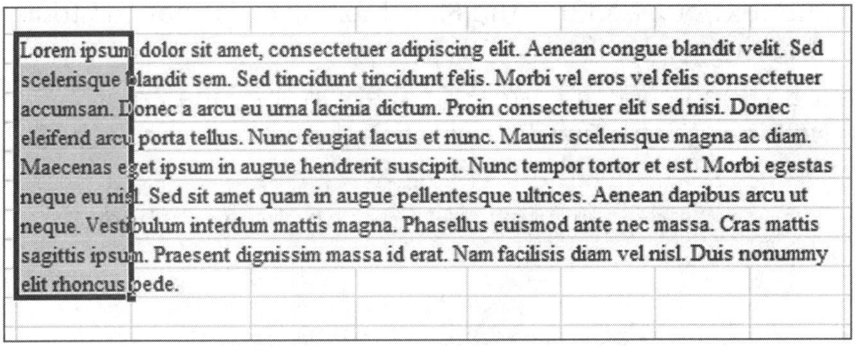

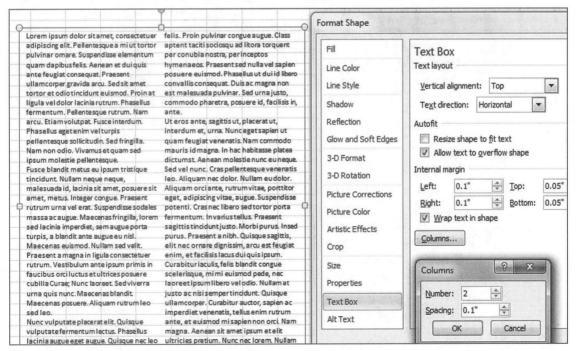

Figure 30.3 -
Fill, Justify will cause the text to fit a certain area.

Using the Justify command is not perfect. It does not work when a cell contains more than 255 characters. If you resize any columns after the justify, you will have to do the justify command again. If some cells have different formatting, they will be lost after the justify.

Using a Text Box

For dealing with long passages of text, you can insert them in a text box in Excel. Follow these steps:

1. On the Insert tab, choose Text Box.
2. Draw a rectangle in your worksheet about the size and shape that you want the text to fill.

Figure 30.4 - *In Excel 2010, text boxes support multiple columns.*

3. Paste (or type) the text.

4. Select the text in the text box and use the Mini Toolbar to format the font size to fit the text box.

5. Right-click the text box and choose Format Shape. On the Line Color category, choose No Line. In the Text Box category, you can specify the number of columns that you want in the text box.

When you click out of the text box, your text will float on the worksheet.

Next Steps

Microsoft Word has offered an equation editor. Since Excel is the application that most often is used to perform mathematical calculations, it makes sense that the equation editor should be in Excel as well. Chapter 31 explains how to use the Equation Editor in Excel 2010.

31

Equation Editor

The Equation Editor from Word 2007 has been ported to Excel 2010. This makes a lot of sense, because you might want to show mathematical equations next to certain Excel models.

An equation has to exist inside of another object, such as a text box or a shape. Although you can insert the 10 sample equations without having a shape first, you will usually have to insert a rectangle or a text box into the worksheet first.

If you use Insert, Shapes, and insert a rectangle, you should first go to the Drawing Tools Format tab and choose a style from the Shape Styles gallery that shows black text on a white background.

Then, with the shape selected, choose Insert, Equation, Insert New Equation.

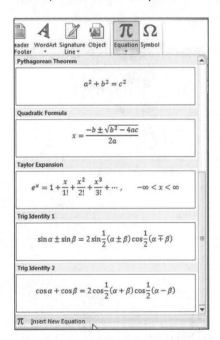

Figure 31.1 - *After selecting a shape, insert an equation.*

Excel starts with an equation of *Type equation here*. Those words are against a purple background. When your cursor is inside the purple background, you have access to the Equation Tools Design tab in the ribbon.

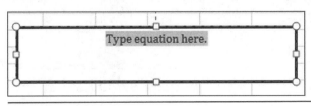

Figure 31.2 - *Type the equation within the purple shading.*

The Equation Tools Design tab offers a large Symbols gallery. Although this gallery starts out with a lot of basic math, there are other choices.

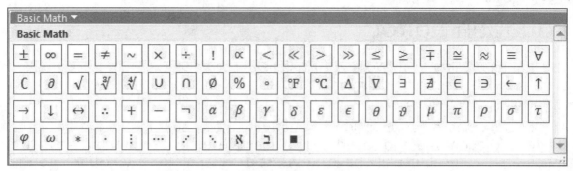

Figure 31.3 - *You can insert symbols into your equation.*

By using the drop-down at the top of the gallery, you can choose from symbols related to Basic Math, Greek Letters, Letter-like Symbols, Operators, Arrows, Negated Relations, Scripts, and Geometry. When you choose a new item from the drop-down, you get a new gallery of symbols.

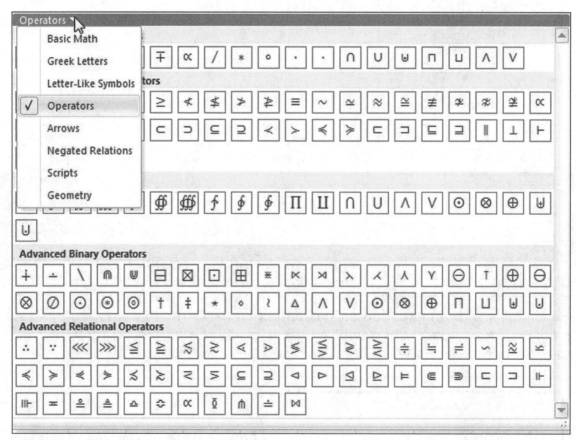

Figure 31.4 - *Change the drop-down to choose from other symbols.*

The right side of the Equation tab of the ribbon features a number of Structure drop-downs. These drop-downs offer various shapes, sometimes around large symbols such as the integration symbol.

In Figure 31.5, a simple structure offers an exponent.

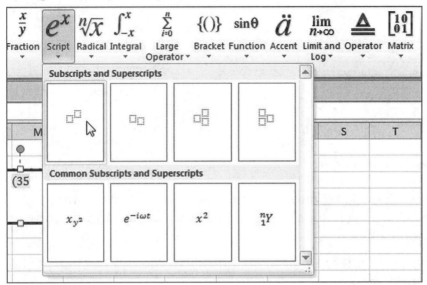

Figure 31.5 - *Choose a structure to add it to the equation.*

In Figure 31.6, you can see that the Equation Editor added two small placeholders to the equation. The insertion point moves to after the placeholders.

 Figure 31.6 - *After you choose a structure from the drop-down, new text box placeholders are added inside the equation.*

To fill in the structure, click the first box and type a character. Then, click the next box. Figure 31.7 shows a *y* that has been typed in the first box. The second box has been chosen and you are ready to type something there.

 Figure 31.7 - *When you click a box, the box becomes highlighted.*

Enter a character for the exponent, and you've completed the structure, as shown in Figure 31.8.

$(35y^3$ **Figure 31.8** - *Type a 3 to complete the structure.*

You can build the equation in a 2D fashion. After you've entered the whole equation, use the Professional icon in the Tools group to convert the equation from 2D to 3D. Figure 31.9 shows an equation in 2D format, and Figure 31.10 shows the equation after clicking the Professional icon.

$(35y^3 + 10y^2 + 15y)/5y$ **Figure 31.9** - *Build the equation in a linear style.*

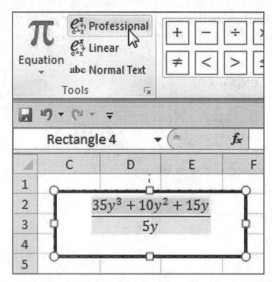

Figure 31.10 - *Then convert to Professional.*

As you work with the Equation Editor, be careful that you stay within the highlighted equation area. If you see the Equation Tools Design tab disappear, you've left the equation.

You can use the font size and font color icons on the Home tab to change the color of characters within the equation.

Figure 31.11 is not a valid equation, but shows a variety of symbols available in the various galleries in the Equation Editor.

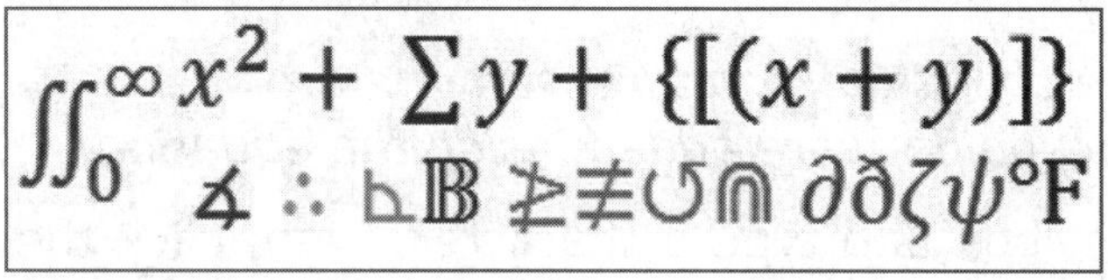

$$\iint_0^\infty x^2 + \Sigma y + \{[(x+y)]\}$$
$$\measuredangle \therefore \natural \mathbb{B} \ngeq \neq \cup \between \partial \eth \zeta \psi °F$$

Figure 31.11 - *A variety of symbols available in the Equation Editor.*

Next Steps

Chapter 32 covers the translation tools available in Excel 2010.

32

Quick Translations

The Review tab offers a translation feature in Excel. Choose any cell and click Translate on the Review tab.

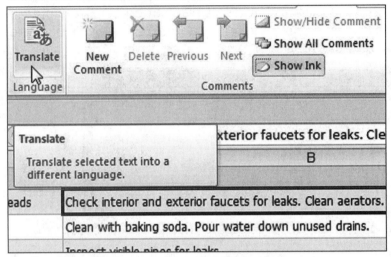

Figure 32.1 - *Select a cell to be translated and click Translate.*

The Research pane will appear along the right side. Choose the From and To languages. Excel will send the phrase out to an online site and return a rough translation of the phrase.

Figure 32.2 - *The original cell is translated to Spanish.*

Caution: This translation service is great for getting a loose understanding of text in a foreign language. Automated translations are not perfect. Hire a human translator if the task is important.

If you choose Translation Options, you can see all the translation pairs available. Excel 2007 had used a site called WorldLingo.com as the default translation source for each pair. Excel 2010 is using a Microsoft translation service instead. If you find that Excel 2007 was translating better, you can switch back to WorldLingo.com for any language pair.

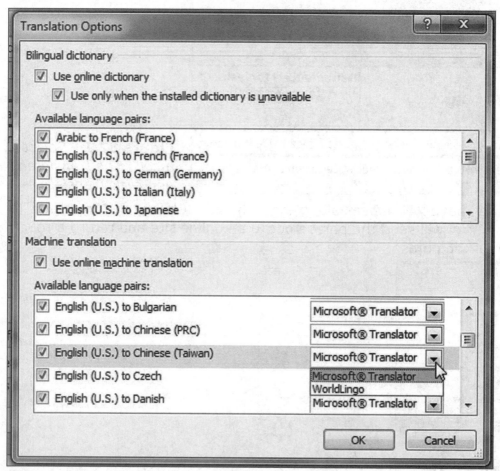

Figure 32.3 - *Choose either Microsoft or WorldLingo as the source of the translation.*

Next Steps

Chapter 33 introduces the new Excel web application.

33

Excel in a Web Browser

This is pretty cool.

Starting in Excel 2010, you can view and interact with your Excel workbook in a browser. You can even do some basic editing in the web browser.

Back in Excel 2007, Microsoft starting touting a server version of Excel. I found few people who could use this version, since the barriers to entry were $15K for a server running SharePoint and an IT guy to figure out how to configure the server and keep it running.

In Excel 2010, the Excel server version is available to anyone with a browser, which basically means everyone with a computer.

Start with a Windows Live Account and SkyDrive

If you don't have one, go out and sign up for a free Windows Live account at Home.Live.Com.

After you are signed in to Windows Live, open the More drop-down in the top navigation and choose SkyDrive. Go through the setup process to sign up for the free SkyDrive service. This gives you a 25 GB storage in the cloud.

Save Your Workbook to the SkyDrive

From Excel 2010, choose File, Save & Send, Save to Web. On the right side of the Backstage view, you will have to enter your Windows Live user ID and password.

After you've signed in to Windows Live, your SkyDrive folders will appear on the right side. Choose a folder and click the Save As icon on the right side of the screen.

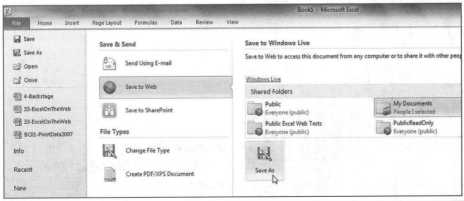

Figure 33.1 - *You can Save As to your SkyDrive.*

On the face of it, this is a great way to make files accessible so that you can work on them from home or on your next business trip. Instead of carrying flash drives back and forth, you can simply keep a copy of the file on the SkyDrive.

View the Workbook on the SkyDrive

On any computer, sign in to Windows Live and choose SkyDrive from the More drop-down. Navigate to the proper folder and find the workbook that you saved from Excel.

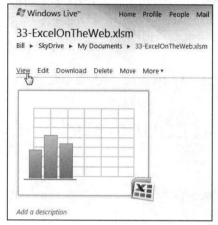

Figure 33.2 - *Your workbook is available on the SkyDrive.*

You will see choices such as Download, but for now choose View.

The results are shown in Figure 33.3. This is a browser! Those are slicers across the top and left side. That is a pivot table and a chart. At the bottom left of the screen, you will see that there are two worksheet tabs that you can access.

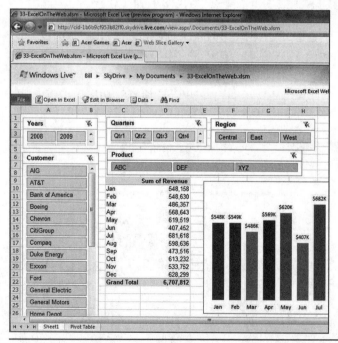

Figure 33.3 - *This is an amazing rendering of the workbook in a browser.*

You are still in View Only mode, but you can do a few amazing things in View Only mode. Try selecting new items from the slicers. In a few seconds, the pivot table and pivot chart update!

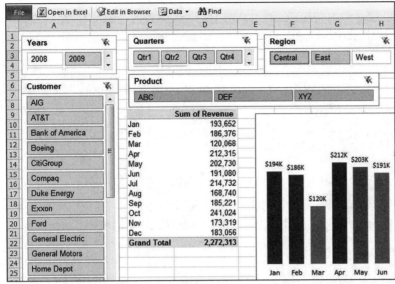

Figure 33.4 - *In View mode, you can interact with the slicers and see new results in the pivot table and chart.*

This is pretty wild. Behind the scenes, Microsoft has the $15,000 Excel Services for SharePoint running on the SkyDrive, rendering your worksheet in a browser.

It gets even better.

Editing the Workbook in a Browser

At the top of the screen, choose Edit in Browser.

A ribbon appears above the worksheet with a File menu, Home tab, and Insert tab.

In edit mode, I typed new labels in J2:J5, some numbers in K2:K4, and a PMT formula in K5. I then formatted cell K5 using formatting commands on the Home tab.

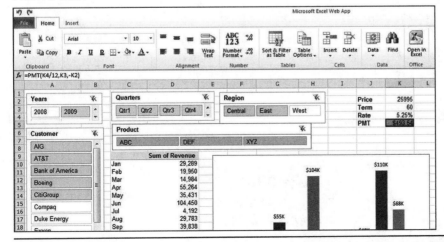

Figure 33.5 - *You can do simple edits in the browser.*

All the while, this feels remarkably like Excel. I tried entering the formula using the mouse and tried entering the formula using the arrow keys to point to the other cells.

Some limitations apply as to what you can do in the browser, but there are an amazing number of things that you *can do* in the browser.

For example, the browser does not support pictures or shapes.

You cannot enter a new array formula, but the browser will calculate array formulas that were entered previously.

You cannot create a new pivot table, but you can interact with slicers for an existing pivot table.

You cannot run macros or have links to external workbooks.

You can adjust row height and column widths. If you have data that is larger than will fit in a cell, you can merge cells so that the entire value will appear.

This is a fairly miraculous browser experience.

If you make changes in the browser, they are automatically saved. When you get back to work, you can enter the SkyDrive version from your Recent Files list. It all works amazingly well.

Figure 33.6 shows the File menu. Figure 33.7 shows the short Insert tab.

Figure 33.6 - *File menu when editing the workbook in a browser.*

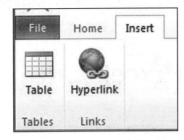

Figure 33.7 - *The Insert tab has only a few commands.*

You can choose Open in Excel. The workbook will download from the SkyDrive and open in whichever version of Excel or Excel Starter that you have installed on that machine.

A Quick Word About Excel Starter

You might have heard of or seen a product called Microsoft Works. This entry-level product often shipped with new PCs and included a basic word processor and a simple spreadsheet. I hated Works because it created files that were not XLS files. Whenever anyone sent me a file from Works, I had to jump through hoops to figure out how to open it.

Starting with Office 2010, Works has been discontinued. Instead, new PCs will ship with something called Office Starter. This product offers Excel Starter and Word Starter.

Good news: Excel starter produces XLSX files that can be opened by anyone with Excel. Excel Starter is really Excel 2010 with much of the rich functionality disabled. People using Excel starter will have most of the Home tab commands plus some spell-checking commands.

The somewhat bad news is that people will start calling you asking for help with Excel and they will not reveal that they actually have Excel Starter. You can spot Excel Starter because the task pane never goes away, and an ad appears in the lower-right corner of the screen.

Next Steps

Chapter 34 discusses the community of enthusiasts at the MrExcel message board.

34

Get Excel Answers from the MrExcel.com Board

If you are an Excel fan, join our community of Excellers at the MrExcel message board.

The board was launched in 1999 as a way to provide answers to questions people have about Excel and Excel VBA.

Since the launch, the community of Excellers at the message board have answered more than 400,000 questions. Every question and answer is archived at the site and is searchable.

If you ever have an Excel question, post your question with sufficient detail. Usually within minutes, others will either ask clarifying questions or provide assistance.

To get the MrExcel message board, follow these steps:

1. Visit www.MrExcel.com.

2. From the left navigation box, choose Message Board.

Figure 34.1 - *Use the left navigation to find the message board.*

3. Using the top-right links, choose to Register. We ask for your e-mail address and for you to verify that you are 13 years old or older.

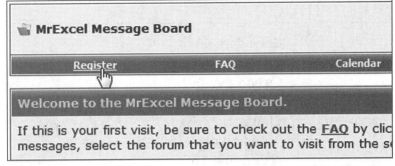

Figure 34.2 - *The Register link is toward the upper-right corner of the site.*

4. After registering, click the Excel Questions forum.

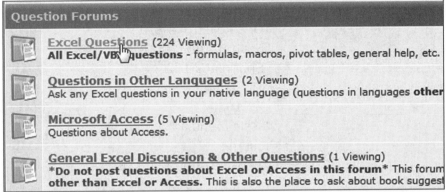

Figure 34.3 - *Other forums exist for Access, the Lounge, and questions in languages other than English.*

5. Click New Thread.

Figure 34.4 - *The New Thread button appears just above the list of topics.*

6. Give your question a really good subject so that people can (a) know whether they will be able to help and (b) find your topic again later. A subject of "Excel Help" is not a good subject because everyone at the board is looking for Excel help.

7. Build your question and click Submit.

> **Tip**: If you need to show an Excel spreadsheet in your post, download the HTML Maker using the links from the bottom of the board.

8. Check back in 5 to 10 minutes. Someone will usually pose a clarifying question. Answer that question. In another 5 to 10 minutes, you will usually have your answer.

Index

Index

Index

Index

Index

Index

- Heading Locked in on Multi Worksheet

- [Alt F 1] Makes a chart.

  Use Default Button at Bottom.

- Sparklines - Tiny Data Intense chart. in a
  Column

- A2 & "_" & A3 = Combined Name

"Ctrl Z" = Undo

- Proper Freelse

- Double Rlick Fill Handle.

- Shift "Group Mode"
- Ctrl

  Click
  Click   ⟩ Tabs at
                Bottom

- Filter. Advance

- Pivot Tables Slicer - Dashboard type stuff

- Magic Cell

  ⊙?? Rights User for Pivot Tasks

- PowerPivot.com
     More Than 1,000,000.

- MS MapPoint

  jjj = Hide Data

  ← Management
  ← Sales Tier 1
                    2
                    3

  - Shaded Worksheet - Hide →
                              ↓

  - Automatic Data on Charts
    outside the Data add
    Text

  - Chart Title Right Click on
    Title Add = Sheet1!D1 $.

VLOOKUP   Put False at the END of ALL VLOOKUP
             STATEMENTS
    · F4 Puts $ in Formula

IF ERROR STATEMENT.

IF Function | = IF (F2 >= 20000) THEN, 2000, 0.0
               |
    = IF | = IF (AND(FIRST CONDITION, SECOND condition)
               | BONUS, 0)
               |
               | =

          1.) = IF (F27= 20000, IF 127 05

SumIF   Use Filter   Turn off "Get Pivot
SumIFS   TABLE"
Aggregate   ONLY Because IT Uses
                              HARD coded. INFO..

- (Edge key ~) Shows ALL Formules in SPREAD SHEET.

- Pivot tables By Customers / options

- Access - Filter By Selection / Auto Filter

Notes

- TRUE VLOOKUP |. MATCH (False)
  HLOOKUP |. INDEX.

  . True statement at the end of a
  VLOOKUP gives you the Next Smallest
  #

. F9 gives you ~~And~~ An ARRAY.

. ALT 10 Adds Excel to words.

. 60m series of Data Table example.

fub@ mrexcel.com

N.D Seinwar

Notes

Notes

Notes

Notes

Also Available from MrExcel.com

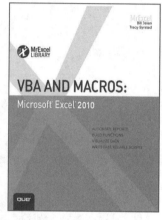